GOVERNORS AND HARD TIMES

GOVERNORS AND HARD TIMES

edited by

Thad L. Beyle

University of North Carolina at Chapel Hill

A Division of Congressional Quarterly Inc.
Washington, D.C.

Cover design: Ben Santora

Copyright ©1992 Congressional Quarterly Inc.
1414 22nd Street, N.W., Washington, D.C. 20037

Printed in the United States of America

Library of Congress Cataloging-in-Publication Data

Governors and hard times / edited by Thad L. Beyle.
    p.   cm.
  Includes bibliographical references and index.
  ISBN 0-87187-710-4
  1. Governors--United States--Case studies.   I. Beyle, Thad L.,
1934--
JK2447.G67 1992
353.9'1313'0922--dc20   92-7805
                                                         CIP

CONTENTS

FOREWORD

In 1981 Jim Florio lost to Tom Kean by only 1,700 votes in the election for governor of New Jersey. After a year of recession, the economy rebounded and practically all of the rest of Governor Kean's two terms in office was a period of boom. State government went on a roll; programs and services were awash in funds. Kean left office, having served the maximum of two terms, a happy man in a prosperous state. In 1989 Jim Florio ran again. This time he won, and overwhelmingly against Rep. Jim Courter. He looked forward to governing and providing policy leadership in the state.

But Governor Florio immediately ran into the recession of the early 1990s. He was faced with an immediate shortfall and the prospect of a court decision requiring increased funding of the state's urban schools. Florio and the Democratic legislature raised taxes by $2.8 billion. And they rolled back state government as well. New Jersey taxpayers and a number of powerful interest groups revolted and in 1991 elected veto-proof Republican majorities to both the state Senate and the state Assembly. Jim Florio was blamed for New Jersey's problems and for the Democratic defeat.

To say the least, Florio's timing was off, while Kean's was on. The latter held office when the economy was up; the former took office as the economy went into decline. Despite the impressive powers at the disposal of the office of governor in New Jersey, the chief executive may not be able to turn the tide if the currents are running in another direction.

I explored the subject of governors and legislatures several years ago, at the end of the 1980s. Given the times that preceded my exploration, it was natural for me in writing about executive-legislative relations to refer to many instances of gubernatorial power, gubernatorial policy success, and gubernatorial popularity. Luckily, however, I hedged a bit. In assessing gubernatorial popularity, the volatility of public opinion was evident, and I noted that a decline in the state's economy, a proposal to raise taxes, or some governmental scandal all could bring a governor down in the polls. In the few years since my observations, the economy, taxes, and scandal all have operated in one place or another to reduce the governors' popularity ratings.

This past is prologue. Hard times unfortunately are now upon the nation, the states, and the governors. The gubernatorial story today—and probably in the years just ahead—is not a pleasant one, not even for legislators, who are institutional rivals, or for those in the opposite party, who are competitors for power. Thus, writing a foreword to a book without a happy ending cannot be a totally enjoyable task. But it is a rewarding one, in the sense that *Governors and Hard Times,* a book of "first snapshots" of ten new governors, is fascinating reading and an important contribution to our understanding of executive leadership in the states. The states are where it's at today, and where it will be tomorrow. And governors are the principal actors on the scene. The effort by Thad Beyle and his colleagues may not be the most up-beat reading, but it is essential reading. Perhaps, we can look forward to a successor volume some years hence, when a new generation of governors has larger surpluses, smaller problems, and an approving public. That is a book that I would certainly like to write.

Alan Rosenthal
Eagleton Institute of Politics
Rutgers University
New Brunswick, New Jersey

1. NEW GOVERNORS IN
HARD ECONOMIC AND POLITICAL TIMES

Thad L. Beyle

The gubernatorial elections of 1989 and 1990 brought twenty-one new governors to the state capitals. Most had had previous experience in state government, but some had not. The inexperienced would have to learn not only about the new job but also about what states do and how they do it; the others would be able to learn about their new job while building on their previous experience.

But no one could be prepared for the state of the states as we entered the last decade of the twentieth century. In effect, the demands on these governors' offices were so great and of such immediacy that they virtually eliminated the advantages experience should have bestowed. The times called for governors who could cope with unmanageable problems with grossly inadequate resources that were rapidly eroding.

The State of the States

Many of these new governors faced very difficult fiscal situations—falling revenues and rising demands for services—which forced them to make almost impossible choices as they entered office. They had virtually no room to further their own agendas through starting new programs or putting new twists on old programs. Many had to make the ultimate of tough choices: not only to cut programs and services but also to raise taxes (revenues) just to keep state government and current programs functioning. For many states, this was the worst fiscal situation in at least a decade, and despite optimistic forecasts by economists and national leaders, it continues to linger and even worsen as the effects of all governmental budgetary cuts are felt.

These new governors entered the highest office in their state when it was clear that the national government, despite presidential and congressional rhetoric to the contrary, was in the process of reducing its commitment to the domestic side of the policy agenda. In addition, the national government was transferring sizable program commitments to the state and local governments without offering enough financial support to assist them in carrying out their new responsibilities. In fact, much of the additional revenue derived from some of the hard fought

1

battles for tax increases at the state level over the past few years was being consumed just by the rising costs of Medicaid and by inflation.

One political bargaining chip governmental leaders in some states have in the early 1990s is redistricting. Once a decade some of those who want to continue their careers in the U.S. House of Representatives have to pay attention to what the governors and the state legislatures are doing. Although redistricting does not immediately affect members of the U.S. Senate, some of the incumbent members of the House will be prompted to set their sights on a statewide Senate race rather than face running in a new district. But the enormity of most states' fiscal problems did not allow state legislators and governors the luxury of using this chip as they might have wished.

Some of the new governors had unique problems to address, some tied to the economic situation, others not. Consider the following examples.

- Arizona turned a very sharp corner in 1986 after some upbeat years under the leadership of Gov. Bruce Babbitt (D, 1978-1987). Since then, the impeachment saga of Evan Mecham, a caretaker replacement, and a legislative bribery scandal (AZ Scam) sharply eroded the credibility of the state and its government. Changes in an electoral process that had allowed Mecham to win in 1986 with 40 percent of the vote led to a nondecision in the 1990 general election. So the malaise in state government continued until a runoff general election in 1991. Just four years after Babbitt, the new governor faced a major challenge to rebuild citizen confidence in state government.

- California has been undergoing massive economic and societal changes that are only now being recognized. The decline of major defense industries and the loss of jobs have been well documented, as has the massive infusion of new people, mostly from ethnic minorities, into the state. What has escaped the notice of many observers is the outmigration of corporations into Arizona, Nevada, Utah, and other states where transportation, housing, and workers' compensation costs are lower; environmental and other restrictions on business are less stringent; health care costs are not so high; personal and corporate taxes are lower; and crime is less rampant. More California firms are considering moving out.[1] The most obvious effect will be on the state's economy and then on governmental revenues—both state and local— continuing the fiscal problems of 1991 well into the future.

- Massachusetts was characterized as an economic miracle and had a governor who sought but did not win the presidency. By 1990, the governor, the Massachusetts Miracle, and state government had been discredited, and the state was hard pressed. New England states in general were in deep economic trouble, which showed politically as three of the six governors who were eligible to seek reelection in 1990 decided not to run. One of the incumbents who ran lost.[2]
- Rhode Island was facing a collapse of the state regulated banks unless quick action was taken. Millions of dollars were involved and thousands of citizens were affected. By comparison, governmental fiscal problems seemed to recede in importance as citizens lost confidence in a range of private and public institutions.
- Texas is under court order to revamp its system of financing public education. No matter how the problem is viewed, the answer has to include major changes in the state's system of taxation. Not only must money be raised for education, but some of the richer parts of the state must help pay for education in the poorer parts of the state.

Several of the new governors brought a new perspective and indeed a new rhetoric. Some observers were baffled: they did not know what they were hearing from the new governors would mean in terms of the state budget, programs, and services. At least two of the governors—Lawton Chiles of Florida and William Weld of Massachusetts—brought the "entrepreneurial government" symbolism to their new jobs, a line of approach suggested by David Osborne.[3] And Pete Wilson in California is proposing "preventive" rather than remedial government programs. Are these only new words and concepts for some old activities, or are they something really new?

Changing Politics in the States

The political nature of the states is undergoing tremendous change, the greatest being the decline—even the loss—of political parties as defining organizations. Certainly, the parties still set the stage for the political campaigns for governor through the various state approaches to choosing candidates. But the expense of the races in California ($53.2 million) and Texas ($50.5 million) only highlights a political fact of life: parties are the vehicle by which candidates and their own individualized partylike organizations play the costly game of winning a nomination and an election. Parties are not winning these contests, candidates and their personal organizations are. Political campaigns usually do not rely on the political party for support. And in 1990, two of the new governors were elected as independents; they did not head any party.[4]

Political campaigns themselves have drifted toward negative advertising and personal attacks so that few voters know what the issues are, let alone what the candidates might do once in office. In most cases, the issues that should have been addressed for the future of the state were not publicized in political ads, nor were they part of the political dialogue. There is evidence that some candidates themselves did not know what the issues were, nor had they considered and debated how they might be addressed. These candidates did not even indicate what they might do once elected to the governor's office.

The costs of running a campaign have become so high that candidates and their supporters make a greater effort to raise money for the campaign than to reach the voters directly. They use radio and television ads to communicate with voters rather than make direct contact. They also rely on their political polls to frame their actions and statements rather than formulate their views on issues and indicate how they will provide leadership.

Once in office, new governors find further evidence of the decline of the political parties as defining organizations. The concept of "power split" depicts what has become a normal situation in many states—split partisan control of the executive and legislative branches. For the past few years nearly three-fifths of the states have been in this situation. The two states with independent governors are the extreme examples of the power split concept.

Further, over about fifteen years, the U.S. Supreme Court has effectively reduced the power of patronage from elected executives at the state and local level.[5] Winning an election does not necessarily provide the winner the opportunity to appoint friends and supporters (political and otherwise) to positions in the new administration.

Some of the new governors are trying to redefine what government and politics are about. As a result, they may change their states' political systems. Yet the current systems could overwhelm them and resist change; individual leadership may not have as much influence as some might hope.

This Book

The contents of this book are a series of "first snapshot" analyses of how well ten of these new governors are faring in their jobs. In all but one case (Virginia), these analyses are based on the governors' first nine or ten months in office; in Virginia nearly two years are encompassed.

The authors are political scientists who have written on and taught about governors, state politics, and policy over the years. They are also members of a select class of "governor watchers" who pride themselves on understanding what is going on in their governor's office as well as in the offices of other states' governors. Several have had experience in a governor's administration or with gubernatorial organizations, such as the National Governors' Association, or in the state legislature.

They agreed to take these "first snapshots" under considerable constraint, not the least of which was a nearly impossible publication deadline forcing them to make their assessments very early in the gubernatorial administration. But, as many observers of political executives know, how the executive weaves his or her way through the early months usually sets the tone of the tenure and how the efforts will be viewed. A governor's legacy is often set in these very early months.

The reader will find considerable variety in these studies as the authors developed their analyses. Some are short and succinct, some are long and detailed, and others fall between these points. As editor, I take full responsibility for allowing this diversity to occur; it made more sense to give the individual authors a general sense of the goals we were seeking and then let them develop their own perspectives than to force them to follow a set format with rigid guidelines. This approach has worked in the past in looking at gubernatorial transitions[6] and gubernatorial reelections.[7] I trust it will again here.

Before embarking on the individual studies of your particular interest, there are two pieces of the book that you may want to sample. First, is my own perspective on the common themes and perspectives these studies bring to readers. Second, in Chapter 2, is Bob Crew's perspective on understanding gubernatorial behavior.

Some Common Themes

The ten governors profiled here lead very diverse state governments. Nonetheless, a reading of the studies in this book allows one to make a number of generalizations. Nine themes are identified in the remainder of this chapter. These will be helpful for interpreting the chapters on the governors.

1. Things are not like they used to be. In most of the states studied there is evidence at the very outset of the administration (if not in the campaign) that a new way of defining and addressing problems is needed in the state. If this is not clear initially, it becomes apparent over the early period of a gubernatorial administration.

Governors are frustrated by the severe national recession, which has lowered revenues and has produced increased demand for services.

They can do little to address this macro-level problem; they can only try to cope with its effect on state government. They are so constrained that they have little time, money, or ability to help needy local governments. They often must reduce state support for local governments and pass responsibility for programs and services on to them.

Governors and state legislatures are forced into making the difficult decision to both cut expenditures and raise taxes. The citizen must pay more for less. In some states, such as Massachusetts, additional revenues could not be raised. Deep budget cuts were required, cuts going to the very heart of what had been business as usual for many years.

2. For some, the situation was well known; for others, the situation was a surprise. The problems of the New England states were obvious, and those running for governor knew what they were getting into—or thought they did. In other states, the serious fiscal problems were initially on the horizon. As they were approached their enormity was glimpsed, and each problem seemed to be followed by a larger one. There seemed to be no end to the fiscal disasters.

In many states, governors and legislatures made patchwork decisions that they hoped would carry the state through the current economic slowdown. These decisions had to be revamped as the crises worsened. Promises of "no more taxes" often turned into arguments over which taxes to increase and who should bear the cost. Program cutbacks and realignments soon became severe across-the-board cuts. In some cases state employees were laid off and/or even terminated, and the outreach capacity of state government was curtailed. To many observers, the functions of state government were being crippled and citizens were being seriously hurt.

The fiscal crises appeared suddenly after a decade of rather steady—in some cases spectacular—growth of state economies and state revenues over the 1980s. State leaders seemed to take such growth as a given and allowed government and governmental programs to grow rapidly, often at a rate much greater than economic and revenue growth. As the pie grew, everyone could be served.

This growth of the 1980s could not be sustained in the 1990s. Decline became the driving force. The costs of maintaining government and programs could not be supported in most states. Most participants could not comprehend the politics of cutback management. They were not prepared to engage in the politics of retrenchment—of taking back after a long period of giving. As the pie shrank, not everyone could be served—and those who were served received smaller pieces.

The politics of the 1980s seemed to give birth to unbeatable incumbents who could continue winning by making certain most everyone of political importance received something. For this, they were rewarded with political contributions to fuel their winning campaigns. The 1990s may very well be the decade of de facto term limits as incumbents return home after short careers in office. These term limits may not be law; they will be imposed by angry voters who have experienced increased taxes and reduced services.

3. In several states, sideshows to the main attraction served as defining events for the new governor. While the fiscal problem was ever present, often other problems also burdened the governor. Their handling of nonbudget problems often had more effect on public opinion than how they coped with their fiscal problems.

In Rhode Island, the collapse of the state's credit unions and thrifts forced the new governor to take immediate action to forestall a banking collapse; in Virginia Wilder's national ambitions and candidacy for the 1992 presidential nomination took the spotlight; in California the fight over gay and lesbian rights brought considerable controversy directly to the governor, after favorable press for his handling of the fiscal problems of the state; and in Illinois a political fight erupted over the selection of a chancellor for the Chicago campus of the University of Illinois—a fight the governor handled with skill and directness.

Finally, in Arizona the AZ Scam scandal in the state legislature made it even more necessary for the governor to succeed. At a minimum, the scandal left a great void in political leadership for the governor to fill.

4. The personality and the style of the new governor affected his or her ability to lead the state. More than in many recent election years, strong individual personalities and the views and styles of those seeking the governorship were important factors in winning and governing. These factors, not partisanship, were the key in several states.

In Connecticut, Lowell Weicker himself was seen as the solution to the state's problems; in Arizona, Fife Symington, the private CEO, became in effect the state's CEO in order to restore confidence in state government. In Florida, Lawton Chiles's strong personality and style were critical to the state. The characterizations of Ann Richards as the tough woman who enjoyed the difficult job of being governor in Texas, and of Virginia's Douglas Wilder practicing confrontation and brinksmanship as the first elected black governor helped set the tone of their administrations.

In California, the style of the new governor, Pete Wilson, was a great contrast to that of the man he replaced. His positive and pragmatic approach to government, his view of government's role, and his teamwork earned him early support and smoothed his way. Republicans in Illinois were pleased to continue their hold on the governor's office, but the personalities and styles of the outgoing and incoming governors were very different. Finally, in Massachusetts, the style and toughness of the new "old money" Yankee in the governor's chair forced politicians of all stripes to rethink the politics of governing.

5. **Some of the new governors are rethinking their approach to state problems.** Obviously, the reality of the situation in many states almost forced a reevaluation of the states' roles and responsibilities. But more is involved. As noted earlier, two of the governors—Chiles in Florida and Weld in Massachusetts—came in as apostles of the themes developed by David Osborne in his recent work on the states.[8] Not only did they take steps that seemed to follow the theory Osborne was suggesting, but their rhetoric in major addresses echoed, if not borrowed from, his writings. In fact, Osborne was a consultant or adviser to them.

In Michigan and Massachusetts, the avowed and demonstrated conservatism of the new governors was a positive and powerful aspect of how they approached their jobs. In Florida, Chiles was able to use difficult fiscal circumstances to achieve other goals he had articulated while running for the governorship: stronger ethics in government and campaign reform.

6. **The federal system is undergoing a radical redefinition.** We are moving from an era of cooperative federalism to an era of "go-it-alone" federalism at all levels.[9] It should come as no surprise that few of the new governors put much faith in the national government as a partner in addressing their states' problems. Although there have been some joint presidential-gubernatorial activities, such as the education summit of 1990 in Charlottesville, Virginia, little help from Washington has been forthcoming—nor is it expected.

In fact, increasing tension appears to be developing between the leaders of the two levels of government. This tension is the natural outcome of the governors' need to cope with unfunded mandates in certain federal programs, to help distressed local governments, and to bear the brunt of public anger over the increased taxes the states must adopt to meet these needs. At the national level, government leaders continue to pay lip service to decreasing the size of the federal deficit while ignoring the fiscal plight of the states.

If the evidence from these case studies is correct, what John Shannon suggested as an important legacy of the Reagan revolution—"fend-for-yourself federalism"—has come to pass with a vengeance. Shannon's term refers to the national " 'hands-off' policy in respect to interstate equalization" of federal aid.[10] Now this concept should be expanded to cover virtually all facets of federal activity because governmental units at each level—national, state, and local—must find ways to go it alone in facing their problems.

Gubernatorial and legislative decision making in 1990 was almost uniquely focused within the state and on its peculiar fiscal situation. In Massachusetts, federal aid was a late budget saver, but only after a part-time worker found an overlooked federal program provision which unlocked the federal coffers for some begrudging assistance. Illinois also was able to develop a new program to assess hospitals and nursing homes for additional funds, a program which the federal government then matched through Medicaid funds; but this loophole will surely be closed.

Similarly, states with severe fiscal problems were cutting back on support and aid provided to local governments. What the federal government was doing to the states and local governments, the states were also doing to their own local governments as those at the bottom of the system attempted to balance their budgets. The impact of this double whammy at the local level is already being felt in many ways as cities and other local units attempt to survive.

Where our federal system is headed as each level continues to cope with its own problems and fashion its own solutions is not known. But what is clear is that there is no overall plan to guide the various actors and units in the system. The individual coping exercises will undoubtedly set the scene for needed reforms to be undertaken once the go-it-alone system reaches maturity and creates its own set of intractable problems. A view from the bottom of the system might suggest that we are not far from that point. Yet we are not near the point of focusing on reform.

7. Despite the "power split" of divided partisan control, legislative-gubernatorial relations were fairly peaceful. Certainly there were difficult fights and almost intractable relations between some of the governors and their legislatures, but the greater story in these studies is how well the governors and the legislatures finally worked together to achieve common goals, at least in the brief initial period. Despite the push-and-shove style of legislative relations practiced by Governor Wilder in Virginia, an accommodation was reached. Governor Chiles in Florida was able to achieve an admirable success rate for his proposals. And although Governor Weld's message and direction in Massachusetts may not have made believers of his adversaries, his strength of resolve and style in coping with a longstanding problem did. Governor Wilson's positive views of governing and solving problems by being inclusive made friends of former gubernatorial adversaries in California.

The story of Connecticut is instructive. Governor Weicker stood strong for the needed income tax against a legislature bent on ducking this awful political liability. This governor without a party was able to have his vetoes upheld in the legislature. Yet although he finally won on the issue, both the governor and the legislature may have lost politically in the end.

8. The role of the political party continues to change. While many decry their decline in our system, political parties do still have considerable impact on state governments.

In Virginia, the rise in strength of the Democratic party among both voters and leaders beginning with the election of Charles Robb to the governorship in 1981 set the stage for the victories by Gerald Baliles in 1985 and Douglas Wilder in 1989. This success reversed more than a decade of Republican control of the governorship in the Commonwealth.

In Arizona and California the strength and consistent ideological fixation of the right wing of the Republican party has caused problems. Conservative Republican Evan Mecham's election as governor of Arizona in 1986 led to a series of political events that has left that state in turmoil. Similarly, in California the need to pay attention—albeit symbolic at times—to the right wing of the Republican party has caused headaches for Governor Wilson.

In two other states, U.S. Supreme Court decisions relating to partisan activities had a direct impact on what happened in 1990-1991. The Illinois case, *Rutan et al. v. Republican Party of Illinois* (1990), changed how patronage was to be handled by governors in general, and specifically by newly elected governor Jim Edgar. No longer could party affiliation be the key variable for hiring and promoting personnel. Because the case was based on the now unconstitutional personnel activities of the administration of Edgar's immediate predecessor, James Thompson (R, 1977-1991), particular and careful attention had to be paid to how hiring and firing were handled.

The Connecticut case, *Republican Party of Connecticut v. Tashjian* (1986), in retrospect was an important step in Lowell Weicker's journey to the governor's chair. Always at the left margin of what was respectable for the state's Republicans, Senator Weicker sought to loosen up the state's primary system so that more voters could participate in the Republican primaries. The Court's decision upholding this strategy opened up the party primary to voters who were not members of the Republican party. In Weicker's case, it was to a broader, more moderate cross-section of voters in the state. His later run for governor as an independent candidate was foreshadowed by his involvement in this case.

Add to these examples the individualized nature of political campaigns and the impact of power splits on gubernatorial-legislative relations. What then is happening to our party system? Russell Murphy, in summing up the situation in Connecticut—and, by extension, in many states—observes that while we watch emerging democracies in the world struggle to establish a political system based on viable political parties, we continue to take steps in this mature democracy to undermine them.

9. The erosion of these governors' popularity was fairly rapid over the initial months of their tenure. As can be seen by the results of some poll results in ten states taken during the latter half of 1991 and early in 1992 (see Table 1-1), most of the new governors had slipped well below a 50 percent positive rating level even before the end of their first year in office. In fact, five of them had higher negatives than positives, while three others had a virtual split in their positive-negative ratings. Only two of these governors had higher positive than negative ratings.

One explanation is that the governors are fairly uniformly doing a poor job in office. While possible in some situations, it is not a plausible explanation for all cases.

More to the point, however, would be an explanation that these governors are doing what they must do to keep their ships of state government afloat. The consequence is that they are forced to take actions that alienate the public. As the most visible and proximate targets of voter and citizen discontent, the governors are feeling a "kill the messenger" wrath.

But, if this is true, for what message are they are being "killed"? In most cases, they have been taking steps to rectify past mistakes, to balance the state's checkbook, and in some subtle and some not so subtle ways to change what state governments are doing (or are expected to do). The nonsupport, often anger, they face might better be directed at those who preceded them, or at national leaders who have not acknowledged the problems of the states, or at the condition of the national economy. In fact, some of the low gubernatorial ratings may be more a reflection of citizen anger at governments in general than an assessment of the governors' specific performance.

Will the governors be "killed" for this guilt by association? Will they become part of a "kill the messenger" legacy in which their chances and attempts to seek reelection or election to higher office are "killed"? Will this phenomenon serve as a virtual term limit imposed by the voters on their gubernatorial leaders?

We will get the first part of an answer in 1992 when the term of Bruce Sundlun of Rhode Island is up. Then in 1993 we will watch the

Table 1-1 Job Performance Ratings for Selected New Governors, August 1991-January 1992

Governor	Election Year	Positive [a] Rating	Negative [b] Rating	Poll
Jim Edgar (R-Ill.)	1990	65%	23%	Marketing Strategies, Inc. (early September); N = 800 adults
Ann Richards (D-Texas)	1990	49	44	The Texas Poll (mid-October); N = 1,004 adults
John Engler (R-Mich.)	1990	44	43	Marketing Resources Group Poll (late August); N = 800 registered voters
Bruce Sundlun (D-R.I.)	1990	42	40	Alpha Research Associates (mid-November); N = 505 registered voters
William Weld (R-Mass.)	1990	41	37	Becker Institute (early October); N = 400 residents
Fife Symington (R-Ariz.)	1991	38	44	*Arizona Republic* Poll (January 9-12); N = 808 residents
Pete Wilson (R-Calif.)	1990	28	67	Field Institute (January 13-18); N = 1,028 adults
Lawton Chiles (D-Fla.)	1990	23	76	Mason-Dixon Poll (December); N = 813 registered voters
Lowell Weicker (I-Conn.)	1990	22	74	*Hartford Courant* (mid-October); N = 500 adults
Doug Wilder (D-Va.)	1989	22	78	Mason-Dixon Poll (January); N = 803 registered voters

SOURCES: *The Political Report* 14 (September 13, 1991): 7-8; *The Political Report* 14 (October 10, 1991): 7; *The Political Report* 15 (January 13, 1992): 7; Mason-Dixon Poll; and individual state chapter authors.

NOTES: All state polls used the excellent-good-fair-poor rating scale except for the Arizona, Illinois, and Michigan polls, which used the approve-disapprove rating scale, and the Rhode Island poll, which used the excellent, above average, below average, and poor rating scale.

D = Democrat, R = Republican, I = Independent, and N = number of people polled.

[a] Positive combines excellent, good, and above average ratings or an approve rating.

[b] Negative combines below average, fair, and poor ratings or a disapprove rating.

saga of New Jersey's Gov. Jim Florio, whose four-year term will be up. For the rest, we must wait until 1994.

Presidential politics is also involved here. Governor Wilder of Virginia, who is constitutionally ineligible to seek reelection, cited his record of balancing the state budget in tough times without a tax increase as one of his major qualifications to replace George Bush. But in the end he bowed out of the 1992 presidential race, indicating that he had to spend more time on difficult state budgetary issues. This echoed the rationale of Gov. Mario Cuomo (D-N.Y., 1983—), who finally decided not to enter the race due to fiscal problems in his state.

Could it be that incumbent governors, especially those who must cope with serious state fiscal problems, cannot be considered as potential presidential candidates because they cannot afford to spend the time and money on a primary campaign? Will our developing go-it-alone federal system also serve to reduce the pool from which we can select national leaders? This development would be ironic, as those being excluded are the political leaders who have the experience of working through the tough set of decisions attending a balanced budget, experience sorely needed at the national level.

Obviously, there are much broader questions involved here than just how this or that specific incumbent fares with the public in the polls and the ballot box. More basic questions are tied to how governors, state legislators, and other public officials at all levels can recapture the faith of the citizens in their elected officials and thereby in their governments.

Hard economic times have brought on hard times for individuals, families, and businesses. With better economic times, will the citizens respond positively and become engaged in politics? Maybe, but some of the problems will be alleviated simply by people being at work and paying more taxes into state coffers. The hope is that the reasons for citizen discontent will not be forgotten in better times and that some of the critical thinking and decisions being made in hard times will be carried over to become a part of a revitalized and energetic system of state government and national federalism.

Notes

1. "California Development," *State Policy Reports* 9 (September 1991): 12.
2. Michael Dukakis (D-Mass.), William O'Neill (D-Conn.), and Madeleine Kunin (D-Vt.) decided not to run for reelection; Edward DiPrete (R-R.I.) lost his bid.
3. David Osborne, *Laboratories of Democracy* (Cambridge, Mass.: Harvard

Business School Press, 1988).

4. Walter Hickel (Alaska) and Lowell Weicker (Conn.). Both had previously run statewide and served in office as Republicans.

5. *Elrod v. Burns* (1976); *Branti v. Finkel* (1981); *Connick v. Myers* (1983); and *Rutan et al. v. Republican Party of Illinois* (1990).

6. Thad L. Beyle, ed., *Gubernatorial Transitions: The 1982 Elections* (Durham, N.C.: Duke University Press, 1985) and *Gubernatorial Transitions: The 1983 and 1984 Elections* (Durham, N.C.: Duke University Press, 1989).

7. Thad L. Beyle, ed., *Re-Electing the Governor: The 1982 Elections* (Lanham, Md.: University Press of America, 1986).

8. Osborne, *Laboratories of Democracy*.

9. Apologies and thanks to John Shannon who first set out this concept in "The Return to Fend-for-Yourself Federalism: The Reagan Mark," *Intergovernmental Perspective* 13 (Fall 1987): 34-37.

10. Ibid., 34.

2. UNDERSTANDING GUBERNATORIAL BEHAVIOR: A FRAMEWORK FOR ANALYSIS

Robert E. Crew, Jr.

Much, if not most, of the writing about the behavior of governors and of other political executives exhibits two characteristics: reliance on only a few (often only one) variables to explain that behavior, and use of anecdotal examples rather than systematic, empirical data. Thus the accomplishments of political executives are attributed to political style, to political skill, or to ingenious strategies; rarely are the effects of all of these—and other—variables combined. Further, much of the analysis that forms the basis of speculation about these executives comes from "reporters' comments, newspaper editorials, biographies and autobiographies, as well as political arguments by [legislators] or the administration." [1] Such data are impossible to evaluate adequately without knowledge of comparable situations and statistics. A framework, or model, is needed that incorporates the major variables identified by research as being important to an understanding of executive behavior. It is also important to pay attention to the nature of the data upon which assessments of executive behavior are based. This chapter proposes a model for the analysis of gubernatorial behavior and suggests which data can be used to test hypotheses about the interaction of the variables contained in the model.

Determining Gubernatorial Success

Despite differences in their approaches, those who study the activities of governors are interested most generally in the success the governors achieve—success in reaching goals set either by the governors themselves or by other interested parties, including constituents, the media, or scholars. The standard, or measure, of success is the subject of energetic debate and varies substantially among interested parties. Within the field of presidential studies, at least two camps exist. The first, identified most closely with Richard Neustadt, defines success somewhat narrowly in terms of maximization of administration goals. The second, identified with Fred Greenstein, celebrates a broader view of success, that of "public harmony and governmental legitimacy." [2]

The debate over the appropriate conceptualization of success is normative, not objective, and must be resolved in the minds of the people involved. Nonetheless, the use of systematic, and where possible empirical, data in discussing gubernatorial success will reduce the number of misinformed judgments made about gubernatorial behavior and improve the quality of explanation.

Several kinds of empirical data may be put to use in the study of gubernatorial success. Some of the richest sources of these data are each governor's State of the State address, inaugural address, and budget messages. Each of these identifies goals of varying specificity, which can be tracked through the legislative, judicial, or administrative process. Measures of administration success can be calculated from these data, and indicators of gubernatorial priorities and positions can be developed. Such measures can be used for comparative purposes, particularly within individual states.

Gubernatorial success can also be examined through the use of systematic data on appointments to administrative, advisory, and judicial positions. Appointments provide governors the opportunity to insinuate broad political and governmental philosophies into the politics of their states and to satisfy campaign promises. Appointments offer researchers a basis upon which to assess gubernatorial success on these levels. Has the governor been successful in moving state courts or agencies in new directions? Have new philosophies been introduced into state government? Have specific groups benefited or been disadvantaged? These and other questions can be addressed systematically through the analysis of data on appointments collected over time.

Finally, systematic examination of gubernatorial vetoes can provide insight into what a governor thinks must be prevented. Some scholars view the veto as an admission of failure on the part of the governor; yet an examination of vetoes categorized by policy area can provide information that complements what is developed from analyses of gubernatorial messages. An analysis of vetoes can fill out the picture of gubernatorial priorities and positions. And studying attempts to override vetoes offers another way to assess gubernatorial success and political strength.

A Framework for Studying
Gubernatorial Behavior

Most studies of gubernatorial behavior focus on success in achieving policy purposes, variously defined. How the governor develops and uses his or her political resources and how he or she shapes political strategies to achieve policy success within a particular environment are also of concern. These issues can be examined within the

Figure 2-1 A Model of Factors Affecting Gubernatorial
Policy Success

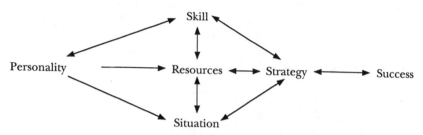

framework of a model of leadership that links policy success to the governor's role in bringing it about. The model is displayed in Figure 2-1. It includes personal, institutional, and environmental variables.

Gubernatorial performance in office is postulated as depending on five separate factors. First is the governor's personality, "the thumbprint"[3] of perception and inclination created as one adapts to the situations of his or her life. Several aspects of personality may be important in examining gubernatorial behavior. These include motivation, character, and cognitive and behavioral styles.

The second factor affecting a governor's performance is political skill. Gubernatorial achievements are dependent on more than intellectual and managerial prowess. A successful governor also possesses the skill and will to engage in the elemental activities of public life: "persuading, bargaining, battling, compromising, co-opting, committing, catering, arm twisting,"[4] and public rhetoric.[5] Experience in government helps one develop these skills[6] and assists one in confronting and dealing with the ambiguities, pressures, and uncertainties of the job.

Leadership success is also associated with a third variable: the nature of available political and personal resources. In the political arena a governor is dependent on party support within the legislature, public approval, and professional reputation.[7] At the personal level the resources are "time, attention and political influence."[8]

The fourth variable that affects gubernatorial performance is the nature of the situation he or she faces. To what extent are conditions favorable to the accomplishment of goals inherent in the particular situation facing a governor? To a large extent, leadership success is structured by the opportunities faced. Thus, one question to be asked about all governors is whether they made the most of their opportunities. Skill in specifying objectives, using political resources, and shaping political strategies must be examined against the backdrop of the existing "political time"[9] and the presence of governmental, political, and personal resources.

Finally, gubernatorial performance is affected by a fifth variable: the governor's design or strategy—that is, the specific means chosen to implement his or her expressed goals and intentions. Governors have their own ways of approaching the opportunities and problems of office, and each has a method of pursuing his or her purposes. "His way is bound to capitalize on what he is good at, to minimize what he is not good at, and to reflect on what he has learned from experience about what works and what does not work." [10]

I suggest that the interrelationship among these variables is the most important focus for scholars and that the skill with which the governor creates unity among them is the key to gubernatorial success. Gubernatorial performance cannot be explained solely by reference to any one of these factors. "A dynamic interaction is always at work. In the final analysis, effective ... leadership that achieves policy goals depends upon how the [governor's] agenda matches the political 'temper' of the times as well as on [gubernatorial] skill in making the most of historical opportunities and political resources." [11]

Politics and Personality

The belief that the personality of an elected official is related to his or her public performance is widely accepted in social science. A rather large body of research has been directed to identifying the important elements of executive personality and to relating these elements to the performance of individual presidents, governors, and other elected officials. Despite the methodological problems associated with this research, it can be useful in analyses of gubernatorial behavior. Indeed, in the absence of some attention to personal differences among governors, analyses of their performance are mechanistic, abstract, and unrealistic. Thus, attention to the topic is necessary. Following are three lines of research that may be useful in bringing attention to the subject.

Cognitive Style. Personality theorists have demonstrated systematic differences among individuals in the way that they assimilate and interpret information affecting their decisions and their view of the world. Some elected officials think in rigid, simplistic categories, conceive of the world in terms of polarized stereotypes, and display a conscious intolerance for ambiguity in their environment. Others display a capacity for "integrative complexity" in their thinking, a capacity that requires finely differentiated and fully integrated representations of an event or environment. These differences have been shown to have implications for a variety of political leaders, ranging from revolutionaries[12] to generals[13] to U.S. senators[14] and may contribute to an understanding of gubernatorial behavior.

The Paragraph Completion Test, the most widely accepted test for determining individual placement on the dimension of personality, has been adapted for use with documentary materials. Thus scholars interested in the relationship between personality and gubernatorial behavior can perform content analyses of gubernatorial speeches, interviews, and other methods of gubernatorial communication.

Gubernatorial Motivation. Common sense suggests that cognition alone cannot account for all executives' behavior; and personality theorists agree. Theorists believe that a motivating force must reside behind each decision and each activity. Leaders differ not only in the way they process information, but also in their fundamental drives; and such differences may have political manifestations and implications. The three drives widely considered to be of political relevance are power, achievement, and affiliation. Research has shown that leaders who score high on each of these motivations behave differently than those who score low.

Thus presidents who score high on the power motive may be more likely to involve the United States in a war,[15] expand U.S. territorial holdings,[16] and enjoy a good relationship with the press,[17] but are at a greater risk of an assassination attempt on their lives.[18] Presidents who score high on the achievement motive may be willing to sacrifice continuity and conviviality to get a job done,[19] and affiliation-driven presidents tend to be more flexible in dealing with issues.[20] However, those motivated by the last drive are also more likely to select advisers who make better friends than expert advisers.[21]

While motivation may be of great importance to gubernatorial leadership, the measurement problems associated with tapping this dimension have been substantial. Fortunately this problem has been mediated by the adaptation of the Thematic Apperception Test—a standard instrument for scoring motivational drives when used with the written materials of leaders.[22] Thus scholars of gubernatorial performance now have an opportunity to examine the extent to which motivation affects performance.

Gubernatorial Character. A third element of personality—character—has been widely touted as an important explanatory variable in the assessment of political leaders, especially American presidents. Character is the way a political leader orients himself toward life and can be arrayed along two dimensions. The first, psychological satisfaction from office, can range from positive to negative. The second, energy invested in the job, is anchored by activity and passivity. As articulated by James David Barber,[23] presidents who exhibit active-positive character traits are better candidates for success than are those with passive-negative traits.

At least one attempt has been made to apply Barber's schema to the study of gubernatorial behavior. In *Florida's Gubernatorial Politics in the Twentieth Century*,[24] David Colburn and Richard Scher place the twenty-one men who held the Florida governor's office from 1900 to 1986 into the categories identified earlier. The authors did not, however, go on to the next logical step and use the placement as an independent variable to explain gubernatorial behavior. Further, their effort illustrates pitfalls that are inherent in the methodology.

First, such analyses are rooted in the examination of childhood and early adult experiences and require substantial biographical data. Most governors, I suspect, have not been the subject of enough early biographical research to provide the data necessary to determine with any security their placement along the two dimensions described by Barber. (This did not, however, deter Colburn and Scher who had biographies or studies of only seven of the twenty-one governors they studied.) Second, the psychological interpretations required in such analysis, "stressing the ways interpersonal experiences shape the person's self-image," are fraught with subjectivity. In the absence of precise rules guiding such interpretations, different scholars are likely to differ on the placement of individual governors. Thus, while the concept of presidential (or gubernatorial) character continues to capture the imagination of some, its usefulness in explaining behavior has yet to be demonstrated.

Nevertheless, attention to the personalities of governors can help explain the larger picture of gubernatorial behavior and should be part of any analysis of gubernatorial performance.

Political Skill

A dominant theme in the literature of executive leadership has been that the potential and limitations of the executive are a function of his or her own behavior and particularly of his or her political skill.[25] Although this theme has been modified,[26] there is still agreement that the success attained by a president or governor will depend to some degree on that person's skill in the political arena. Thus, in analyzing the performance of individual governors, some attention must be directed to an assessment of the political skills they use in their efforts to achieve their goals.

Two problems emerge for researchers interested in relating political skill to gubernatorial success. The first is how to decide on what skills are required. The second is how to determine the extent to which a governor possesses those skills. Since more attention has been devoted to the first of these problems than to the second, some consensus has been achieved regarding the required skills. Although this consensus comes in the absence of supporting research, most scholars refer to one of two sets of skills when identifying those necessary for political success: the effective use of informal sources of power (persuasion, bargaining, and negotiation)[27] and, in an age of mass communication, positive presentation of self.[28] In the absence of an alternative list, these skills seem to have achieved some acceptability and should be examined in any analysis of gubernatorial performance.

Political Resources

There is an old saying in the South, "You can't make chicken salad out of chicken manure." This saying certainly seems relevant to executive leadership. Many scholars argue that success is directly related to the nature of the resources, or capital, available for addressing governmental problems. "Given low levels in [gubernatorial] capital, even the most positive and most active executive could make little impact." [29]

According to Paul Light, political resources come in two "packets": internal and external. The internal packet includes the resources of time, information, expertise, and energy. The external packet reflects the incumbent's political strength and includes party support in the legislature, public approval, electoral margin, and professional reputation.[30] Some of these resources, particularly the external ones, are quantifiable and quite easily brought to bear on an analysis of gubernatorial performance.

For example, some measures of party support in the legislature—the distribution of Democrats and Republicans—are easily collected and others—key votes, nonunanimous support—can be calculated from sources that exist for virtually all states. Electoral margins are also easily gotten, and data on public approval are increasingly available. It is essential to use these data when examining the performance of individual governors. Gubernatorial success starts with party, and party support is related in some degree to the nature of the governor's electoral margin. The size and loyalty of the governor's legislative coalition are major explanatory variables and contribute to a systematic explanation of gubernatorial behavior. Use of data measuring these variables in a ume series analysis of several governors will contribute to a theoretical understanding of the institution within a particular state.

The Context

The first scholars who attempted to explain the success of political executives focused on differences in character and skill. These analysts placed the executive at the center of attention and assumed that differences in their will or skill accounted for variations in success. Typical of this genre are Richard Neustadt's *Presidential Power*, Barbara Kellerman's *The Political Presidency*, and the work of a long line of organizational theorists who have used the "trait" approach.

While individual variations in the skills of leadership undoubtedly account for some of the differences in success, there are "bounds to what even the most skilled [governor] can accomplish under some circumstances—indeed under 'normal' circumstances." [31] All governors accept the mantle of leadership at a unique time and face a particular constellation of political and economic circumstances. These circumstances may be so complex and intractable that they defeat even the most capable governor. Thus, analysis of these circumstances is clearly important to an understanding of gubernatorial behavior and may result in a lowered standard of gubernatorial performance and less disappointment with "failures" of leadership.

Two elements of the environment in which governors operate are of particular importance to their performance. These are the general economic conditions of the state and the overall political situation. Variations in these factors can be identified fairly precisely.

State Economic Conditions. Gubernatorial priorities and strategies are constrained or enlarged by economic circumstances. Declining revenues and a stagnant economy often limit new initiatives and reduce service levels. Abundant economic resources may have opposite effects. Further, the nature of changes in these resources—their trend—is also important. An economy buoyed by optimistic predictions has a different effect on gubernatorial strategies than does an economy about which there are gloomy predictions.

Data describing variations in economic circumstances help establish precisely the nature of the situation within which an individual governor labors. Used in a time series, these data reduce the tendency to exaggerate or to downplay the importance of such circumstances.

The Political Environment. The nature of the political environment within which a governor operates can be described at two levels. Both can be measured fairly precisely. Analyses of gubernatorial behavior should be placed in their context.

At one level the political environment can be conceptualized as the distribution of partisanship and political ideology within a state and as a sequence of changes in the nature of the "political time" [32] during which the governor serves. At a more immediate level we can examine the distribution of political power within the legislature and the executive office, the extent of the governor's electoral mandate, her or his personal popularity and professional prestige, and the occurrence of short-term events that affect the nature of political opinion. Most such events are conceptualized as political resources and will, therefore, be treated later in this chapter.

The distribution of partisanship within a state's populace is a broad constraint on gubernatorial activity. While a specific distribution of Democrats and Republicans within the electorate may not be transferred into an analogous distribution within governmental institutions, a governor's actions are likely to be different if 65 percent of the population identifies with the Democrats than if 35 percent does. Public opinion polls that discern the distribution of partisanship within states are now widely available. Although the time series is short in some states, in others (such as Minnesota, Iowa, and California) such polls have been conducted since the 1940s. Analyses of gubernatorial behavior can be placed in the context of the existing distribution of partisanship and in the context of any changes that are occurring.

Gubernatorial behavior can also be placed in the context of a time series distribution of citizens along the liberal-conservative ideological dimension. This abstraction is the most widely used and accepted measure of political attitude. It focuses upon the "degree to which the government should assume interest, responsibility, and control over [various] sectors of endeavor." [33] The distribution of such attitudes has obvious implications for the behavior of governors. Like the measure of partisanship, the distribution of ideological predispositions within a state is usually available, and for some states a fairly long time series is available.

Explanations of gubernatorial behavior will also be enhanced by consideration of the "political time" during which the governor serves and by examination of the extent to which this time is changing. The political history of any state is characterized by periods of dominance by specific coalitions representing geographical regions, ideological predispositions, or political cultures. Stephen Skowronek labeled such periods political times; they exhibit a "distinctive set of institutional arrangements and approaches to public policy questions." [34] These arrangements and approaches affect mightily the nature of gubernatorial strategies and actions. Different political challenges face a governor at different political times, and the quality of gubernatorial performance may be related to the changing shape of the dominant political order. Therefore, some attempt must be made to characterize political times and to assess their implications for gubernatorial success.

Efforts to analyze the effect of political time on gubernatorial activity will take both quantitative and qualitative forms. The nature of the legislative environment at various points in time can be characterized by placement of the legislature along a quantitatively derived centralized-decentralized continuum. The measure is an index constructed by standardizing the sum of two standardized variables: the number of committees and subcommittees in the state legislature, and the percentage of state representatives and senators having served some specific number of years in these bodies.[35] Beyond this, attention can be focused on the personalities in positions of influence within both state government and state political parties, the interrelationships among political elites, and the ideological predispositions and policy preferences of these elites. The results of this latter analysis will be less precise than the quantitative analyses suggested earlier. But its contribution to an understanding of gubernatorial behavior will be as great.

One other element of the political environment is also important to an understanding of gubernatorial behavior and performance: the unexpected event that triggers a political reaction and attracts the public's attention. Research on the presidency reveals that six kinds of events are likely to engender such a reaction: threats to peace, domestic disruptions, political scandals, the conduct of diplomacy, policy initiatives, and incidents that focus on the personal and political health of the incumbent.[36] Systematic efforts to identify and relate such events to gubernatorial performance will enhance explanations of that performance.

Strategy

To achieve their goals "in the face of uncertainty, surprise, ambiguity, inadequate information, and centrifugal forces, public executives need a ... set of premises deliberately chosen to provide direction to their thinking, choices, and administrative behavior."[37] This set of premises is referred to as a strategy and is a major variable in the equation linking public executives to successful performance in office. Indeed, one observer of presidential performance argues that "if a president does not want to leave his legacy to chance or be merely a caretaker in office, he must take a self-conscious strategic approach to the presidency."[38]

All governors employ some form of strategy to guide their actions. The strategies can be defined by scope, character, and timeliness. One strategy assumes that the size of the governor's agenda is related to success and that "each extra proposal submitted reduces the probability of passage for every proposal."[39] A second strategy is based on the assumption that the governor is more effective at some points in his term than at other points.[40] A third posits a direct causal link between the substantive nature of policy proposals and the response they generate. An empirical measure of the size of the governor's agenda can be calculated by a simple count of the measures proposed in the messages given by the governor. The time at which proposals are introduced by governors can be divided into categories such as honeymoon/first year, midterm election year, post-midterm election year, and gubernatorial election year. The type of policy represented by the governor's initiatives can be categorized by distributive, regulatory, redistributive, and constituent policies using the procedures in the work of Robert Spitzer.[41]

Use of these, or other, conceptualizations of gubernatorial strategy will permit the examination of the contribution of strategy to gubernatorial success.

Conclusion

This chapter advances two unremarkable propositions: that the understanding of gubernatorial behavior will be improved by the integration of several perspectives and that the conclusions drawn from such analyses will be made more meaningful if they are based on systematic and empirical time series data. It suggests a framework for use in combining five variables that are often employed separately into an explanation of gubernatorial performance. The scholarship on this topic should focus on the interaction among these five variables; gubernatorial performance cannot be adequately assessed in the absence of attention to each.

Notes

1. Gary King and Lynn Ragsdale, *The Elusive Executive* (Washington, D.C.: CQ Press, 1988), 4.
2. Bert Rockman, "The Leadership Style of George Bush," in *The Bush Presidency,* ed. Colin Campbell and Bert Rockman (Chatham, N.J.: Chatham House, 1991), 156.
3. David Keirsey and Marilyn Bates, *Please Understand Me* (Del Mar, Calif.: Prometheus Nemesis Books, 1978), 27.
4. Barbara Kellerman, *The Political Presidency* (New York: Oxford University Press, 1984), xi.
5. Jeffrey Tulis, *The Rhetorical Presidency* (Princeton, N.J.: Princeton University Press, 1987).
6. Richard Neustadt, *Presidential Power* (New York: Wiley, 1964).
7. Paul Light, *The President's Agenda* (Baltimore: Johns Hopkins University Press, 1982).
8. Laurence Lynn, *Managing Public Policy* (Boston: Little, Brown, 1987), 39.
9. Stephen Skowronek, "Presidential Leadership in Political Time," in *The Presidency and the Political System,* ed. Michael Nelson (Washington, D.C.: CQ Press, 1984).

10. James Young, Foreword to Erwin Hargrove, *Jimmy Carter as President* (Baton Rouge: Louisiana State University Press, 1988), xiii.
11. Hargrove, *Jimmy Carter,* xxiv.
12. P. Suedfield and A. D. Rank, "Revolutionary Leaders: Long-Term Success as a Function of Change in Conceptual Complexity," *Journal of Personality and Social Psychology* 34 (1976).
13. P. Suedfield, R. Corteen, and C. McCormick, "The Role of Integrative Complexity in Military Leadership," *Journal of Applied Social Psychology* 16 (1986).
14. P. E. Tetlock, "Personality and Isolationism, *Journal of Personality and Social Psychology* 41 (1981).
15. D. G. Winter, *The Power Motive* (New York: Free Press, 1973); and Winter, "Leader Appeal, Leader Performance and the Motive Profile of Leaders and Followers," *Journal of Personality and Social Psychology* 52 (1987).
16. Ibid, *The Power Motive.*
17. H. W. Wendt and P. C. Light, "Measuring Greatness in American Presidents," *European Journal of Social Psychology* 6 (1976).
18. Ibid; Winter, *The Power Motive.*
19. D. G. Winter and A. J. Stewart, "Content Analysis as a Technique for Assessing Political Leaders," in *The Psychological Examination of Political Leaders,* ed. M. G. Hermann (New York: Free Press, 1977).
20. Ibid.
21. Ibid.
22. Richard Donley and David Winter, "Measuring the Motives of Public Officials at a Distance: An Exploratory Study of American Presidents," *Behavioral Science* 15 (1970): 227-236.
23. James David Barber, *The Presidential Character* (Englewood Cliffs, N.J.: Prentice-Hall, 1977).
24. David Colburn and Richard Scher, *Florida's Gubernatorial Politics in the Twentieth Century* (Tallahassee, Fla.: University Presses of Florida, 1980).
25. Neustadt, *Presidential Power*; Kellerman, *Political Presidency.*
26. George Edwards, *Presidential Influence in Congress* (San Francisco: W. H. Freeman, 1980); George Edwards, *At the Margins* (New Haven: Yale University Press, 1989); Lynn, *Managing Public Policy*; Hargrove, *Jimmy Carter.*
27. Neustadt, *Presidential Power*; Kellerman, *Political Presidency.*
28. Samuel Kernell, *Going Public* (Washington, D.C.: CQ Press, 1986); Tulis, *Rhetorical Presidency.*
29. Tulis, *Rhetorical Presidency.*
30. Light, *The President's Agenda,* 34.
31. Tulis, *Rhetorical Presidency,* 146.
32. Skowronek, "Presidential Leadership."
33. Angus Campbell, Phillip Converse, Warren Miller, and Donald Stokes, *The American Voter* (New York: Wiley, 1960), 194.

34. Skowronek, *Presidential Leadership*.
35. Mark Peterson, *Legislating Together* (Cambridge, Mass.: Harvard University Press, 1990), 316.
36. Charles Ostrom and Dennis Simon, "Promise and Performance: A Dynamic Model of Presidential Popularity," *American Political Science Review* 79 (June 1985).
37. Lynn, *Managing Public Policy*, 130-131.
38. James Pfiffner, *The Strategic Presidency* (Chicago: Dorsey, 1988), 156.
39. Richard Forshee and Russell Renka, "The Price of Ambition: Presidents, Agenda Size and Legislative Success," 8 (paper presented at the annual meeting of the American Political Science Association, Washington, D.C., 1991).
40. Neustadt, *Presidential Power*.
41. Robert Spitzer, "Presidential Policy Determinism: How Policies Frame Congressional Response to the President's Legislative Program," *Presidential Studies Quarterly* 13 (Fall 1983).

3. ARIZONA: THE CEO APPROACH OF J. FIFE SYMINGTON III

Ruth S. Jones and Katheryn A. Lehman

John Fife Symington III was elected governor of Arizona on February 26, 1991. To an outsider, the governor's patrician-sounding name might seem out of sync with the popular image of heroes of the rough-and-tumble western frontier. Yet, in a state where George Herbert Walker Bush III is exceptionally popular and where individualism and free enterprise are as sacred as flag and country, Symington is right at home.

Fife Symington is one of the new breed of governors. He is young (born in 1945), earned a B.A. in liberal arts from Harvard in 1968, and served four years as a lieutenant in the U.S. Air Force. He is a businessman, not a lawyer, and his experiences are those of the private, not the public, sector. He had held no elected public office, nor had he served in any state or local governmental agency, prior to running for governor. Hence, he was an entrepreneurial businessman launching a new career when he took office on March 6, 1991, as the nineteenth governor of Arizona.

Symington began his Arizona entrepreneurial activities with a brief partnership in a development company and swiftly rose to chairman of the board of the Symington Company, his own commercial and industrial development enterprise. At the time of the gubernatorial campaign, his personal assets were estimated to be at least $12 million.[1] His campaign capitalized on his successful business career; one of his primary campaign themes was that he would bring the skills and know-how of private sector success to government.

During his twenty-year residency in Arizona, Symington engaged in the usual range of community activities for a young businessman on the rise—arts councils, charitable foundations, hospital boards, and civic commissions. He also served as a member of the board of directors for two financial institutions, a health care facility, and several community associations.

The Symington family name is well known in political circles outside Arizona (the Democratic branch in Missouri and the governor's family in Maryland). However, Fife Symington's involvement with the

Arizona Republican party, primarily in the area of fund raising, has been relatively recent and brief. Still, he is not without strong ties to the state's Republican establishment. He is married to Ann Pritzlaff Symington, the daughter of a former Republican member of the Arizona House of Representatives and state Senate and former U.S. ambassador to Malta. Symington's success as a local real estate developer, experience as a party fund raiser, and access to established party leaders proved to be a powerful combination during his campaign.

The State Context

It is not surprising that the voters of the state were attracted to Fife Symington and his message of bringing business leadership and management to government. After boom years early in the decade, the Arizona economy leveled off during the second half of the 1980s. Despite optimistic predictions about the inevitability of renewed growth in this dynamic sun belt area, state revenues continued to fall short of even conservative predictions, state budgets have been repeatedly cut, and services have generally been kept at an unchanged level.

Arizona's problems go beyond those generally associated with the country's economic downturn. The state ranks thirty-fifth in annual income per capita and is in the top one-third in terms of state and local revenue. Arizona's population grew by 35 percent during the 1980s. Although ethnic minority groups comprise 29 percent of the state's total population, they account for 39 percent of the change in population during the last decade. Moreover, 40 percent of children under five years of age are members of minority communities.[2]

The state has experienced both the positive and the negative consequences of rapid growth. Throughout much of the 1980s, high-tech industries brought to Arizona a disproportionate share of well-educated professionals, especially engineers. And Arizona continues to rank above the national average in job growth, which in turn attracts new residents. However, job growth has not led to absolute economic prosperity. From 1987 through 1990, while jobs were growing at about 2.5 percent, the state ranked fiftieth in per capita personal income growth! The state has failed in its last three major efforts to attract up-scale industry, and the boom trend of attracting high-tech development has given way to growth in low-wage industries. For Arizonans steeped in the lore of growth and development, times are frustratingly difficult.

The problems accompanying rapid population growth are visible in every sector of society. Crime rates, environmental pollution, drug use, and gang activity continue to increase while the state languishes in the bottom one-fourth on such measures as average expenditure per pupil, prenatal health care services, and high school graduation rates.

Prodded by a court order to increase services for the chronically mentally ill, the state recently moved from last place to a tie for thirty-eighth. But the increase in funding for mental health came at the expense of other, equally pressing, social services.

In sum, the economic woes of the state are not unique. However, because of such rapid and sizable population growth, demands for services have outdistanced the ability, the willingness, and the capacity of the state to respond. The new governor faces the task of leading a state where per capita personal income is declining and the caseloads of social workers are growing. The negative impact on the state budget is obvious, and the governor will be sorely challenged to reverse the trend.

The Electoral Context

Although managing the state's economic growth will be central to the success or failure of Symington as governor, the politics of the state cannot be ignored. Nowhere is this more obvious than in the electoral context within which the 1990 campaign was waged.

Arizona politics was anything but usual at the end of the 1980s and the beginning of the 1990s. The 1986 election was the first election in nearly two decades in which there was no incumbent candidate (elected or elevated through vacancies). Evan Mecham, who had scored a stunning upset in the Republican primary, was elected with slightly less than 40 percent of the vote in the general election. After two years in office, Mecham was impeached and the Arizona secretary of state, Rose Mofford, became governor according to the constitutional provisions for succession. Although Mofford had almost fifty years of experience in Arizona government, she was unable to establish herself as the state's political leader. In January 1990, she announced she would not be a gubernatorial candidate.

Because the Republicans viewed Mofford as vulnerable, a field of primary candidates had emerged early. The Democratic heir apparent was generally considered to be the young political veteran and mayor of Phoenix, Terry Goddard. Forty-one percent of the state's registered voters turned out for the primary, and Goddard received 84 percent of the Democratic vote. From the field of five candidates, Symington won the Republican primary with 44 percent of the vote (Evan Mecham was runner-up with 24 percent).[3] Symington had positioned himself in the political mainstream while his opponents generally represented the conservative wing of the Republican party.

When the general election campaign began, the odds were in favor of the well-known Goddard over the newcomer Symington. Both candidates presented strong action plans and they differed sharply on few issues. They did differ, however, on a ballot issue initiative which called for state spending on education to increase $100 per child per year for ten years. Goddard supported the increase; Symington opposed it. Backed by a coalition of prominent members of the educational and business communities, the initiative enjoyed overwhelming support among potential voters until the last weeks of the campaign. Then, a group opposed to "throwing money at the problem" organized an effective drive against the increase. Quickly, the school issue became a symbol of the differences between the gubernatorial candidates: Goddard was pictured as the tax-and-spend liberal and Symington as the spokesman for fiscal restraint.

Vying for the attention of the electorate throughout the campaign was the continuing saga of the Keating Five, particularly Sen. Dennis DeConcini and Sen. John McCain, as well as Charles Keating himself. The state was blanketed with coverage of the financial insolvency and junk-bond dealings of Keating's California-based Lincoln Savings and Loan and the collapse of his vast development empire which was rooted in the Arizona-based parent company, American Continental.[4] During the campaign, both Arizona senators were the focus of publicity for allegedly inappropriate, if not illegal, efforts to intercede with federal regulators on Keating's behalf. Although the impact of this intrigue on the campaign can never be determined, the continual local media coverage served as a reminder that candidates, officials, and campaigns may not always be what they seem.

On election day, with 59 percent of registered voters voting, the school initiative was soundly defeated and Symington, who had been behind in the polls almost the entire campaign, pulled off a tremendous upset by edging out Goddard, 49.6 percent to 49.2 percent (a 4,293 vote difference). Seven write-in candidates collectively received 1.1 percent of the votes, the majority (1.0%) of which were received by the Stop Abortion party candidate (a Mecham Republican loyalist). Under a new law passed in the aftermath of the impeachment of plurality-elected Governor Mecham, a runoff election was required.

The Runoff

The pundits had a field day trying to explain the election's outcome. One obvious theme was that the disgruntled Mecham supporters had thwarted Symington's majority by supporting the write-in candidates. Another explanation was that Goddard, seeing his lead erode, became more negative. He charged, for example, that many of Symington's real estate "successes" were in deep trouble and questioned his "management expertise." He also attacked Symington's failure to disclose his taxes and his assets, suggesting that he had something to hide. However, Goddard could not make headway with these attacks; in fact, one view is that they backfired because they were out of keeping with Goddard's heretofore squeaky clean image.[5] Other explanations focused on the differences in campaign spending, increased Republican voter registration, higher Republican turnout, and strong opposition among Republicans to the unsuccessful Martin Luther King, Jr., holiday ballot propositions.

In its haste to ensure against another plurality-elected governor, the legislature enacted (and voters approved) a runoff, but it failed to address any of the practical issues involved with implementing the runoff election. Thus, rules for the runoff were unclear and it took several weeks before a date (February 26) could be set and procedures established. In the meantime, Symington called for a moratorium on campaigning over the holidays and left for a California vacation. Goddard, who took no PAC money, had been outspent $2.3 to $1.3 million.[6] Since he was unable to match the deep pockets of Symington and his family, Goddard spent the month of December scurrying for money. Whereas the general campaign had been rather ho-hum up to the last few weeks, the runoff campaign began where the mud slinging had left off and got progressively dirtier. *Political Hotline* called it a race "too crass to call" and *USA Today* referred to it as "the campaign from hell." [7] Goddard, behind in the polls and underfunded (he raised only $500,000 for the runoff), became particularly shrill. Symington added another $1.1 million to his campaign outlays and countered with a hard-hitting, sophisticated negative media campaign.[8]

After all this, only half of the registered voters participated in the runoff election. Symington again was victorious, this time with a 44,000 vote margin and 52.4 percent of the vote.

But the politically weary electorate could not yet escape uninspiring state politics. On February 5, three weeks before the election, a sting operation, to become known as "Az Scam," resulted in the indictments of seven legislators and numerous party leaders, consultants, and lobbyists. Viewers of the evening news were bombarded by video clips of legislators counting their bribes, making deals, and stuffing money in gym bags. Then came the long, drawn out series of events involving legislative resignations and replacements, plea bargains, public apologies, sentencing, and, for some, incarceration. With the legislature in turmoil, if not immobilized, and the executive branch in transition, state politics was in total disarray. Certainly, the time was ripe for a new, take-charge executive.

From CEO to Governor

During the interim between the general election and the runoff, Symington began identifying potential staff members and set them to work preparing for the transition and a fast start after the inauguration on March 6. His inaugural speech was short and direct. He pledged "to restore confidence in the fairness and competence of state government." He called Arizona a state of opportunity where "industry and talent can make their mark," and he set the theme for his administration: "Our goal will be to improve the delivery of services and increase the dollars that actually serve people by streamlining government." [9]

Once in office, Symington quickly announced the names of the core of his staff, most of whom were former campaign workers, business associates, or former legislators. In general the team was young but experienced in diverse political arenas within the state. In later high-level appointments and in naming members to more than two hundred state agencies, boards, and commissions, Symington drew most heavily on former business contacts and experts, often non-Arizonans, who were expected to streamline government agencies. With a few notable exceptions, his appointments met little opposition.

One new twist the governor put on the appointment process was the development of a comprehensive database, which would include the more than nine hundred job applications he had received. He urged all administrators seeking to fill civil-service-exempt positions to use the database. In the governor's view, this was a rational process for making quick, efficient appointments; several administrators viewed it as a form of intrusion.[10]

The Legislative Branch

A late-arriving governor might have been at a severe disadvantage with a strong legislature that had already developed a full head of steam and was rolling toward enacting its own legislative agenda. However, Az Scam had taken a toll on the legislature, not only in terms of personal energies and damaged reputations, but institutionally as well. Six of the indicted legislators resigned their positions; the seventh had to be formally removed from office by her legislative colleagues. Not only did replacements have to be appointed, but several scandal-tainted members had been committee chairs or co-chairs, and the legislative leadership had to be restructured.

To compound the problem, the leadership of the legislature was relatively new. The 1988 election had swept several seasoned veterans from office and produced an unusually large crop of new legislators, many of whom represented the Mecham faction of the Republican party. The 1990 election produced a divided government. The House Republicans maintained a majority (by one seat), but the Democrats won a four-seat majority in the Senate. This was only the fourth time in state history that the two houses had been held by separate parties.

With ten new faces in the thirty-member Senate and the GOP Senate caucus left with only seven incumbents, and with a fragmented Republican party holding a precarious majority in the House, legislative politics was in disarray.

By the time Symington took office in March, legislative regulations on the introduction of bills made it impossible for the governor to start on his own legislative agenda. However, he took an aggressive role in shaping the bills already before the legislature. For example, after months of unsuccessful efforts by the legislature and former governor, Symington negotiated the buyout of a poorly conceived state contract for the private construction and ownership of a hazardous waste disposal plant. The press hailed the buyout as a solid double, but not a home run for the governor. It solved a very thorny issue *and* advanced his efforts to privatize components of state government. The buyout involved a $44 million payment to be financed by the sale of two state prison facilities. The facilities would then be leased back over twenty years at an estimated cost of $100 million. Many legislators viewed this creative financing as crazy financing and remain opposed to such long-term leasing arrangements.[11]

The governor also was centrally involved in the budget process. Although Mofford had submitted a governor's budget in January, Symington worked with his party leaders to reshape the House budget proposal to reflect his own priorities. Senate Democrats proposed their own budget, which called for larger overall expenditures in such areas as education, health services, courts, and universities. Within a slightly lower total request, the House/governor's budget sought larger expenditures for corrections, the Arizona Health Care Cost Containment System, commerce, and tourism. In the final days of budget negotiations, the governor's insistence on a $72 million carry-forward remained controversial; the Democrats proposed $25 million. Ultimately the budget resolution was passed without a major revenue increase (service fee increases were the method of choice) and with a $51 million carry-forward. The governor signaled early that he would take a major role in establishing the state budget, and he did.

However, the governor encountered some rough waters as he navigated his way through the first legislative session. Symington used his veto power generously: nine times. Some blamed his political inexperience for the fact that he vetoed Republican bills without informing the Republican leadership of his intentions. Others viewed it as simply typical CEO behavior that did not distinguish between the norms of the private and the public sectors. In one, independent managerial decision making is an asset; in the other, it creates ill-will and political debt. Similar insensitivity to relationships between such agencies as the Corporation Commission and the Real Estate Commission prompted one political reporter to write, "I see signs of the closed, arrogant, chief executive officer mentality in his methods." [12]

Similarly, in the waning hours of the session, Symington insisted that his nominee for director of administration be considered. The governor was warned repeatedly that the Democratic Senate would not vote to confirm because the Democrats wanted to carry the nomination over as leverage against his threat to use the line-item veto against certain Democratic measures. However, the governor forced the issue, the vote was taken, and the Senate denied confirmation.[13]

The governor also irritated Republicans and Democrats alike with such actions as ordering gold-embossed napkins, spending $2 million to replace the executive aircraft, and almost depleting the entire state computer account (earmarked for upgrading existing systems throughout state government). To many, these are examples of an attitude that conveys: "Do as I say, not as I do." The computer purchases were doubly vexing. Not only did the governor use the state account rather than the governor's account to bring high-tech communication systems to his top-level agency people, but he also purchased Apple computers when the state is pledged to an IBM environment. The fact that the purchases were made during the time Arizona was trying to woo Apple to move part of its operation to the state may not have been coincidental. Poor politics, but good business.[14]

Assessments of Symington's first foray into the legislative process were mixed, but the positive outweighed the negative. One senator who wished to remain anonymous initially characterized Symington's leadership style as "my way or no way," but acknowledged that the governor learned during the process and was accessible and willing to listen. Another characterized him as a well-briefed chief executive and a tough bargainer who occasionally got too involved or involved too soon. As for Symington, he confessed "the most difficult part [of] this session was personal relations." [15]

His second session may be even more difficult. The governor must cope with a strong "no new taxes" faction within his own party while trying to stretch state revenues to meet the ever increasing needs of a rapidly growing population. He has done his homework. For example, he has identified numerous revolving fund accounts in state agencies that he feels could be more efficiently managed if brought into the regular budget process. However, this is certain to provoke a turf fight and will sorely test the governor's ability to maneuver in dangerous waters.

The legislature, reacting in large part to Az Scam, created a task force on election reform, its primary focus being campaign finance. The

governor has definite ideas about changes in campaign finance regulation, and they do not necessarily parallel those of reform-minded
legislators. The governor expressed hope that the election law task force
would follow basic principles based on the fundamental premise that
"money does not buy elections; instead it is the necessary tool by which
candidates deliver their messages to the voters." [16] This is the same
well-financed candidate-turned-governor who balked at disclosure
during the campaign: "I continue to say that whether you are a public
or a private citizen, how much money you're worth or your tax returns
are really your personal business." [17] As a candidate with close ties to
the business community and whose wife and mother loaned him $1.3
million during the campaign, Symington's credibility in matters of
campaign finance reform may be suspect. If the governor refuses to call
the special session the legislature is expecting, campaign finance reform
is certain to be high on the legislative agenda in January.

Executive Initiatives

Other substantive policy issues will arise from the governor's
initiatives. Early on, the governor created a nonpartisan task force on
State Long-Term Improved Management ("Project SLIM") to bring
total quality management to state government. Describing the program
as "a crucial element of Arizona's management revolution," the
governor acknowledged that promoting a new way of thinking in state
government would not be easy but said "it *will* happen." He argued,
"Economic conditions and widespread frustration with tax increases
and runaway spending *demand* it be done." [18] Project SLIM is the
most visible example of the impact of Symington the CEO on
Symington the governor. And the governor is expected to use the
recommendations of the task force to further his agenda of streamlining
government.

Similarly, Symington appointed a task force on education that was
charged with studying the full range of K-12 issues, from open
enrollment to school funding. The governor is on record advocating the
creation of a market-driven education system as "the most basic,
axiomatic thing" Arizona can do to improve its schools.[19] However, any
task force recommendation on school funding that involves property
taxes is sure to be controversial. The same is true for recommendations
for open enrollment and for permitting public money to go to private
schools if, in return, private schools adopt public school standards.

Finally, many of the governor's hopes for economic development
depend on more trade ties with Mexico and Japan. During the 1991
session, Symington got emergency authority to spend $100,000 to open
a trade office in Mexico City, and he has plans for a trade office in

Japan. However, these programs are necessarily long-term invest-
ments, not quick fixes. The test will be whether the short-term outlay
to develop external interest and markets can be sustained during times
of fiscal austerity. The governor may be taking a page from President
Bush. If his "foreign" policy for economic development shows some
successes by 1994, "domestic" issues may become secondary in the
minds of the electorate.

Clouds on the Horizon

Six months into his governorship, an internal memo of the
Resolution Trust Corporation (RTC) that focused on Symington, the
businessman, became public. The leaked memo alleged that in 1983
Symington, as a director of Southwest Savings and Loan, had influenced the thrift's board to invest $40 million in one of his development
projects. Moreover, the RTC memo pointed out that Symington
personally invested only $432 in the project but earned more than $8
million in development fees. Arguing that Symington engaged in
"blatant self-dealing" and spent Southwest funds with "reckless abandon," the memo urged that Symington be sued to recover millions of
dollars.[20] Rumors of a congressional inquiry continued to circulate.
Within the same month, businessman Symington was forced to
renegotiate financing on four development enterprises or risk losing
them; several already were delinquent in payments. By the end of the
month, the Symington Company was removed as manager of one of the
partnership properties, which subsequently was destined for a trust
sale.

The governor and his supporters immediately set out on a
program of damage control, charging that the leak was politically
motivated and designed to discredit Symington. In an effort to set the
record straight, the governor quickly and repeatedly pointed out that
(1) after serving on the thrift's board for twelve years, he resigned in
1984, five years before the thrift went under; (2) he did not actually
vote in the board's decision to enter into a direct equity arrangement
with the Symington Company; (3) the fees he received for development
activities were commensurate with industry norms; (4) the property
that was the focus of the RTC memo remains a viable investment; (5)
and finally, by the late 1980s the bottom had fallen out of the Arizona
real estate market, forcing all but one thrift into insolvency and creating
difficult times for all major real estate developers. In short, his forceful
argument was that he had acted legally and in good faith and that his
"troubles" were the result of the depressed economy generally and the
collapsed real estate market more particularly, not illegal, improper, or
poor business management.

The situation was not the most favorable for a governor who campaigned on a slogan promising to run state government as he ran his own business and pledging to adopt new ethical standards for his administration. The business community worries that if the "economic development" governor's effectiveness is called into question, new investors, site locators, and business prospects might look less favorably on the state.

Certainly, the situation placed Symington at personal risk. For example, he personally guaranteed the $9.2 million construction loan on the RTC-targeted property. Symington wrote in an *Arizona Republic* article, "My entire net worth is at risk in the project." [21] There was less certainty about his political vulnerability. The publicity and the threats of a congressional inquiry and possible lawsuit over his personal business dealings were less than welcome. Arizonans are more likely to recall that a $432 investment yielded an $8 million profit than that the direct equity investment by Southwest Savings and Loan in the Symington Development Corp. was typical of joint ventures during the boom days of the 1980s.

Adding fuel to the fire, reporters began to draw parallels between the Symington and Mecham administrations. In October, the governor created two highly charged controversies with shoot-from-the-hip pronouncements from which he quickly had to distance himself. One involved the unwarranted suspension of two top officials in the Department of Public Safety, and the other called for abolishing a constitutionally established higher education agency, the Arizona Board of Regents. Adding to these fiscal and political woes, a newspaper story about the possibility of a personal relationship between Symington and a former campaign worker suggested more potential headaches. She was appointed to a $60,000-a-year position for which she had no background and in which her competency has been seriously challenged. Hence, questions about the governor's personal and professional judgment have been raised.

Damage to Symington's long-range success remains a possibility. However, this is the same state electorate that within a five-year period lived through the recall movement and impeachment of a governor and then, at the next election, cast almost a quarter of the Republican primary votes for the same man; made up the electoral base for two of the "Keating Five" senators (DeConcini and McCain); recognized Charles Keating as a local community leader; voted down two ballot initiatives for a Martin Luther King, Jr., holiday; endured the state's first runoff campaign for governor, which was both tedious and dirty; and was entertained or repulsed by nightly TV stories about AZ Scam, bribe taking, and malfeasance within the legislature.

The Future

J. Fife Symington III faces many of the same problems as other governors of the 1990s. He has pledged to promote efficient, private-sector-style management techniques and to resist efforts to raise taxes while retaining an acceptable level of governmental services. The Arizona economy does not seem destined to rebound as more optimistic forecasters had predicted. Arizona is a relatively young state and the rapid pace of scandal and change in state government has left both the electorate and the elected reeling. It is difficult to predict political or economic conditions for any state, but Arizona in the early 1990s seems particularly volatile.

The new year began poorly for Symington. In January 1992 he traveled to Washington to present his side of the RTC story and quell the negative publicity associated with his personal business difficulties. In January the governor also announced salary increases totaling more than $70,000 for his top staff members. But in response to widespread criticism, Symington quickly announced that he was rescinding most of the raises, despite initial attempts to justify the increases. Then, less than three weeks later, the governor announced that eight staff positions in his fifty person office had been cut, and that the remaining staff would be furloughed for twelve days before July 1. And, an 11.2 percent pay cut for remaining staff was an attempt to address an estimated $250,000 in cost overruns in the governor's office.[22] Finally, on January 31, the governor filed his financial disclosure report, and the next day the press reported the apparent omissions of loans and corporate associations.[23] Symington's activities during January did not enhance his image as a decisive, efficient manager but led many to wonder about his campaign pledge to run state government like a business.

The future may hinge on how easily Symington can transfer experiences and successes back and forth between his two primary environments: the CEO's management-oriented board room and the elected official's political back room. He will need all his management skills and business know-how and the support of his network of leaders within the economic community if the state is to recapture the boom days of the 1980s. Yet his relationships with the legislature as well as with factions of his own party and with independent agencies and local governments call for strategic politics, including negotiation and com-promise in the partisan trenches. In this setting, "capital" is not monetary gain measured by profit and loss; it is the demonstrated ability to sustain an effective set of coalitions within the norms of a highly partisan political system.

After less than a year in the governor's office, Symington has set several key ventures (SLIM, school reform) into motion, and the public is waiting to see results. His relationships with the legislature improved during his first foray into the policy-making arena, and both sides learned from and about each other. But the legislative agenda contains a host of problems for which there is no consensus about solutions—a daunting challenge for even the most experienced of politicians.

The clouds on his personal horizon threaten to darken Symington's image as a successful business leader.[24] In the event that the new governor's greatest political strength—his image as a successful businessman opposed to traditional politics—begins to tarnish, his salvation may depend on how quickly and fully he embraces the tenets of old-style governmental leadership and partisan politics.

Barring another political scandal, however, Governor Symington can be expected to continue his efforts to reduce state government spending, eliminate "needless" government regulation, increase reliance on private industry, and encourage economic growth. His successes or his failures may be attributed to the techniques he brought from the board room or the lessons he learns in the partisan, legislative caucus rooms. The state desperately needs strong leadership that will provide a measure of stability and restore faith and confidence in state government. Rank-and-file citizens, like most stockholders, are more interested in *what* he does than how he does it. And in that respect, Symington, the CEO, is right at home.

Notes

1. Susan Schmidt, "Symington 'Smeared' by Leak of S&L Memo," *Arizona Republic,* September 13, 1991, A1, A6.
2. Phyllis Gillespie, "Ranking Arizona," *Arizona Republic,* July 21, 1991, A18; and *Insight,* Arizona State University, Center for Business Research, August 1991.
3. All election statistics are from *The Official Canvass,* published by the office of the Arizona secretary of state.
4. Sam Stanton, "McCain Circling His Wagons," *Arizona Republic,* October 3, 1990, A2; and Sam Stanton, "Letter Puts Light on Keating Case," *Arizona Republic,* October 5, 1990, A11.
5. "Gloves Likely to Come Off in Runoff," *Arizona Republic,* November 11, 1990, A1; and J. Brian Smith, "Fighting Fire with Fire," *Campaigns and Elections* 12 (May 1991): 48.
6. Mary Jo Pitzl, "Symington Seeking to Slow Campaign," *Arizona Republic,* November 20, 1990, B1; and campaign contribution and expenditure reports filed in the office of the Arizona secretary of state.

7. Smith, "Fighting Fire," 48.
8. "Democrats Hammer Symington as Polls Show Goddard Closing," *Arizona Capitol Times,* February 13, 1991, 3.
9. From the inaugural address of Governor Symington, March 6, 1991.
10. "Governor Asks for More Input in Filling Patronage Positions," *Arizona Capitol Times,* July 24, 1991, 9; and "1,000 Candidates Swim in Job Pool," *Arizona Republic,* July 20, 1991, B7.
11. Pat Flannery, "Symington Collects Many Hits in Rookie Season as Governor," *Phoenix Gazette,* June 24, 1991, A1, A6; and "Symington Cuts ENSCO Knot; State's on Its Own Again," *Arizona Capitol Times,* May 8, 1991, 1.
12. Francie Noyes, "Public Official Symington Still Acts Like Business Executive," *Scottsdale Progress,* October 9, 1991.
13. Pat Flannery, Randy Kiell, and Mike McCloy, "Appointee Is Victim in Budget Vote," *Phoenix Gazette,* A1, A14.
14. "DPS Plane—Plans Disclosure Burns Dems, Symington Too," *Arizona Capitol Times,* May 22, 1991, 16; and Flannery, "Symington Collects Many Hits," A6; and Mary Jo Pitzl, "Computer Buy by Administration Called End Run," *Arizona Republic,* October 3, 1991, B1.
15. Flannery, "Symington Collects Many Hits," A6.
16. "Committee Outlines Election-Law Blitz," *Arizona Capitol Times,* July 24, 1991, 11.
17. "Symington Takes Bi-Partisan Tack at First 9th Floor Press Confab," *Arizona Capitol Times,* March 6, 1991, 3.
18. "The First Hundred Days of the Symington Administration," office of the governor of Arizona, June 1991.
19. "School Choice Progresses," *Arizona Republic,* September 8, 1991, C4.
20. "The Esplanade: A Whodunit," *Arizona Republic,* October 6, 1991, A18; and Susan Schmidt, "Symington Suit Urged," *Arizona Republic,* September 13, 1991, A6.
21. Fife Symington, "Governor Details His Esplanade Role," *Arizona Republic,* September 29, 1991, C1, C3.
22. Mike Phillips, "Governor's Staff Cut; Survivors Get Furlough," *Scottsdale Progress,* January 29, 1992, 6.
23. Mary Jo Pitzl, "Governor 'Creative' in Report," *Arizona Republic,* February 1, 1992, B1.
24. Kim Sue Lia Perkes, "Approval Rating of Governor Sliding," *Arizona Republic,* January 23, 1992, A1, A4.

4. CALIFORNIA: PETE WILSON, A CENTRIST IN TROUBLE

Richard W. Gable

Five months after becoming governor of California Pete Wilson joked about the deficit Gov. George Deukmejian left him. In his imagination he called his predecessor and asked, "Duke, is there perhaps something you forgot to tell me?" "I didn't forget," Deukmejian replied in this fantasy conversation. "Actually, I've never liked you, Wilson."

Wilson inherited from a governor of his own party a shortfall which quickly mounted to almost 25 percent of the general fund budget—a $14.3 billion deficit. Remarkably, his victory was the first in-party succession since 1930, even though Republicans held fourteen of the seventeen governorships in this century. During those sixty years one Republican governor died in office and was succeeded by his lieutenant governor, who was elected in his own right. Earl Warren was elected three times; when he resigned to sit on the U.S. Supreme Court, he also was succeeded by his lieutenant governor, who was then elected in his own right. Thereafter, the governorship alternated parties with Democrat Pat Brown, Republican Ronald Reagan, Pat's son, Jerry Brown, and George Deukmejian, who left Wilson the greatest fiscal crisis in California's history.

Previously, when Deukmejian succeeded Jerry Brown in 1983, he too inherited a projected deficit, but it amounted to only $1.5 billion (less than 7 percent of the budget). Brown was running for the U.S. Senate when he left office and did not want to call for a tax increase in his last budget. Ironically, his opponent in that Senate race accused him of hiding the deficit by "papering over holes in the budget." That opponent was Pete Wilson, who proceeded to support a tax increase of $7 billion to balance the budget during his first year as governor.

The deficit was only one of many problems Wilson faced when he assumed office. There were also the recession and unemployment; the effects of a five-year drought, a major earthquake, and a disastrous freeze; a population explosion; mounting traffic congestion; the need for environmental protection; an inadequate educational system; and serious social problems (the plight of children, poverty and homelessness, crime, drugs, soaring health care costs, and so on). To cope with these problems Wilson had to work with a legislature controlled by Democrats in both houses during the year in which new legislative and congressional district lines had to be drawn.

Few governors approached this job in California better equipped by virtue of a varied career in government. The governor's race was Wilson's eighth electoral campaign. Over a quarter of a century he was elected three times as a California assemblyman; two times as mayor of San Diego, the state's second largest city; and to the U.S. Senate in 1982 and 1988. He was supported by a wide spectrum of Republicans in the gubernatorial primary, including archconservatives who had other preferences, because he was seen as the strongest candidate to win the general election. As governor he could veto reapportionment bills that would preserve control by the Democrats during the next decade.

The Campaign

Wilson won the 1990 election with less than a majority of the votes cast for governor. Fewer than 200,000 votes separated him from his opponent, Dianne Feinstein, a former mayor of San Francisco. Neither was an exciting campaigner. It was a ho-hum race that turned out only 58.7 percent of the voters. Wilson outspent Feinstein $25.2 million to $19.8 million.

In Washington, Wilson had been a relatively obscure senator. Because he was out of the state during his Senate years and because Feinstein had waged a strong primary campaign, she began the gubernatorial race somewhat ahead of him. There was little to distinguish them on certain major issues. Both were pro-choice, pro-gay rights, and pro-death penalty. They were both environmentalists and supported care for the young. While they differed on financial issues, both refrained from pledging "no new taxes."

Wilson departed from traditional Republican opposition to government programs and increased spending by announcing an attractive program for "preventive government." In the face of limited resources he proposed using more funds for programs that would prevent social problems from developing, such as prenatal and early childhood care for the poor, children's mental health care, student mentoring, and school-based health clinics. Less money would be spent for programs meant to cope with existing problems.

Feinstein was a tough campaigner, but her effort was poorly organized. As the campaign progressed she fell behind. Her relative lack of funds hurt. The Republicans carried on an intensive voter registration campaign; the Democrats made little effort to register their supporters. Wilson's team also encouraged absentee voting and waged a vigorous get-out-the-vote effort. In the final week Feinstein climbed in the polls to within two points of Wilson, but it was too late.

The outcome was so close that victory was not declared on election night. Wilson received 3,763,151 votes (49 percent), Feinstein got 3,497,875 votes (46 percent), and three other candidates divided the remaining votes.

Voters were also confronted by a record number of ballot propositions; they balked. They turned down five tax propositions, five environmental propositions, and nine bond propositions totaling almost $5 billion, including previously popular prison bonds. (Only a bond measure for veterans passed.) Just five months earlier, in the June primary, voters had approved $5 billion in bonds.

One proposition that did pass might have failed without Wilson's support. He alienated legislators of both parties by backing Proposition 140, a measure which limited their terms and cut the budget for both houses by 40 percent. Feinstein opposed the proposition while Wilson capitalized on the rising public dissatisfaction with the lawmakers. (The legislators challenged the constitutionality of the proposition. A year after the election the California Supreme Court upheld it, assuring that the state would have an all-new legislature by the end of 1998.)

Political analysts felt Feinstein lost the election as much as Wilson won it. Her campaign was erratic and unfocused until the last week, when she made a populist appeal similar to that of her successful primary campaign. Observers noted that her TV spots did not convey a clear message. Wilson portrayed himself as a centrist who was tough on crime. His ads stressed leadership and used images designed to enhance his appeal to women as well as men, thus stealing some of Feinstein's gender appeal. More than anything, Wilson droned on without making any mistakes.[1]

The Transition

The governor-elect moved swiftly and surehandedly to prepare for taking over the governorship. The day after the election Wilson designated his longtime friend and political aide, Bob White, as transition director and chief of staff. White had been with Wilson since his early days in Sacramento.

Wilson's active and well-informed wife, Gayle, who was intimately involved in his most recent campaigns, also participated in transition planning. She would become a key adviser to him in office.

The transition office was set up the Friday after the election and was quickly staffed with about forty people, far fewer than the governor would have when he moved into the Capitol. Wilson would have to make more than four hundred key appointments to set up his administration. In addition, the state's 375 boards and commissions would require another 2,600 appointments as terms expired.

Two weeks after the election Wilson made his first, and most important, cabinet appointment. Thomas Hayes was named state finance director the same day the independent Commission on State Finance announced a projected budget deficit of $14.3 billion for the next fiscal year.

Hayes was a respected bureaucrat Deukmejian had appointed to the post of state treasurer after Jesse Unruh died while serving in that position. Previously he was in the nonpartisan position of auditor general. Hayes then ran for treasurer but was defeated by Jerry Brown's sister, Kathleen.

The policy director, Loren Kaye, formerly Deukmejian's deputy cabinet secretary, began working on programs to implement Wilson's campaign promises. Policy teams were appointed. They talked to administrators, interest groups, public advocates, industrialists, and academics and reported back suggestions to be considered by Wilson, White, and his eventual cabinet.

Early appointments to several offices suggested the possibility of a new breed of Republican leadership in California. In mid-December Democrat Maureen DiMarco was appointed to a new cabinet-level post of secretary for child development and education. This was Wilson's first step to fulfill a major campaign pledge for preventive government. She was president of her local school board and immediate past president of the California School Boards Association. Bright and aggressive in school affairs, she was an outspoken critic of Deukmejian's education policies.

Later in December Wilson acted to meet his commitment to be an "environmentally sensitive and activist" governor and reorganize the state's environmental oversight functions. Conservationist Douglas Wheeler was appointed to head the state's Resources Agency, which encompassed departments managing fish and wildlife resources, state parks, forests, and the coastline. He was vice president of both the World Wildlife Fund and the Conservation Foundation in Washington, D.C., and had been executive director of the Sierra Club. In January Wilson delivered on another campaign promise by proposing the creation of a California Environmental Protection Agency merging three independent boards.

After his inauguration Wilson continued to make appointments that contrasted with those his Republican predecessors had made. Andrew Mecca, a Democrat, was appointed director of the Department of Alcohol and Drug Abuse Programs. Mecca grew up in a family of drug abusers and admitted to having smoked marijuana during college.

He was also the chairman of the California Task Force to Promote Self-Esteem and Personal and Social Responsibility, a body cartoonist Gary Trudeau had satirized in "Doonesbury."

Later a former crack addict who had been on skid row was appointed deputy director of the Policy Council within Mecca's department. Askia Abdulmajeed had overcome his drug dependency to become a community affairs representative at the Union Rescue Mission in Los Angeles, where Gayle Wilson met him during the election campaign.

Most of those appointed were Republican, often white men, although a white woman was appointed secretary of the State and Consumer Services Agency, an Hispanic was named secretary of the Youth and Adult Correctional Agency, and an Asian was appointed to the Board of Equalization. Many selected for the top positions came from outside the state. Wilson especially relied on his Washington experience for appointees. He did not keep many of Deukmejian's appointees.

The last cabinet-level position was not filled until the governor had been in office a hundred days; some supporters criticized this delay. (The Senate has a year in which to confirm appointments.) Generally, Wilson's appointees were not expected to encounter political trouble. However, two of Wilson's preinaugural appointments generated criticism.

Deukmejian's director of the Department of Food and Agriculture, Henry Voss, was asked to continue in that position. He was former president of the largest farm lobby in the state, the Farm Bureau Federation. His initial confirmation was approved in the Senate by only one vote. The Senate president said that Voss's reappointment would encounter opposition because of his controversial order to spray malathion in urban areas to combat the Mediterranean fruit fly. Environmentalists complained that the department had been biased in favor of agriculture and the chemical industries at the expense of public health. To calm these fears Wilson explained that he was going to take the regulation of pesticides away from Food and Agriculture and put it in the new California Environmental Protection Agency. Voss was not happy losing that jurisdiction.

Another appointment, to the U.S. Senate seat Wilson was vacating, drew even more fire from fellow Republicans. A dark horse, state Senator John Seymour, was named. He was a relatively unknown legislator who had chaired Wilson's 1988 Senate reelection campaign. Their friendship dated back to the early 1970s when both were mayors (Seymour was mayor of Anaheim).

Seymour came to the state Senate in 1982 as a conservative. He helped unseat the Senate's moderate Republican leadership to install a right-wing regime. He was closely identified with the huge Irvine Company, which owns much of Irvine County, the most conservative county in the state. Over time he shifted politically. He switched to a pro-choice position on abortion and became an environmentalist, opposing offshore oil drilling. These shifts put him closer to Wilson but alienated conservative Republicans. They questioned Wilson's selection and wondered about Seymour's electability; he had just lost a primary race for lieutenant governor. (Seymour must run for election to the Senate in 1992, when the term he filled expires.)

The Inauguration

Wilson explained his philosophy of preventive government in his inaugural address: "No longer can we be satisfied with reactive and remedial efforts. Even in this time of unprecedented fiscal constraint, we must find a way to at least begin to move to a mode of anticipation and prevention. . . . Prevention is far better than any cure." [2]

For example, he argued that it is better to provide prenatal care to fifty or sixty women who will give birth to healthy babies than to provide, for the same cost, neonatal care for only one unhealthy baby; that it is better to teach a child to value himself more than a quick high than to pay for costly and uncertain drug therapy; that it is better to keep pregnant women from using drugs than to take care of addicted babies; that it is better to keep teens in school than to counsel teen mothers or chase down drug gang members; and that it is better to prevent crime than to punish it.

Wilson's words dramatized the contrast with his Republican predecessor. Deukmejian had been a low-key, uncharismatic, caretaker governor. He was honest, dedicated, and hard-working, but his style was passive and reactive. He had few clear policy objectives and left much unfinished business. Wilson appeared to be proposing active, remedial programs to tackle serious problems. Deukmejian had an intransigent resistance to new taxes. Wilson never expressed opposition to new taxes and laid out an ambitious agenda that would require new spending.

Two days after his inauguration Wilson began to transform his campaign promises into policy with a State of the State address to the legislature. He returned to his pledge to increase the prison time of "thieves, thugs, rapists, killers and drug-runners who prey on innocents" while highlighting his preventive and remedial concerns with measures to improve the physical and mental health of children and pregnant women. Democratic legislators had more praise for Wilson's speech than his fellow Republicans did. One Democrat called it the best speech heard in a decade and another expressed surprise to hear support for health programs Deukmejian had rejected. The anticrime measures drew support for emphasizing the protection of women and their children—longer sentences for rapists and for drug dealers who knowingly sell drugs to pregnant women and children.

Wilson supported a substantial spending increase in family planning, asserting that contraceptive services help avoid the "massive human and financial costs" of unwanted children. By contrast, Deukmejian wanted the program to stop providing birth control services and other medical care to low-income women. However, Democrats were critical of Wilson's determination to cut the Aid to Families with Dependent Children (AFDC) program. At the time it paid a single mother with two children a monthly average of $694; Wilson proposed a cut of $61. (Later he made a serious gaffe when he defended the cut: "They will have less for a six-pack of beer." His effort to repair the blunder did not help. He said the example "might have been 7-Up, it might have been Coke, it might have been cigarettes.") Other cuts were going to be necessary as the dimensions of the budget deficit became known. Wilson estimated it would be $7 billion; the Commission on State Finance put the figure at $10 billion.

A fence-mending dinner followed the State of the State address. Wilson hosted legislators, their spouses, and a few key aides in an elegant dinner that cost $40,000. Wilson toasted the lawmakers: "I am proud to be in your company. Here's to the California Legislature." Satirist Mark Russell, who was a featured speaker, then skewered the politicians: "People are saying at last we have a governor with more sparkle than Deukmejian. Oatmeal cookies have more sparkle than George Deukmejian." [3] (Eight years earlier Russell had commented on Deukmejian's inaugural party: "The Deukmejian gala—there's an oxymoron for you. Boy, I'll bet the oatmeal flowed 'till 9:30." [4])

A few days later Democratic Assembly Speaker Willie Brown praised Wilson by comparison with Reagan and Deukmejian; those predecessors had seen government itself as the root of the state's problems. He averred, "Pete Wilson, on the other hand, has a vision of state government as a necessary part of the solution to these problems. That fact alone should make for a far more productive relationship with the legislative branch."

The next week Wilson attended the reunion of the self-esteem task force. This commission had been created through the effort of John Vasconcellos, the influential Democratic chair of the Assembly Ways and Means Committee, who would be a key player in budget negotiations. Wilson said that the commission's report and his preventive government proposals had "a very high congruity" with one another. He also declared February to be "Self-Esteem and Responsibility Month." He said, "We can't expect 'Doonesbury' to do it all." [5]

The New Administration

Wilson hit the ground running. A workaholic, he kept up a frenetic pace, functioning on five hours of sleep a night. Amy Chance, a *Sacramento Bee* reporter, described one week:

> He traveled to Washington, D.C., to attend an annual dinner studded with political stars, taped two television talk shows, went on to Los Angeles for the Academy Awards, held a meeting with rape victims to promote tougher anti-crime legislation, met with a farm worker's family in Visalia to dramatize the devastation wrought by California's freeze, spoke to a gathering of county sheriffs in Sacramento and held a press conference to endorse a no-fault auto insurance plan.[6]

He enjoyed an immediate and extended honeymoon with the legislature and reporters, who were prepared to welcome almost anyone after Deukmejian. In appraising Wilson's first hundred days, the independent *Sacramento Bee* editorialized: "Wilson has acted like a governor who believes government can and must play an important role in protecting and improving the quality of life of the state's citizens, and who relishes the job of making that happen. For California, that's a refreshing change." [7]

But Wilson faced overwhelming problems. The recession was beyond his control. During 1990 welfare rolls increased 10 percent, to include 58,000 families. Unemployment, which had usually been below the national average, surpassed it in January and continued to rise, reaching 7.6 percent in July. The economy was heavily dependent on the defense industry while defense expenditures were being reduced and military bases closed.

Population growth in the 1980s was two and one-half times the nation's rate. An increase of another 20 percent—from 30 million to 36 million—was projected for the next decade. The Council on Growth Management was created, not to tackle the causes of growth but to mitigate its adverse effects—air and water pollution and loss of open space, for example—and to deal with local governments that continue to encourage growth for revenue. Managing growth itself might not be possible.

Nor would accomplishing law and order be easy. California has the fastest-growing penal system in the industrialized world. During the 1980s the prison population increased by 220 percent. In a decade the state spent $3.8 billion for prison expansion, but the prisons are still at 180 percent of capacity. The annual budget to house 100,000 prisoners runs $3 billion (7 percent of the total state budget). Yet violent crime was up 11 percent during the 1980s. The prison population is projected to grow to 175,000 by 1995 and billions of dollars more will have to be spent.

A fourteen-point program designed to help preserve forests, wetlands, rivers, and wildlife was unveiled on Earth Day in April 1990. The program would formally establish the California Environmental Protection Agency. The agency's jurisdiction would encompass three existing boards for integrated waste management, water resources control, and air resources; the toxic substances regulatory program in the Department of Health Services; and pesticide regulation in the Department of Food and Agriculture. Wilson's environmental agenda included a proposed $628 million bond measure to acquire and develop parklands, but that may encounter voter resistance if their treatment of bond measures in the November 1990 election is any indication.

The Budget

During his first year as governor, Wilson was scarcely able to tackle the many problems the state faces because of California's overwhelming fiscal problems. The success of a large part of Wilson's administration will depend on his ability to construct a budget that copes with the deficit and provides funds for new and established programs. The commitment to a new policy of preventive government attracted state and national approbation, but its many elements would require new expenditures. At the same time, most remedial programs would have to be continued. The needs of children, to whom much of the preventive government policy would be directed, also would include improving the quality of public education, which was assured 40 percent of the budget by Proposition 98 on the 1988 ballot.

A few days after the 1990 election Deukmejian boasted: "I am proud of the fact that while I inherited a budget deficit from my predecessor, I will leave my successor ... a balanced budget and a Triple A credit rating." Yet the legislative analyst Elizabeth Hill saw a revenue shortfall of between $.5 billion and $2 billion by the end of the 1990-1991 fiscal year. Within weeks of that statement Deukmejian called a special session of the legislature to deal with the worsening fiscal condition of the state. He asked for a $1 billion cut in spending during the rest of fiscal 1991—1 percent across the board for all state agencies and almost $550 million from the allocation to public schools.

The legislature did not act on Deukmejian's request, preferring to see what Wilson would propose in his budget message after the inauguration. In the meantime projections worsened. By early December Hill reported the deficit might grow to $5.9 billion over the next eighteen months.

Soon after his inauguration Wilson submitted to the legislature a $55.7 billion budget for fiscal 1992, a 2.3 percent increase over the previous year's budget of $54.4 billion. He estimated that the deficit over the rest of fiscal 1991 and all of fiscal 1992 would be $7.1 billion. Therefore, he proposed $1.7 billion in new taxes and $5.3 billion in cuts. Taxpayers would pay more for motor vehicle licenses, higher taxes on liquor, and new sales taxes on snack foods, newspapers, and periodicals. The taxes were distasteful to the Republican governor, but he insisted he could not cut government services any more deeply.

Increases were not proposed in personal income tax, bank and corporation tax, or sales taxes. The spending cuts were spread across the board, with schools and welfare hit hardest. At the same time Wilson proposed $180 million in new spending for his preventive government programs. One legislator complained: "There's something here for everyone to hate." Wilson agreed.

By the end of March Wilson said the budget crisis had become a "budget emergency." The projected deficit was now $12.6 billion, $3.6 billion by the end of fiscal 1991 and another $9.0 billion in the next fiscal year. Standard and Poor's had placed the state on credit watch. Wilson offered to meet with the legislative leaders every day until a budget was formulated.

Budget cuts alone would not be sufficient. Wilson explained that shutting down the University of California's nine campuses and California State University's twenty campuses; opening prison gates, releasing all felons, and discharging all guards; and eliminating every job in state government would not close the gap. Tax increases as well as selective cuts would be needed.

Wilson's proposals were middle of the road. He wanted a sales tax increase of 1¼ percent, a figure that was acceptable to business leaders but not to conservatives who objected to any tax increase. Nor was the increase acceptable to liberal Democrats, who complained that the burden would be heaviest on low-income people. Instead, liberal Democrats wanted tax rates to be raised on high incomes and on corporations. Furthermore, the spending cuts were not as deep as conservatives wanted and hit programs the liberals liked, although the process did protect middle-class priorities, such as prisons.

When the May revision figures came in the budget gap became a chasm—$14.3 billion. The national recession had eroded the state tax base and put greater burdens on health and welfare programs. The level of debate became more heated, not only between the parties in the legislature but also between the governor and conservative Republicans, especially in the eighty-member Assembly. The Republicans held thirty-one seats there, enough to block the budget and appropriation bills, which in California need a two-thirds vote for passage. The Democrats, of course, could block efforts to cut or eliminate state programs, but the governor and the Republicans maintained control over spending levels.

As the new fiscal year began on July 1, there was no final budget, but some agreement had been reached. Cuts of more than $5 billion had been approved. Public schools were assured the funding guaranteed by Proposition 98 plus an additional $400,000 and funding was included for the governor's preventive programs to benefit women and children. Assembly Democrats agreed to cut AFDC by 4.4 percent, half the governor's original demand, and they were willing to discontinue automatic inflation adjustments for welfare recipients, but only for five years.

Wilson was also supporting $7.2 billion in new revenues. He had to remind his party members in the legislature that Governor Reagan, during his first year in office, had supported the largest tax increase in California history until that time. The Proposition 13 babies (the name applied to many of the conservative Assembly Republicans first elected in 1978) continued to oppose new taxes. When asked if he would twist arms, Wilson replied he would "break arms if it's necessary" to get support. After heavy lobbying by the governor, enough Assembly Republicans joined Democrats to pass the increase in sales and alcohol taxes and vehicle license fees.

Both houses approved moving certain health programs to local government and using $1.6 billion of the public employee retirement fund to help balance the budget. But more revenue was needed, and the governor and legislature were divided over how to raise it. Some Democrats wanted to raise taxes on individual incomes over $250,000 ($500,000 for couples), to produce another $1.4 billion; others wanted to raise both upper-income and business tax rates from 9.3 percent to 10 percent. Another Democratic proposal would levy new taxes on gas, electric, and water utilities, raising up to $1.9 billion. This proposal was an expansion on Wilson's plan to boost taxes on telephones and cable TV to raise $900 million.

Negotiations for added revenues became intense. Assembly Republicans were adamantly opposed to the income tax hike. Wilson agreed to an increase in the income tax rate for the wealthy, but in return he demanded reforms in the workers' compensation system for which his business supporters were pressing. Earlier in the year Wilson had insisted that workers' compensation claims for stress-related illness be at least 50 percent attributable to the workplace and that good-faith personnel actions, such as discipline or layoffs, be immune from stress compensation actions. The Democrats argued that the budget should not be held hostage for workers' compensation reform sought by the California Chamber of Commerce and the California Manufacturers Association. Wilson threatened to veto the entire spending plan unless the legislature approved the workers' compensation changes and the tax increases he wanted.

The logjam broke two weeks into the new fiscal year. A $2.3 billion tax bill was approved and the governor accepted less than a major overhaul of the workers' compensation system. The top tax rate was raised from 9.3 percent to 10 percent for individuals earning $100,000 (couples earning $200,000) and to 11 percent for individuals making $200,000 (couples, $400,000), while Wilson settled for a change in the workers' compensation system which simply prohibited workers from filing stress-related claims in their first six months on the job. The workers' compensation reform effort was getting so complicated that he did not want further delay in enacting a budget that was already two weeks late. Before signing the budget, the governor used his line-item veto to cut $191 million from the spending plan. The $55.7 billion spending plan included a $1.2 billion reserve for emergencies.

A First-Year Appraisal

One year is not enough time in which to appraise any governor, much less a governor who faced in his first year the problems confronting Pete Wilson.

He began well. In his State of the State address alone he made more proposals than his predecessor had in most of his eight such addresses. After California's budget was signed David S. Broder wrote in the *Washington Post:* "Wilson is California's first activist governor since Pat Brown in the early '60s." [8] Wilson's leadership contrasted markedly with that of his three predecessors.

Viewed by some observers as a Tory reformer, Wilson embarked on a program of preventive government while attempting to carry on most of the remedial programs already in place. Surrounding himself with able longtime political loyalists, he undertook to lead a state once headed by a governor who saw government as part of the problem. As a pragmatist, Wilson regarded government as part of the solution. He was willing to use political leverage as a tool to achieve policy goals. He was also willing to compromise.

In the process, Wilson was prepared to take risks. A few of his early appointments were dramatic moves to capture public attention. Several were unlike the traditional appointments a new governor often makes. Yet by the end of the year the creation of the proposed cabinet-level Child Development and Education Agency that was to be headed by Maureen DiMarco was stalled by legislative bickering over reapportionment.

Wilson's greater risk was his willingness to raise taxes, although until the final crunch, when income tax rates were raised, the taxes were of the kind Republicans have usually been willing to tolerate. Actually, many of Wilson's fellow Republicans would rather have balanced the budget entirely with spending cuts, while the Democrats opposed most cuts and would have preferred most revenues to come from income and corporation taxes rather than sales taxes. Not only did conservative Republicans criticize the reliance on new revenues, but they also resented the alliances the governor made with the Democrats to win support for his tax increases. Thus, his leadership of the party, if not of the state, was questioned by some critics.

State employees, both unionized and not, have become increasingly critical of Wilson. As mayor of San Diego he had clashes with organized labor. As governor, his first confrontation with unions was with teachers over his initial effort to modify the Proposition 98 guarantee for school funding. Proposals to lay off thousands of state workers and to cut pay and benefits drew heated responses and threats of strikes. Efforts to modify the makeup of the governing board of the Public Employees Retirement System and to use pension funds as another budget-balancing move also alienated state employees.

In spite of inevitable criticisms from various sectors, midway in his first year Wilson was seen as a centrist—moderate, pragmatic, positive, and upbeat. He had succeeded in bringing elements of both parties together to raise taxes and balance the budget. He saw himself as a consensus builder. Energetic and gregarious, he often made two or three public appearances a day. Although occasionally awkward, he escaped serious criticism for his early missteps. There was little doubt that he regarded the job as fun. And there was more fun to be had nationwide. Wilson appeared to have his eye on the White House.

Any governor of a state as large as California attracts nationwide attention. By midyear Wilson earned that attention because he appeared to be a different kind of Republican from recent state and national GOP leaders. Broder called him "the most interesting and important American politician outside the White House today. He is attempting nothing less than a redefinition of conservatism by tackling head-on the domestic problems shunned by the last two Republican presidents. If he succeeds ... American politics will be fundamentally changed." He concluded, "He is playing for high stakes—with a possible 1996 White House bid in balance." [9]

Robert Reinhold described Wilson in the *New York Times* as a person "widely touted in Republican circles as a Presidential contender but who often challenges Republican orthodoxy. . . . Not in a quarter of a century . . . has California seen such an active, involved Governor. . . . [The budget resolution] was testimony to the skills and stamina of Mr. Wilson." [10]

But as an active centrist, Wilson was on a hazardous course in California. A centrist leader has room to maneuver when both the right and the left are moderate or do not hold strong ideological positions. But when the right is rigidly conservative (as are many in Wilson's party) and the left is vigorously liberal and dominates the legislature (as in California), a centrist must steer down a very narrow path.

Wilson's centrism and consensus building were viewed by the conservatives in his party as betrayal. Raising taxes instead of cutting more from the budget was regarded as giving in to the opposition. Certain appointees—Seymour and others—as well as some policies— such as his pro-choice stand and support of gay rights—were immediately denounced. In their September convention many Republicans walked out on Seymour. Wilson chose not to appear. Resolutions were passed condemning his policies without mentioning his name.

Wilson had to rebuild his support on the right. At the end of September he vetoed controversial legislation that would have added sexual orientation to a law prohibiting job discrimination because of race, gender, religion or national origin. Earlier in the year he had hinted that he would sign such legislation, but the Republican convention had demanded a veto. The action was presented to the public as an effort to protect small business from excessive litigation. The left became alienated. The veto spawned demonstrations and protest from many more than just gay-rights activists. A *Los Angeles Times* poll found that 46 percent of the respondents disapproved of the veto, while 40 percent approved. [11]

Wilson's problems mounted. In early October he vetoed a bill that would have provided an additional thirteen weeks of unemployment benefits to the state's one million jobless people. The same day unemployment figures were released showing California's jobless rate at 7.7 percent, up from 7.3 percent the previous month. The governor asserted that the cost of extending benefits would be too high for business and government.

Later in the month, on the same day the U.S. Senate narrowly approved the appointment of Clarence Thomas to the Supreme Court (after the Clarence Thomas/Anita Hill Senate hearings), Wilson vetoed legislation that would have provided compensation to victims of employment discrimination, including sexual harassment. Ironically, the legislation, authored by a female Republican senator, was designed in cooperation with business interests to encourage the resolution of discrimination complaints out of court and would have imposed limits on punitive damages.

Moreover, the state's fiscal condition continued to deteriorate. By the end of October state tax revenues were below projections because of the continuing recession. Also, expenditures were up because of recession-related social needs. The state could have a $2 billion deficit by the end of fiscal 1991-1992 and an additional deficit of $3 billion by the end of fiscal 1992-1993.

Overhanging all of these problems was reapportionment. California gained seven congressional seats, more if the alleged undercounting in the census were acknowledged. These had to be reapportioned along with eighty Assembly and forty Senate electoral districts. After enacting the fiscal 1991-1992 budget the legislature devoted the remaining time in the term to reapportionment. The governor vetoed three plans that were drafted by late September, and the Democratic leaders failed to obtain an override. The California Supreme Court then accepted the governor's request that the justices redraw district lines. They immediately appointed three retired judges, two Republicans and one Democrat, to act as "court masters" and supervise the process. A similar procedure had been followed in 1973. These court masters were to be "guided by the procedures and criteria" developed by the earlier masters and to conform to the requirements of the federal Voting Rights Act. The court was to deliver its maps by the end of January so that the 1992 elections could be conducted in the new districts.

The court masters acted expeditiously. They conducted hearings, prepared recommendations, and delivered a report in early December. The Supreme Court accepted the report and issued it on schedule in late January 1992. The Republicans were elated with the results: few Republicans will be displaced, most districts will be more competitive, and minority representation will be enhanced. The path to Republican control of the legislature by or before the end of the century may also have been laid. The reason conservatives had accepted Wilson as a gubernatorial candidate was primarily to prevent a Democratic governor from approving a reapportionment plan drafted by a Democratic legislature.

Wilson may find his job a little less fun—and his prospects for the presidency in 1996 have been dimmed. Back in 1988, when he first considered running for the governorship, political consultant Stu Spencer warned him that the state was "ungovernable." Given the problems he faces and the need to work with a Democratic legislature while wooing his conservative party members, the label seems accurate.

Indeed, Wilson's prospects for reelection as governor in 1994 are fading. His ratings have fallen precipitously. In early February, Mervin Field's California Poll reported that 36 percent of the respondents said he was doing an excellent or good job, 31 percent said he was doing a fair job, and 12 percent said he was doing a poor or very poor job; 21 percent were undecided. In September, even before his veto of the gay rights bill, the poor/very poor rating had risen to 33 percent while the excellent/good rating had dropped to 29 percent; only 6 percent of the respondents had no opinion. By January 1992 the poor/very poor rating continued to rise—to 35 percent (nearly triple what it had been one year earlier) while only 28 percent of the people polled gave his performance an excellent/good rating. In all cases the fair ratings ranged between 31 percent and 33 percent.

Wilson's current rating is much more negative than similar ratings given his three immediate predecessors after their first year in office. In contrast to the 28 percent still saying Wilson is doing an excellent/good job, Deukmejian was rated as doing an excellent or good job by 43 percent, Jerry Brown by 53 percent, and Reagan by 42 percent. At the other extreme, 16 percent rated Deukmejian's performance as poor or very poor, 9 percent for Brown's performance, and 15 percent for Reagan's, in contrast to the 35 percent who rated Wilson's performance poor or very poor. The fair ratings for the three previous governors ranged between 32 percent and 36 percent; the no opinion ratings were 6 percent or 7 percent.[12]

Wilson's conservative party members have not been particularly kind to him. The need to cater to their strong views has made Wilson appear opportunistic, without firmly held beliefs and policies. Wilson needs to win stronger support from members of his own party in the legislature. Now that the Supreme Court has delivered reapportionment maps that provide Republicans an opportunity to gain control of the legislature, Wilson will have justified his election in the eyes of his party. But to live up to early appraisals of his governorship and to deliver his announced programs, he will need more Republican moderates in the new districts. After alienating the Democratic leadership during the reapportionment battle, he will not receive the support they gave him to reduce the first year's budget deficit. The needed two-thirds majority to pass a budget will be very difficult to achieve.

Wilson will also need an improved economy both to help balance the budget and to implement his program of preventive government. That is not happening. By the end of January 1992 the Wilson administration announced that the fiscal 1992-1993 budget it had proposed could be as much as $6 billion in the red if enacted by the legislature. Director of Finance Hayes said, "Actual economic conditions are worse than we projected." [13] Thus, Wilson's future is uncertain. He needs a party that will support him, a legislature with which he can work, and a rapidly improving economy. His leadership is going to be tested.

Should Wilson be reelected in 1994, he will face even greater problems. In mid-November 1991 the Department of Finance reported that during the rest of the decade tax revenues—when adjusted for inflation and population growth—will lag far behind the cost of California's current level of education, health care, and other social services. Even if California's economy recovers, the cost of such services by the year 2000 will grow from the present $43 billion to $105 billion a year. Revenues are projected to be only $85 billion, leaving a deficit of $20 billion. Because of high immigration and high birth rates in the last decade, there will be fewer working-age Californians to pay the taxes needed to support the rapidly growing youth and elderly populations. With or without Wilson, California faces troubled times ahead.

Notes

1. Rick Kushman, "Not too pretty, experts say of fall campaign," *Sacramento Bee,* November 8, 1991, A5.
2. *Sacramento Bee,* January 8, 1991.
3. James Richardson, "Gov. Wilson serves up food, wine and good will," *Sacramento Bee,* January 11, 1991, A3.
4. *Sacramento Bee,* January 5, 1991.
5. *Sacramento Bee,* January 25, 1991.
6. Amy Chance, "Wilson's first 100 days full of trials," *Sacramento Bee,* April 14, 1991, A1.
7. *Sacramento Bee,* April 21, 1991.
8. David S. Broder, "Pete Wilson: Playing for High Stakes," *Washington Post,* July 28, 1991, C7.
9. Ibid.
10. Robert Reinhold, "California's Governor Gets a Fast, Deal-Making Start," *New York Times,* July 25, 1991, A1.
11. Reprinted in the *Sacramento Bee,* October 6, 1991.
12. William Endicott, "Wilson's rating plummets drastically after year in office," *Sacramento Bee,* January 28, 1992, A3.
13. Robert B. Gunnison and Vlae Kershner, "State facing big deficit for '92-'93," *Sacramento Bee,* January 29, 1992, A1.

5. CONNECTICUT: LOWELL P. WEICKER, JR., A MAVERICK IN THE "LAND OF STEADY HABITS"

Russell D. Murphy

He won with only 41 percent of the vote and thus became the first third party candidate ever elected governor of Connecticut.[1] And as governor he continues his independent ways. No sooner had he taken office in January 1991 than he proposed a broad-based personal income tax—a tax that for decades had been unmentionable among state politicians, but a tax the new governor nonetheless insisted was necessary and succeeded in getting enacted.

The governor in question is Connecticut's Lowell P. Weicker, Jr., and with his election it is no longer business as usual in the state. Some may even wonder whether the state any longer qualifies, as many claim it once did, as the "land of steady habits."

The answer, in brief, is that it does. While the state may have abandoned some of its habitual ways, it has done so selectively, and it is not at all clear that it has done so permanently. True, the new governor is something of an anomaly, both in Connecticut and elsewhere. But he is by no means unique.[2] Nor were his independent candidacy and subsequent victory surprising, even in a state that is usually counted among the strongest of the strong party states. And, finally, there is more continuity than discontinuity in the Weicker story, and there is no evidence, at least to date, that a major restructuring of Connecticut politics is in the offing.

On a Path Well Trodden

He planned to remain in the Senate, Lowell Weicker announced in 1985, and he wanted to end, "once and for all," the rumors he would seek the Republican nomination for governor.[3] As it turns out, the senator was largely true to his word. He remained in the Senate until 1988, when he lost his bid for a fourth term. And he never did seek the Republican nomination for governor. Instead, he formed a new political party—which he called A Connecticut Party—and ran on his own.

Weicker's decision, made public on March 2, 1990, probably came as little surprise to most Connecticut voters. For one thing, it had been rumored for months that he would run. For another, although nominally a Republican, Weicker had developed a reputation as an independent and a maverick during his eighteen years in the U.S. Senate. Nor was his decision to challenge the major parties very risky or reckless. Indeed, the timing and the times were more than favorable. Connecticut's major parties are by no means moribund. But they have struggled of late and on occasion have stumbled. And as he has done over his long and controversial career, Weicker skillfully exploited both his reputation as a maverick and what, for the moment, at least, was a political and governmental system in disarray.

Weicker embarked on his independent course with a number of important political assets, not the least being a substantial electoral base outside the two major parties. He owed much of his success over the years to his appeal to unaffiliated voters—a sizable and significant group in Connecticut. In 1988, for example, unaffiliated voters were the second largest group of registered voters in the state—roughly 600,000, compared with 698,000 Democrats and 489,000 Republicans.

His appeal to this group is not difficult to understand. His carefully nurtured image as someone who could be counted on to do what was best for the people, not the party, was one factor. His behavior was another, including his much publicized attacks on the Nixon and Reagan administrations and his proposals, during the early 1980s, to give unaffiliated voters the right to vote in Republican party primaries.

His efforts to broaden participation in Republican primaries are instructive. At the time, Connecticut law required that anyone voting in a party primary be a registered voter of that party, and the Democrats, who controlled the state legislature, rejected Republican-sponsored legislation to change this. But Weicker and his allies won in federal court, which ruled the state's restriction on primary voting an unconstitutional burden on the party's freedom of political association.[4]

The publicly stated reason for the reform was straightforward enough, namely that by reaching out to disfranchised, unaffiliated voters, the Republican party would be much more attractive to them. Unstated, however, were the strategic calculations that made such a gesture especially attractive to Weicker and his allies—the likelihood, for example, that unaffiliated voters would produce more centrist candidates than might otherwise emerge from the nominating process,[5] and the likelihood, further, that these voters would strengthen Weicker's hand within the party. In fact, strengthening Weicker's hand was probably the major reason for the initiative in the first place—and, more concretely, to forestall future challenges of the kind Weicker had survived the year before.

An Errant Republican

The challenge had come from what is commonly called the Republican right. The challenger was Prescott Bush, brother of George Bush. Bush ran against Weicker for the Republican nomination for the Senate. Weicker won the state convention's nomination. But he made it clear that, had he lost, he might have run as an independent. Bush, though eligible to contest the nomination in a primary, declined to do so, citing the need for party unity.[6]

Weicker's response to the Bush challenge was fully in character. Long before 1982, his reputation as a rogue Republican had been well established. Indeed, his repeated and highly publicized refusal to be a team player was what provoked the challenge in the first place. His record in this regard was clear. He had become something of a national celebrity as a member of the Senate Select Committee on Presidential Campaign Activities (the Watergate Committee) for his persistent criticisms of the Nixon administration. That was in 1973, two years after he had entered the Senate. Thereafter his party unity scores declined markedly, as did his support for Republican presidents (see Figures 5-1 and 5-2). Indeed, for most of his Senate career, Weicker's presidential support scores more closely approximated those of the Democrats than those of the Republicans.[7]

Weicker's independent strategy worked quite well as long as Democrats nominated fairly liberal candidates, which they did in each of Weicker's first three Senate elections. In 1970, 1976, and 1982, disaffected Republicans (and many moderate Democrats as well) had nowhere else to go. But his independent strategy failed in 1988 when Democrats nominated a more centrist candidate, Attorney General Joseph Lieberman. Lieberman won, albeit by fewer than 10,000 votes.

More to the point, Lieberman was openly and actively supported by conservative Republicans; had Weicker sought the Republican nomination for governor two years later, he surely would have encountered the same intense opposition. A maverick in a collective body such as the U.S. Senate is one thing. A maverick alone in the statehouse is quite another, especially one bent on using the office to reshape the party in his own image. And few doubted that Weicker would try to do so.

Yet Weicker might have won the Republican nomination had he sought it in 1990. Despite his difficulties with the Republican right, he was still a force within the party. But given the opposition, an independent campaign was simpler and politically less costly. And it minimized the number of compromises that would otherwise be needed, allowing him to structure his campaign (and his administration)

Figure 5-1 Presidential Support Scores in the U.S. Senate, 1971-
1988: Lowell Weicker and Average Senate Republican
Scores

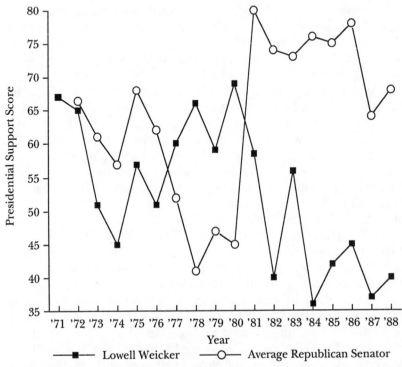

SOURCE: Based on data in various years of *Congressional Quarterly Almanac* (Washington,
D.C.: Congressional Quarterly Inc.).

unencumbered by political compromise and free of those who did not
share his political philosophy. Besides, if history was any guide, the
Republican nomination probably wasn't worth all that much. With the
exception of Weicker himself, Connecticut Republicans had fared
poorly over the past forty years in statewide elections. During that time,
only two Republicans had been elected governor—John Lodge, who
served from 1951 to 1955, and Thomas Meskill, who served from 1971
to 1975.

Spending and the Burden of Incumbency

Had it been in the realm of the possible, the Democratic
nomination would not have been worth much more to Weicker, at least
not in 1990. Even at the time, it was clear the Democrats were in
trouble. The party had lost organizational vitality, as well as voters'

Figure 5-2   Party Unity Scores in the U.S. Senate, 1971-1988: Lowell Weicker and Average Senate Republican Scores

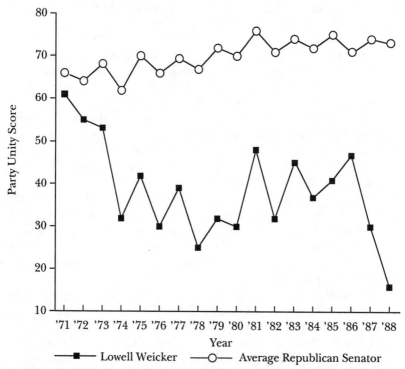

SOURCE: Based on data in various years of *Congressional Quarterly Almanac* (Washington, D.C.: Congressional Quarterly Inc.).

confidence. As a result, it could not deliver the votes as it had under the leadership of former state and national (under President John F. Kennedy) Democratic party chair John Bailey.

The trouble had begun even before Bailey's death in 1975. Indeed, Weicker owed his initial statewide success in 1970 to a factional dispute within the Democratic party. It was the Vietnam era, and the so-called McCarthy wing of the party denied Senate incumbent Thomas Dodd renomination for a third term. Dodd ran as an independent; he divided the Democratic vote between himself and the party nominee, Joseph Duffey, thus allowing Weicker to win with 41 percent of the vote.

The problems continued. In 1989, for example, Republicans and moderate Democrats, in what for Connecticut was an unprecedented move, joined together to oust the Speaker of the House of Representatives, a liberal Democrat from New Haven. And although Democrats controlled both the General Assembly and the governor's office, there were, during the 1989 and 1990 legislative sessions, public and politically embarrassing disagreements between the General Assembly's Office of Fiscal Analysis and the governor's Office of Policy and Management over the size of the state's budget deficit.

The deficit, as it turned out, was the Democrats' greatest liability in 1990. And it was substantial—some would say staggering—no matter who did the counting. In February 1989, for example, Gov. William O'Neill announced a $882.0 million projected deficit in a proposed $6.8 billion fiscal 1990 budget. A month later, the legislature enacted a $247 million package of new and expanded taxes to cover a projected deficit in the then *current* fiscal year. In May, the legislature added an additional $700 million in new taxes when it adopted the 1990 fiscal year budget—striking increases, given the size of the state budget at the time.[8]

Nor was it simply the magnitude of the projected deficits and tax increases that proved so unsettling. It was also the suddenness with which it all had happened. Only five years before, the major problem, ironically, had been substantial budget surpluses. Citizens understandably wondered why the state's fortunes had deteriorated so drastically and in so short a time.

The explanation lay partly in the state of the state's economy. Like many other states in the Northeast, Connecticut had experienced a significant slowdown in its economy during the late 1980s. As a result, the yield from the state's major revenue sources, sales and corporate profits taxes, declined. So too did federal aid, at least in relative terms, which increased still further the pressures on an already overtaxed budget.[9]

But there was another factor as well: namely, the extraordinary growth of state expenditures during the 1980s. In current dollar terms, state expenditures more than doubled during the decade, from roughly $2.9 billion in 1980 to approximately $7.0 billion in 1990, one of the largest percentage increases in the country.

There were a number of reasons for this. Inflation was one, population growth another.[10] But by far the most striking aspect of the growth was the expansion of existing programs and the addition of expensive new ones. One of these was a hurried and costly program to repair the state's physical infrastructure after the collapse of the Mianus River Bridge on heavily traveled Interstate Route 95.[11] Another was a state-mandated and state-subsidized increase in teachers' salaries.[12] And there were major increases in state aid to localities,[13] as well as major additions to the state workforce and a range of social programs, including programs for rental assistance, subsidized prescription drugs, and daycare centers.

Much of this expansion took place during the prosperous mid-1980s. The times were such that existing taxes generated enough revenue to sustain annual growth rates in the 10 to 15 percent range, while at the same time producing politically embarrassing budget surpluses. But even at the time, there were Cassandras who warned of fiscal doom, and critics complained that state officials were more interested in short-term electoral gain than in long-term fiscal responsibility.

And there were cynics as well, those who insisted that the long term was precisely what some state officials had in mind. The logic was sufficiently straightforward. New and expanded programs, according to this view, strengthened the political base for state spending. This, in turn, increased the likelihood, in the event of an economic downturn, that the state would be forced to rethink and restructure its revenue system—and, quite possibly, adopt what had hitherto been unthinkable, namely a broad-based personal income tax.

Even had they wished to, it is unlikely that state officials would have been able to manipulate both the economy and spending decisions as effectively as cynics would have it. But whether they wished or attempted to do so, the sudden and stunning turnaround in the state's fiscal condition was a stark reality. And it had profound political consequences, undermining as it did public confidence in the O'Neill administration's ability to manage state government. The search for alternative leadership soon began in earnest.

Victory

Citing "political realities," incumbent governor William O'Neill announced on March 20, 1990, that he would not seek reelection. The realities were hard indeed. For months, the once popular governor's support in the polls had declined, tracking quite closely the decline in the state's fiscal situation. And the fiscal situation continued to worsen, prompting challenges not only from the Republican party but from within his own party as well. And two weeks before the O'Neill announcement—and doubtless a factor in that decision—Lowell Weicker had announced that he would run for governor as an independent.[14]

The fiscal crisis and what to do about it dominated the campaign from the outset. It was a central issue, for example, in the struggle for the Democratic nomination between Third District Representative Bruce Morrison and New London State Representative William Cibes. Morrison, a liberal New Haven Democrat who himself was something of a maverick, had entered the race early, in the fall of 1989. Cibes declared much later, following O'Neill's announcement and reportedly with the blessing of O'Neill and his political associates. Morrison went on to win both the convention nomination and the subsequent challenge primary, the latter with 65 percent of the vote. And he won, according to most observers, because of his stand on the income tax. Morrison publicly opposed it—ironically, given his general political leanings; Cibes, on the other hand, insisted that an income tax was the only viable alternative for the state.[15]

Taxes remained the dominant issue, along with the worsening condition of the state's finances. But no matter how bold their claims for dealing with the crisis, none of the candidates endorsed the income tax or tax increases generally.[16] And while each of the candidates gestured in the direction of spending cuts, none, including Weicker, presented a plan that would have resolved the state's fiscal crisis. In August, for example, Weicker released a plan that he claimed would eliminate the state's fiscal problems by the following June. But it was not at all clear that the measures he proposed would do so, at least not those that caught the eye of the media—a reduction, through attrition, in the number of state employees, for example, and lower expenditures on consulting fees and computer purchases.

The principal focus of Weicker's campaign, it is fair to say, was Weicker himself and his personal qualities as a strong, no-nonsense leader. The message, in brief, was that Weicker was a newcomer to state government and hence could not be blamed for the state's fiscal problems. His newcomer status, however, did not mean he was a political novice; nor was he simply a political idealist unaccustomed to tough political challenges. Voters were told to expect the same kind of firm, principled leadership he had given them throughout all his years in public service. Whatever needed to be done, it was said, could best be done by Weicker himself—leaving unspecified what it was that needed to be done.

The appeal succeeded. Weicker won the election, although by a far narrower margin than had earlier been predicted—with 41 percent of the vote to Republican John Rowland's 38 percent. As in the past, he had support from across the political spectrum, and even his hardcore Republican supporters, though a minority within the party and within the electorate, contributed to his narrow victory. But he won principally because of independents and Democrats. Indeed, a majority of Democrats voted for Weicker, not for their own party's candidate. Had it not been for a last-minute appeal by Democratic party leaders, Morrison would have fallen below the 20 percent threshold needed under state law to qualify the Democrats as a major party in the next election.

Taxation and the Burden of Incumbency

Weicker had not specified during the campaign how he planned to deal with the state's fiscal problem. What he planned to do, however, quickly became apparent in his February 1991 budget message, in which he advocated the adoption of a state income tax. Throughout the campaign, he had steadfastly refused to embrace the tax. But at the same time, and despite his reputation for straightforwardness, he had been the least specific in his opposition. For those given to reading political signs, he had signaled the likely direction of his administration within weeks of his election. In late November, he appointed William Cibes secretary of the Office of Policy and Management, the governor's chief budget and fiscal office. Cibes was a knowledgeable and respected former state representative, the co-chair of the General Assembly's Finance, Revenue and Bonding Committee, and, most significantly, an outspoken champion of the income tax.

It is not at all clear when or why Weicker changed his mind on the income tax. Cynics claim he never did. Supporters point to a continuing decline in the state's fiscal condition, and argue that this, in effect, forced the governor's hand. Just before the election, for example, the governor's office reported a projected $1.5 billion deficit in the fiscal year 1992 budget. Three weeks later the figure was revised upward, with the announcement that in 1991-1992 the state would spend $2.1 billion more than it collected in revenues. Whatever the reasons, Weicker made the income tax his cause. An intense political struggle ensued.

The struggle lasted well beyond the end of the regular 1991 legislative session. On three occasions, the governor vetoed legislative budgets that would have relied on an expanded sales tax to deal with the fiscal crisis.[17] In each instance, the legislature refused to override the veto. Nor were the governor's income tax plans any more successful. Although the House at one point approved the tax, the Senate quickly rejected it. The stalemate lasted until August, when three critical votes in the Senate's antitax coalition switched. Even so, it required a vote by Lt. Gov. Eunice Groark, the only other member of Weicker's Connecticut party in state government, to break a tie. Within hours of the Senate vote, and following intense lobbying by the governor and the House leadership, the House, by a two-vote margin (75-73), approved the Senate bill, ending the longest and most bitter budget stalemate in the state's history.

Parties, Personalities, and Accountability

Controversies such as Connecticut's prolonged and bitter debate over the income tax can have profound and lasting consequences for political systems, and an altered political system may be Lowell Weicker's principal legacy for the state. But the implications are not clear. True, Weicker was the key player in the income tax debate and

Table 5-1 Connecticut General Assembly Final Vote on Income Tax, August 22, 1991: Percent Distribution by Party

Vote	Senate		House of Representatives	
	Democrats (N = 20)	Republicans (N = 16)	Democrats (N = 87)	Republicans (N = 61)
Yes	80	13	87	17
No	20	87	13	83

SOURCE: Based on data in the *Hartford Courant*, August 23, 1991, 13.

the income tax is at present the principal line of political cleavage in the state, as it probably will be for some time. Despite this, there is no evidence that either the tax issue or Weicker himself is producing a major restructuring of the state's political system or a new state order. In fact, it seems that Connecticut politics is largely business as usual.

The usual business includes, to begin with, the politics of the income tax. The issue is hardly a new one. It dates from at least 1971 and has long been a point of contention within the state.[18] A majority of voters has generally opposed the tax, as have, until recently, most state legislators, many of whom feared the tax would make it impossible to control the growth of a state government they felt was already out of control. But there has been intense support as well, among public employee unions, state teachers' groups, the media, academics, and most liberals. And there has even been support among business people, many of whom viewed the income tax as an alternative to the state's 13.8 percent corporate profits tax, the highest in the nation.[19]

More important politically, the division has been largely along party lines. Democrats have generally favored the tax, Republicans have generally opposed it. There have been important exceptions, most notably in recent times Governors Ella Grasso and William O'Neill, and with them, a sufficiently large bipartisan antitax coalition in the General Assembly to sustain any veto.[20] For the Democrats, this gubernatorial opposition was key; without it, Democrats in the General Assembly voted overwhelmingly in favor of the tax (see Table 5-1).

In an important sense, then, the debate over the income tax transcended Weicker. Had Weicker not been involved, it is true, the debate might well have been different. The governor's personal style and his lack of a legislative party may have prolonged the debate and made it more painful and bitter than it need have been. But Weicker or no Weicker, there would have been an intense political struggle during the 1991 legislative session. The fiscal crisis was too profound for it to have been otherwise.[21]

It is business as usual in other important respects as well. For one thing, although the major parties lost the governorship, they maintain control of the state's other elected constitutional offices. The secretary of the state, for example, is a Republican; the attorney general, the treasurer, and the comptroller are Democrats, as is a majority in both the House and the Senate.

Second, in staffing his administration, Weicker has generally chosen seasoned political figures, not political outsiders or political amateurs. In an effort, perhaps, to compensate for his own lack of experience in state government, Weicker's appointees have had broad experience in the state. Many of these are Republicans, but there are notable Democrats and independents as well.[22] This is in fact precisely what he insisted he would do. Shortly after his election, he announced he would "throw out the old system that made party loyalty more important than expertise in the running of state government . . . and would select state officials solely on [an] objective basis with no political litmus test." [23]

In an important way, however, the promise was an empty one. Party loyalty is important only if there is a party to begin with; in Weicker's case there was none, except in a narrow, technical sense. And although party loyalty could not be a factor, personal loyalty could, and this became the political litmus test for Weicker's administration. Most of his appointees, it turns out, are longtime Weicker supporters.[24] In other words, although there is no party, there is the person, and this is critical to an understanding of once and future politics in Connecticut.

Weicker's political coalition is still highly dependent on Weicker the person. There has been no effort to build the kind of political infrastructure that would be needed for the Weicker phenomenon to survive Weicker himself—to institutionalize, as it were, Weicker's charisma, or, more modestly, his appeal to the current generation of Connecticut voters. Moreover, there has been no major shift in voter registration toward Weicker's Connecticut party, and even Weicker "loyalists" remain active locally in the Democratic and Republican parties.

All this, of course, may change between now and the 1994 gubernatorial election, and at some point new electoral alignments and new organizational entities may begin to emerge. But this seems unlikely. And even if they do, it is unlikely that Weicker himself will be either the architect or the builder of such a new political order. His interests seem more short term and personal.

The more likely outcome is that politics will continue as usual. This means that Weicker will remain an independent force in Connecticut. It means, in addition, that political parties, both as ideas and as institutions, will continue to experience hard times. Weicker has benefited from these hard times. But, as a maverick, he has contributed to them as well, without, however, providing the kind of continuous institutional alternative that is essential to electoral accountability. There is an irony in this. At the very time emerging democracies across the world are struggling to create political parties, efforts to undermine them in mature democracies, Connecticut included, continue unabated.

Notes

I would like to thank my Wesleyan colleagues Donald M. Russell and Marc Eisner for their many helpful comments. And the acknowledgments would not be complete without a special welcome to Clare Marie Murphy, whose joyful arrival on November 3, 1991, was timed just perfectly.

1. There had been independents in the statehouse before, but Weicker was the first elected by direct popular vote. The last third party governor was William T. Minor of the American Party (1855-1857). Minor, however, was selected by the state legislature, having failed to win the then constitutionally required majority of the popular vote. This constitutional requirement was abolished in 1901. The last serious third party candidate was Bridgeport's storied Socialist mayor, Jasper McLevy, who won 26 percent of the vote in 1938. McLevy's fame rests partly on his unorthodox theological views regarding municipal services. "God put the snow there," he reportedly once said to citizens demanding that the city plow the streets. "God will take it away."

2. One is reminded of other independents who had difficulty with the Republican party—New York City's Fiorello LaGuardia and John Lindsay, for example, or, in an earlier time, Theodore Roosevelt (who had been elected president as a Republican in 1904). Like Weicker, Roosevelt was a large, blustery man, with an even larger personality. And like Weicker, he broke with the Republican party to form a party of his own. (As a third party candidate in 1912 he lost to the Democrat, Woodrow Wilson.)

3. *New York Times,* December 9, 1985, II, 4.

4. *Republican Party of the State of Connecticut v. Tashjian,* 599 F. Supp. 1228 (1984). The District Court decision was upheld by both the Circuit Court and the Supreme Court, the latter in a 5-4 decision. See *Tashjian v. Republican Party of Connecticut,* 770 F.2d 265 (1985) and *Tashjian v. Republican Party of Connecticut,* 93 L.Ed. 2d 514 (1986). The Weicker proposal was limited to primaries for statewide state offices, and for the U.S. House of Representatives and the U.S. Senate. It did not extend to primaries for the state legislature or for local offices.

5. Which, some suggest, is precisely why Democrats rejected the proposed

changes, preferring instead that the Republicans continue to nominate "right of center" candidates. This general possibility may also have been what Justice Antonin Scalia had in mind when he suggested that a specially convened Republican convention, whose actions had prompted the attempt to change state law, "may have been dominated by officeholders and office seekers whose evaluations of the merits of assuring election of the Party's candidates, vis à vis the merits of proposing candidates faithful to the Party's political philosophy, diverged significantly from the views of the Party's rank and file." *Tashjian v. Republican Party of Connecticut,* 93 L.Ed. 2d 514 (1986), 538 (Scalia dissenting).

6. Under Connecticut law, a candidate who receives 20 percent of the convention vote is eligible to challenge the convention's nominee in a party primary. Bush received 35 percent of the vote. Weicker's remarks are reported in the *New York Times,* April 9, 1982, II, 2; Bush's decision in the *New York Times,* July 28, 1982, I, 2.

7. During his final year in the Senate, Weicker's presidential (Ronald Reagan) support score was 40, his opposition score 50. By contrast the average presidential support score among Democrats was 47, the average opposition score 45. Weicker also refused to support the Republican convention's 1986 gubernatorial nominee. Instead, he helped engineer a challenge primary, which his candidate eventually won. Despite his reputation as a maverick, Weicker reportedly had been of considerable help to local Republican groups throughout the state. As one former town chairman put it, he was "always available," even when a small turnout was expected, and he was sensitive to local political conditions, insisting he would not impose himself if this would hurt his local Republican supporters.

8. Connecticut had the distinction, dubious or otherwise, of having had the highest growth rate in state revenue during the 1980s—174 percent, according to one estimate. *Economist,* June 22, 1991, 26.

9. In absolute terms, federal aid actually increased, albeit at a much slower rate than it had in the past. The increase, in constant (1982 = 100) dollars was from $954 million in 1980 to $983 million in 1987.

10. Inflation aside, state spending rose by some 43 percent between 1980 and 1987. And although the state's population grew, expenditures grew even faster, in per capita, constant dollars, from $1,103 in 1980 to $1,546 in 1987.

11. Like many other states, Connecticut had neglected its physical infrastructure during the 1960s and 1970s. See, for example, U.S. General Accounting Office, "Effective Planning and Budgeting Practices Can Help the Nation's Deteriorating Physical Infrastructure," *Report to the Committee on Environment and Public Works,* U.S. Senate, November 18, 1982, (GAO/PAD 83-23) (Washington, D.C.: Government Printing Office, 1982).

12. Between 1980 and 1989, average salaries for Connecticut teachers rose, in constant dollar terms (1982 = 100), from $18,909 to $27,609, the largest

such increase in the country. In 1980, the state ranked seventeenth nationally. In 1989 it was second only to Alaska.

13. At the same time, local revenues, exclusive of revenues from the state and federal governments, also continued to grow, albeit at a somewhat lower rate than the state's.

14. The timing of the announcements was of considerable significance. Despite the decline in his popularity, Governor O'Neill remained a candidate until the end of March. Had he not delayed so long, it is likely First District Congresswoman Barbara Kennelly would have entered the race. Kennelly is the daughter of former state (and national) Democratic party chairman John Bailey and a former secretary of the state. By most accounts, she would have been a formidable candidate and some even speculated that Weicker would not have run had Kennelly been the Democratic candidate. In late February, however, Kennelly announced that, rather than running for governor, she would seek a fifth term in the House. She announced her plans, as she put it, "to cool potential 1st District suitors . . . one of [whom had] raised over $100,000 to run for a seat he claims I will not be seeking." *Congressional Quarterly Weekly Report,* February 24, 1990, 614.

15. More precisely, Morrison promised that he would veto any income tax measure unless voters approved it in a referendum.

16. Only the Republican candidate, Fifth District Representative John Rowland, ruled out the tax. Morrison maintained the position he had taken in the Democratic primary, while Weicker, refusing to endorse the tax, refused to rule it out entirely. Weicker "promise[d] the state no new taxes if the state promise[d] [him] no new problems." At the same time, he declared that, given the economic downturn in the state, "imposing an income tax would be like pouring gasoline on a fire." *New York Times,* August 11, 1990, I, 27.

17. At 8 percent, the state sales tax was already the highest in the nation. The legislature's 1991 proposed $7.7 billion budget included some $960 million in new revenues, most of which would be derived from a much expanded sales tax. Under the legislature's plan, the sales tax would have been extended to such previously exempt items as motor vehicle repairs, haircuts, laundry and dry cleaning, newspaper and magazine subscriptions, roofing, siding and external sheetmetal work, house painting and wallpapering, and 900- and international number phone calls. In addition, the exemption on adult clothing would have been reduced from $75 to $25 and a new 10 percent tax would have been added on high ticket "luxury items," such as automobiles over $30,000, boats over $100,000, and jewelry and furs over $10,000. The tax measure eventually signed by Weicker included not only the income tax but the tax on most of these previously exempt items—albeit at a 6 percent, rather than 8 percent, rate.

18. An income tax had been enacted in 1971 but was repealed within weeks because of intense public opposition.

19. An added reason for business support was the fact that some 40 percent of sales tax revenue came from businesses' purchases of goods and services. *Hartford Courant,* July 1, 1991, 4.

20. In 1991, the opposition also included the president pro-tem and the majority leader of the Senate, two of only four Senate Democrats to vote against the tax.

21. The choices were draconian—a substantial tax increase, an equally substantial cut in state spending, or some combination of the two. None of these was a politically attractive option. Now that the tax is law, it is unlikely to be overturned, at least not before the 1992 legislative elections. A special session of the current legislature is a possibility, as is a legislative vote to repeal the tax. But it is highly doubtful that there are sufficient votes in the House or the Senate to override what would be a certain gubernatorial veto.

22. As already noted, his secretary of the Office of Policy and Management is former Democratic State Representative William Cibes. His lieutenant governor and only other member of A Connecticut Party to seek office is Eunice Groark, a Hartford Republican, with close ties to the State's insurance industry. The commissioner of administrative services is a former candidate for the Republican nomination for governor, Reginald Smith. Smith withdrew from the race to support Weicker. The commissioner of consumer affairs is a Democrat, Gloria Schaffer, a former secretary of the state who was defeated by Weicker in the 1976 U.S. Senate election.

23. *New York Times,* December 30, 1990, XII-CN, 1.

24. There have been public charges that, despite his promises, political cronyism remains very much a part of Connecticut politics. According to one press report, a lobbying firm set up shortly after Weicker's election by a long time friend and political ally has, with the help of the governor's office, since prospered. *Hartford Courant,* July 24, 1991, 1.

6. FLORIDA: LAWTON M. CHILES, JR., REINVENTING STATE GOVERNMENT

Robert E. Crew, Jr.

In the early spring, the 1990 campaign for governor of Florida promised to be only moderately interesting. The incumbent, Republican Robert Martinez, was attempting to become the first Republican governor in the state's history to be reelected. Martinez had several assets. He was very well financed, he was supported by George Bush (whose son, Jeb, had been a member of the Martinez cabinet), and he was able, because of Bush's support, to bring to Florida on his behalf virtually the entire U.S. cabinet. (After his defeat, Bush would appoint him the nation's drug czar.) During the course of his administration, however, Martinez had distinguished himself by flip flops: first he opposed new taxes; next he supported a new sales tax on services; and then, after this tax had passed the legislature and was being widely criticized, he switched his position and opposed the tax. Similar incidents had given him a reputation for catering to public opinion polls and for changing his position to suit whatever was popular at the moment. Thus, there was some feeling that he was vulnerable. However, the field of Democrats that emerged to challenge Martinez was nondescript. It was led, or perhaps *fronted* is a better word, by a congressman whose major accomplishment had been to be fired into space on one of the *Challenger* voyages. The other "serious" candidate was a state senator from South Florida. Political observers were, therefore, ambivalent about the possible outcome and about the nature of the impending campaign.

This scenario changed dramatically on April 4, 1990, when Lawton Chiles, former U.S. senator and chair of the Senate Budget Committee, announced his entry into the race. Walkin' Lawton, as he is called in Florida—because of his walk of the length of the state in his first campaign for the Senate—had retired from the Senate in 1986, citing "burnout" in the office. He had spent the intervening years in positions at Florida State University and the University of Florida. His declaration of candidacy "hit Democrats like a lightening bolt," [1] delighting despondent professional Democrats who were questioning the ability of their party's candidates to defeat Martinez, and galvanizing Floridians. Within days of his announcement polls showed him to be 34 percentage points ahead of his Democratic challengers and 6 points ahead of the Republican incumbent. While these leads fluctuated substantially during both the Democratic primary and the general election, he won the primary by 39 percentage points, and the general election by 14. He took office in January 1991, with what he described as a mandate to "reinvent the way government works in Florida." He emerged from his first legislative session with solid accomplishments and a challenging agenda for the future.

Policy Goals and Priorities: Themes and Accomplishments of the Administration

Chiles's primary and general election campaigns both involved discussion of and debate on a variety of issues. They included his stance on abortion, his concern for the treatment of children in Florida, his use of the drug Prozac for depression, his interest in the environment, his opposition to the incumbent's corrections policy, his concern with the manner in which the Florida lottery was being managed, and how the state should finance its service and infrastructure needs. However, at its base, the Chiles campaign was more about the way in which his administration would run state government than about what it would do substantively. Chiles felt that nothing short of a transformation in the way state government did business was adequate to the problems faced in Florida. Allowing that the former governor had tried to be a good manager of the existing system, he declared, "We're going to try to do something that is totally different—we want to change the system." [2]

Two issues emerged as the heart of his campaign and of his administration to this point: (1) the need to "restore faith and trust in state government"; and (2) the need to "rightsize" government, to decentralize and "provide more competition in our government services." These issues reflected Chiles's feeling that Florida's government was on the verge of becoming "beached on a bloated and inefficient bureaucracy" and his concern that public officials were "driven by an insatiable desire to perpetuate themselves in office by depending on exorbitant contributions from those having special interests in legislation." [3] His logic was that until these issues were resolved, state government would not have the credibility to attack other important problems, in particular the financing of state government.

Restoring Faith and Trust in State Government

Chiles and his running mate, Buddy MacKay, a highly regarded former member of the U.S. Congress, made a dramatic attempt in their campaign to address the issue of confidence in government. To "restore the covenant" between the people and elected officials they agreed to accept campaign contributions of no more than $100 from any single contributor. This tactic was meant to signify their independence from "special interests" and to give them an administration "free to decide on the basis of the merits of each case." [4]

Even though Chiles had used similar limits in earlier Senate races, this action was viewed—in the face of the $10 million dollar campaign chest amassed by his incumbent opponent—as political gimmickry, and perhaps suicide. However, Chiles and MacKay were able to raise enough money to run the kind of campaign necessary for two well-known candidates, and the tactic became a positive issue for the challengers. It was a major element in the Chiles-MacKay victory.

Chiles continued to emphasize the theme of strengthening the bond between public officials and citizens in both his inaugural address and his State of the State address to the legislature. In the latter he proposed major legislation that (1) limited campaign contributions to $500 per contested statewide, legislative, and multicounty election; (2) called for the reporting of gifts to public officials that exceeded $25 in value; and (3) gave new investigatory authority to the state's Ethics Commission. He lobbied the legislature very hard on these issues and met personally, before he was sworn in as governor, with the joint House/Senate committee that was working on the ethics bills even before the session began. Each of these pieces of legislation was enacted, giving Florida some of the most stringent campaign finance and public ethics laws in the nation.

Rightsizing State Government

The second major focus of the Chiles campaign and administration has been concern for changing, in a fundamental way, how Florida state government operates—for, as he puts it, "rightsizing" state government. Used as a catch-all term during the campaign, rightsizing came to include several beliefs about government. They were: (1) the federal government cannot solve the state's problems and should not be relied on to do so; (2) state government is too big; (3) state agencies are performing some roles better left to other governmental entities and are not performing more appropriate roles—they are trying to micromanage rather than to set standards and measure outcomes; (4) state government is providing services and "products" for which the private sector or community organizations may be the better supplier; (5) state government, the legislature as well as the executive, is using outmoded or inefficient procedures in budgeting, procurement, and personnel; and (6) in the absence of competition and leadership, state bureaucracy is flabby, uninspired, and unconcerned about "customer" satisfaction.

These principles are not that novel. Indeed, some of them had been a part of Chiles's philosophy of government for years.[5] Further, at least some of his political allies in Florida—in particular, the state commissioner of education—had already begun the "restructuring" Chiles supported. However, the rhetoric that accompanied his discussion of these principles and the manner in which proposals to implement them were packaged gave them a new meaning. In the eyes of many academics and journalists, Chiles is reinventing government. (Much of Chiles's view of government appears in the recent book, *Laboratories of Democracy*, by David Osborne; he and Doug Daniels, the former economic development director in Michigan, were widely cited as Chiles's inspiration on state government reform.)[6]

Chiles packaged his commitment to the reinvention of state government in a series of proposals that he made to the state legislature, in his review of the budget, and in his support of proposals and ideas that came from other sources. His initial legislative proposals included efforts to reduce the size of the government workforce, to create productivity incentives for state agencies, to give local communities more control of education, to expand local influence over the allocation of state dollars spent for corrections, and—in perhaps the most visible and controversial of his actions—to reform the state's career service system. The last effort involved the use of the state's sunset laws to "abolish" the existing career service system and to begin the construction of "a more efficient operational system to deliver services to Floridians." Chiles also appointed a Commission on Government by the People to study and "provide the road-map for right-sizing our government," and he called for the creation of a Department of Elder Affairs (previously authorized in a constitutional amendment) to be used as a model to decentralize, empower, and provide more community participation and control of services. Virtually all of his legislative proposals were enacted into law. Further, the legislature authorized pilot programs to increase management flexibility and efficiency in the Department of Revenue and the Division of Workers Compensation within the Department of Labor and Employment Security.

Given the nature of its focus, the impact of rightsizing could not be expected to be seen immediately. Chiles, in his initial budget, asked for and received reductions in virtually all state agency requests—including the office of the governor—and a cut of $700 million from the 1991 fiscal year agency requests. Indeed, the total state budget passed reflected a 5.9 percent increase over the previous year, the lowest percentage growth in a Florida budget in fifteen years. However, the vast majority of actions designed to implement the rightsizing agenda have emerged over the months following the first legislative session.

One early step was the creation of a nine-member panel charged with reviewing state agency plans for the use of $32.5 million that the legislature cut from agency budgets and then set aside for productivity improvements within state government. In early September, this panel met to consider the proposals submitted by the agencies. Most of the awards went to staff training, computer purchases, and salary adjustments. Examples of the proposals ranged from the mundane (the secretary of administration proposed $199 bonuses for employees in some pay grades) to the revolutionary, at least in the Florida environment (computer hardware, software, and telephone lines to permit the Department of Highway Safety and Motor Vehicles to take driver's license and vehicle registration renewals from citizens without requiring them to go to Highway Patrol stations).

In October, when no dramatic proposals had yet been made to reinvent government, Chiles began to come under fire from some journalists for a lack of leadership, or, as one paper put it, for "stealth leadership." During the course of the month Chiles, who was using various channels to prepare recommendations, responded with a series of initiatives from his office, from a special cabinet task force and from the Governor's Commission on Government by the People. In combination, these efforts produced a reorganization plan that Chiles claimed would save the taxpayers of Florida about $7 million and generated a variety of proposals designed to reduce the number of employees and improve operational efficiency within state government. The recommendations included the following:

1. Abolish the Department of Highway Safety and Motor Vehicles, transferring the Highway Patrol to the Department of Law Enforcement and shifting the driver's license, registration, and titling functions to the Department of Agriculture and Consumer Services.

2. Abolish the Department of General Services, moving its purchasing, construction, and building-management duties to the various agencies and the Department of Administration (DOA). DOA would be renamed Department of Management Services, and personnel functions would be transferred to the agencies.

3. Reorganize dramatically the Department of Health and Rehabilitative Services, shifting more authority back to local communities and breaking the agency into smaller units.

4. Reorganize the Department of Natural Resources (DNR) into an agency that manages state lands; units unrelated to this function would be transferred to other agencies, and DNR would come under the control of the governor, rather than the cabinet.

5. Mandate a seventy-two hour cooling-off period between the passage of a state budget and final enactment to allow legislators and the public to object to spending priorities.

6. Allow the governor's office to hold back 5 percent of each agency's general revenue budget in a special reserve fund and set spending priorities for trust fund money, which constitutes nearly 60 percent of the state budget.

7. Give the governor line-item veto authority for spending in bills other than the budget (in 1990, more than $129 million was spent in such bills).

8. Abolish line-item budgeting in state government.

9. Establish a system of measurable performance standards for all agencies of state government, and create a commission to audit the performance of agencies and collect and publish data relevant to the performance of state government.

Although these efforts were viewed positively and would have been pursued in the next legislative session, the recommendations were quickly caught up in the debate concerning efforts to deal with the state's rapidly deteriorating budget situation. State revenue projections made public early in September forced new attention on the need for tax revision, the issue the governor had hoped to delay until his rightsizing efforts had bought him the credibility needed to change the tax system in a way that would increase revenues.

Chiles's initial response when faced with the revenue shortfall was to ask state agencies to recommend to him and the Florida cabinet reductions amounting to 6 percent of their budgets. The impact of such reductions was dramatic—much lower levels of service, lost jobs, and higher costs for services. Thus, a chorus of calls came in for convening a special legislative session in January 1992 so that the dwindling coffers could be refilled. Chiles stuck to his position that "the public has no confidence in state government's ability to handle money sensibly and that putting new revenue 'patches' on the system would be useless."[7] A poll published on October 18 supported this contention. Only 11 percent of the state's population said that the state should enact new taxes or tax increases to avoid budget cuts.[8]

Facing Chiles's determination to go through with the budget cuts, an attorney representing six foster children whose support from a program housed in the Florida Supreme Court faced a cut persuaded a Florida circuit court judge to enjoin the governor and the cabinet from making this and the other cuts needed to balance the budget. The judge argued that only the legislature, not the governor and the cabinet, had the authority to cut money from the state agencies once their budgets had been approved. In particular, the judge ruled, the governor and the cabinet did not have the authority to include the judicial branch as a state agency, and therefore to cut the disputed program's budget.[9] (Unlike other state agency heads, the state's chief justice had been unwilling to face the tough choices imposed on him by the governor's call for a reduction and had refused to make the necessary cuts in his budget.) The circuit court judge suggested that Chiles call a special session of the legislature if he wanted to balance the budget at the moment.

Supported by a statement from the Speaker of the House that he would not call a special session because there was no legislation ready to raise taxes or to amend the existing budget, Chiles appealed the decision to the state supreme court, placing that court in a classic conflict of interest. The supreme court immediately overturned the circuit court ruling and permitted Chiles and the cabinet to designate the cuts necessary to balance the budget. However, the court reserved the right to study the case in detail and to decide the issue at a later time. On October 22, Chiles delivered on his pledge to try to reduce the size of state government before raising taxes and moved to impose a $579 million cut in the state's budget. Four other members of Florida's constitutionally created cabinet (which consists of six officials elected to other state offices) also voted to approve the cuts. At the same time Chiles began talking explicitly about the need for a revised tax structure, including new business taxes and the removal of sales tax exemptions.

On October 29, the state supreme court ruled that the statute authorizing the governor and the cabinet to cut spending when the legislature was not in session violated the constitutional doctrine of separation of powers. The court said that only the legislature can change laws it enacts and that the legislature had unconstitutionally delegated its authority to the governor and the cabinet. Chiles responded on November 1 by issuing a call for a special session of the legislature to be convened December 10 through 17. The purpose of the session would be to cut the state budget by $622 million. At this point new revenue estimates indicated a need for larger cuts. Modifying his strategy to separate the issue of governmental reform and budget reform, he also gave legislators a long list of government reorganization and budget reforms. In issuing the Call, he reiterated his position that a quick fix—raising just enough revenue to get through the current emergency—would be unacceptable.

To keep the pressure on the legislature, Chiles, on November 22, submitted a budget for 1992-1993 that anticipated the situation the state would be in if no action were taken on his reorganization efforts and if no revenue increases were produced. This budget was $358 million below the 1991-1992 level and would lead to draconian cuts in state services. Saying, "This is not the budget I believe our people should have," Chiles made it clear that if the legislature began his government reform process in the special session of December 10, he would be ready in late December with an "investment" budget that would meet the needs of the state.

The special session proved to be somewhat less tractable than the first regular session had been. At least part of the reason was that Chiles proposed a larger, more complicated agenda. His proposals included reorganization plans for the Department of Health and Rehabilitative Services, abolishment of the Departments of General Services and Highway Safety and Motor Vehicles, and reorganization of the executive branch. From the moment the governor placed his reorganization proposals on the agenda, he began to get resistance. Prominent members of both bodies of the legislature complained that there was not enough time in the session (seven days) to do justice to the complicated legislation associated with government reorganization. In the end, Chiles admitted that he had overstuffed the session and settled for a promise of major action on reorganization in the next regular session. He did, however, get agreement on the issue that had been most controversial in the early stages of his administration, an overhaul of the state's career service system. The legislature made changes in that system that gave managers more authority to change job classifications and to reassign workers to more productive roles. It also followed his lead in making the budget cuts necessary to balance the budget, although there were some differences in the two plans.

Furthermore, the fragile peace hammered out between Democrats and Republicans in the Senate at the beginning of the regular session broke down during the special session. At a crucial point in the negotiations, the Republicans banded together and enlisted one Democrat in their effort to sabotage the budget. The Senate president responded by making the vote on the issue a matter of principle; she removed all Republicans and the wayward Democrat from the chairs of committees and subcommittees and recalled to the capitol two senators who were out of town. She was successful in getting the budget approved (by two votes), but incurred the enmity of all Republicans and perhaps ensured the end of bipartisan control of the Florida state Senate.

Thus Chiles's efforts to reduce spending and improve the operational efficiency of state government as a prelude to improving the state's tax and revenue systems are joined with that issue.

Other Issues

While the issues of restoring the public's trust in their elected officials and rightsizing the government have dominated the Chiles agenda, this focus has not been exclusive. Chiles has demonstrated interest in other problems. His primary concerns are identified in Table 6-1. The table also provides a scorecard of his legislative success with these issues.

Lawton Chiles succeeded in accomplishing most of the major goals that he set for the first year of his administration. He has also clearly articulated an agenda for the future and seems determined to pursue it. What factors have contributed to the success he has achieved to this point, and how are they likely to affect the future direction of the Chiles administration?

Politics and Personality: Political and Managerial Style

Political Style

At least some of Chiles's success thus far can be attributed to his political style. The central elements of this style were evident when he was elected governor of Florida. They had been honed during his twelve years in the Florida State Legislature and his eighteen years in the U.S. Senate. "He is a very religious man, and an earnest one, but congenial enough in temperament not to be cloying." [10] He was one of the most active members of the Senate prayer breakfast group and had "close relations with like-minded colleagues on both sides of the aisle." [11] His values are honesty and humility, and many observers attributed his victory to his ability to get Floridians to trust him. "Former aides, longtime allies and even new converts say that Chiles easily projects sincerity [and] genuineness ... that few modern politicians can muster." [12]

If there has ever been an ideological centrist in politics, Lawton Chiles is it. As a U.S. senator, he generally ended up near 50 percent on all the rating charts, and he describes himself as a "fellow who sort of comes out in the middle." [13] His position on issues seems to reflect small town values, so he is not predictable according to the usual

Table 6-1 Major Components of the 1991 Legislative Program of Governor Lawton M. Chiles, Jr.

Proposal	Outcome
Campaign Reform	
Limit campaign contributions to $500 per contested election.	Passed
Prohibit campaign solicitation in public buildings.	Passed
Prohibit contributions to candidates during legislative session.	Failed
Cap spending at $2 million for cabinet races and $5 million for governor's race in return for public financing of campaign.	Passed
Ethics Reform	
Require quarterly reports by givers and receivers of gifts worth more than $25.	Passed
Prohibit payment of contingency fees for lobbyists who get an appropriation of public funds for their clients.	Failed
Provide automatic penalties for constitutional officers who fail to comply with disclosure requirements of the 1976 Sunshine Amendment.	Failed
Strengthen Commission on Ethics by giving it power to initiate investigations.	Passed
Rightsizing State Government	
Reduce by 5 percent agencies' salaries and benefits (eliminate 4,500 to 5,000 positions—over $163 million).	Passed
Return one-half of these savings ($81.5 million) to agencies for productivity improvements.	Passed at $32 million
Cut $700 million from agency requests to the General Revenue Fund.	Passed
Initiate sunset law governing state career service system.	Passed
Human Services	
Create Department of Elder Affairs in state government.	Passed
Fund "Healthy Start" health care for pregnant mothers and children in need ($91.5 million).	Passed at $90 million
Increase fees paid by hospitals and doctors to pay for indigent health care.	Failed

Education

Support Secretary of Education Betty Castor's recommendation to reform education system:

    a. Eliminate categorical programs. — Passed

    b. Give more authority to local schools. — Passed

    c. Put more people and dollars into classrooms. — Passed

Increase college tuition by 20 percent for in-state students and 25 percent for out-of-state students. — Passed

Environment and Growth Management

Eliminate the High Speed Rail Transportation Commission. — Passed

Eliminate the subsidy for the Center for Urban Transportation Research. — Passed

Fund Preservation 2000 (purchase of land to protect integrity of environment). — Passed at $270 million

Create Everglades pollution clean-up plan. — Passed

Corrections

Pass Community Corrections Partnership Act (provide community-based sanctions and treatment programs; funds provided by state to participating counties). — Passed intellectual orthodoxies. Indeed, his ability to pick out, issue by issue, the concerns of his constituency is viewed as the quality that distinguishes Chiles from other politicians.[14] He is willing to listen, is open to new perspectives, wants to learn things for himself, and is flexible in the positions he takes. Two examples illustrate his openness and inquisitiveness.

The first example comes from his initial campaign for the U.S. Senate in 1970. His basic campaign tactic was to walk the length of Florida, talking to "the fellow who doesn't ask anything from anybody, works like a dog and makes eight to twelve thousand dollars a year." [15] While the walk was an obvious attempt to gain attention, Chiles claimed to have gained an entirely new perspective on politics as a result and made a dramatic change—from hawk to dove—in his position on the Vietnam War.

The second example took place during his campaign for governor, when his inquisitiveness was demonstrated in a way that frustrated his campaign staff and brought into question his political savvy. Abandoning to a large extent the orthodoxy of modern campaigns—flying from one media market to another for "photo ops"—Chiles spent hours in conversations with small groups concerned with or knowledgeable about a particular topic. These "program days" consumed much of the campaign as Lawton and his wife, Rhea, studied the successful programs of local governments and nonprofit groups throughout the state. Furthermore, these activities were likely to take place out of the view of reporters, who quickly tired of genuine discussions of the problems faced by the citizens of Florida. While this tactic drove his campaign staff to distraction, he claims that it permitted him to develop a real feel for the pulse of public concern and to inform himself about the intricacies of particular policy issues. It was also a powerful argument against "slick" politics. He continues to use this mechanism under the title "with the people days."

Chiles is something of an idealist and a sentimentalist. His conception of government and politics hearkens back to a happier, more hopeful time when there was a "covenant" among the people to help and protect each other. He proclaimed his inauguration a "jubilee" where "our most valued possession, our sense of family, our sense of belonging is returned." His politics is rooted in an appeal to these feelings and to small town, Democratic values. He believes strongly that a serious weakness of the American political system is the disruption that special interests create in this "family" fabric.

Despite his small town, laid back style, Chiles is no political pushover. He has demonstrated ambition, has taken risks to advance himself,[16] and has exhibited a willingness to fight to gather the reins of executive power in his own hands.[17] His assertiveness has come as a surprise to some who questioned whether his "earnest search for a centrist position . . . was the most effective way to galvanize others into following his lead." [18] However, he seems personally secure and is clearly confident in his own abilities. He claimed in his inaugural address that "in my life anything that I've been able to believe I could do, I've been able to do." A growing list of examples of battles joined with other important players in Florida politics demonstrates Chiles's willingness to play political hardball.[19] They include:

1. An attempt to change budgetary rules to give himself unprecedented control over budgetary spending decisions during tough economic times—after the legislature had decided on the budget and he had issued his line-item vetoes.
2. A battle with the Public Service Commission Nominating Council for power to go beyond the council's choices of who should sit on the powerful utilities regulatory agency.
3. An attempt to get legislative approval for "lump sum" budgeting—in essence, turning over an agency or program to the executive branch to manage without giving the legislature, or anyone else, a say in how operations are run.
4. A battle with the state Democratic party's central committee over control of the selection of the state Democratic chair.

Organization and Management

The political style described above created several organizational imperatives and has had a demonstrable impact on the way in which Chiles has organized the Executive Office of the Governor (EOG) for purposes of pursuing his policy agenda. The structure exhibits two characteristics: it attempts to maximize control over administration policy and attempts to give Chiles access to divergent opinions about this policy. The organizational chart for the governor's office is presented in Figure 6-1.

Given his inquisitive style, a hierarchical organization designed to shield the governor from all but the most "important" matters would be inappropriate. Chiles and Buddy MacKay, his lieutenant governor and most important adviser, are described as "having their fingers in everything and Chiles is said to want to be in contact with the person working on a problem, not his or her boss." [20] Further, given his long tenure in Florida politics, Chiles can call on the advice of a host of

Figure 6-1 Executive Office of the Governor, State of Florida, January 1991

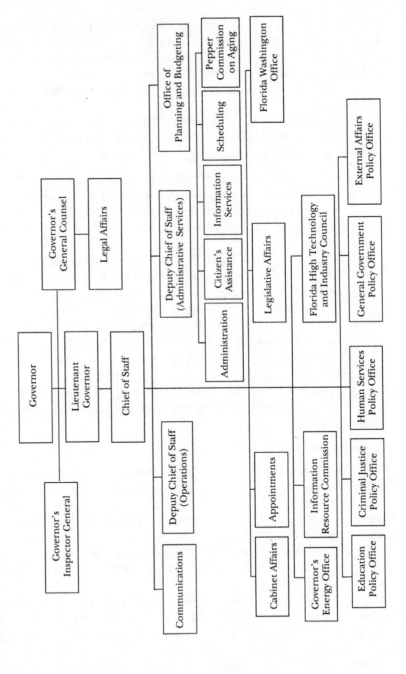

contacts within the political and governmental structure and from the private sector. Thus, while there is a chief of staff in the EOG, Chiles sees that role as "a traffic cop to keep things straight." [21]

As is generally the case in this type of organizational arrangement, reports of jockeying for power and of friction among Chiles's top lieutenants have circulated. Such friction could be relieved if a tight chain of command was established. "Chiles obviously prefers to let the jockeying continue. His stated reason is that this lets him have direct access to divergent opinions. The system also maximizes his control over the administration's policy." [22]

Despite Chiles's insistence on being at the center of decisions involving his administration, his style is not that of a rapid-fire decision maker. "In his efforts to reach decisions, he prefers to avoid confrontations and appears cautious because he keeps his thoughts to himself as long as he can." [23]

The governor also insisted that the EOG had to have a policy orientation—that it had to "be the source for the initiation and development of new ideas and possibilities for the government as a whole." [24] To accomplish this imperative, five policy groups have been created to extend the vision of the governor in five major areas. These are education, criminal justice, human services, general government, and external affairs. The staff assigned to these groups will "perform in the classic general staff capacity, in that they will represent the Governor in direct dealings with departmental secretaries." [25]

Finally, to better coordinate the administration's actions, Chiles has installed Lieutenant Governor MacKay as the "chief of operations ... the inside guy who makes [government] work." [26] MacKay holds weekly meetings with all state agency heads. Further, in the important area of growth-management, MacKay is the person to whom the five agencies most intimately involved with these issues report on a day-to-day basis. Placing the lieutenant governor in this operational position is quite unusual in American politics. It reflects the importance of the lieutenant governor in the administration. But further, because of the close relationship between himself and his lieutenant governor, it demonstrates Chiles's interest in making the EOG a focal point for policy development.

The organizational mechanics reinforce the political style of Lawton Chiles and provide him the opportunity to meet head on one of the frustrations that led him to resign from the Senate: the inability to act forcefully on what he saw as major problems. Indeed, one of the unexpected pleasures of the office of governor to Chiles is the forum it provides for leadership. For most of his political life Chiles had viewed the office as a hassle. "I didn't realize that the fact that you can execute when you're the governor, that you can initiate, makes all the difference." [27] While such naivete about the nature of the office is somewhat surprising, Chiles is clearly ready to use the governorship aggressively. As he said in his State of the State address, "I am determined to provide strong leadership. I may be wrong but I don't intend to be in doubt." He reiterated this point when faced with the furor surrounding the budget cuts made in October. And he was clearly frustrated when the State Supreme Court overruled his attempts to cut the budget and forced the calling of a special legislative session—so frustrated that in response to a question regarding the value of a governor who had so little budget authority, he said, "Well, I would not want to hold it [the governorship], but I'll have to serve out my time. It isn't the contract I thought I had." [28]

Political Skill

Bargaining and Negotiation

Adeptness in maneuvering in the political community of which the executive is a part—be it in Washington or Tallahassee—is clearly one element of success. Indeed, according to the most influential book on political leadership in America, "The successful exercise of [executive] power is the product of skillful bargains with other politicians." [29] Fortunately, according to the governor's former chief Senate aide, Chiles loves this process and the activities involved, the maneuvering and compromising.[30] As a senator, Chiles did not have a reputation as a big time political "operator." However, as chairman of the Senate Budget Committee, he "made more of the position than most thought possible," [31] uniting Senate Democrats around the Reagan budgets. Further, he was successful in rallying a near majority in opposition to the MX missile. Michael Barone attributes Chiles's success in these episodes to his conciliatory manner, "the fact that his own proposals never sound dangerously liberal" and to the fact that he was not perceived as ambitious. Alan Ehrenhalt suggests it was due to his "laid back, folksy manner." [32]

Whatever the basis, Chiles demonstrated substantial skill in the use of informal techniques of power in his dealing with the legislature throughout the first session. While refusing to "horsetrade," he personally went to the Senate chamber to buttonhole senators on behalf of his campaign reform measures and regularly sent the lieutenant governor to the floor to lobby on behalf of his bill to create a Department of Elder Affairs. His negotiations on both of these issues were successful.

Chiles also showed evidence of another useful negotiating skill: knowing when to cut your losses. The best example came in what had been a three-year legal battle with the federal government over the contamination of the Everglades. When Chiles took office, the suit had already cost the taxpayers of Florida $6 million and showed no signs of ending. In May, Chiles stunned even his own staff and settled the suit by accepting blame on behalf of the state. In response he gained control over the cleanup of the wetlands and over curbing future use by farmers and developers.

Public Rhetoric

Gubernatorial success is based to some extent on the "artful wielding of informal power through bargaining." [33] But in an age when the doctrine that a governor ought to be a leader of public opinion has become an unquestioned premise, gubernatorial success is also dependent on the skillful use of rhetorical appeals on behalf of objectives. No one who knows or who has watched Lawton Chiles over the course of his political career would claim that he is a great political orator. In fact, in what surely must have been the unkindest cut of all, one political columnist compared his speaking style unfavorably with that of George Bush.[34] Chiles recognized his limitations on this dimension in his inaugural address. He explained why he "sometimes has trouble behind a podium" with the story that he was descended from a Methodist circuit rider preacher about whom it was said that he "was a fine worker but not particularly gifted as a pulpiteer."

Yet Chiles has demonstrated great skill at political communication. As a U.S. senator he was very effective at the tasks of public leadership: "at defending himself publicly, at promoting policy initiatives statewide, and at inspiriting the population." [35] "Because of his sincerity and inspiration, criticism slips off Chiles like cold butter melting on hot pancakes," [36] and he is often referred to as a teflon candidate. The glare of publicity that focuses more directly on a governor than on a U.S. senator, and the seriousness of the budget crises in Florida, has tested these skills to the limit.

During the campaign, Chiles did prove to be more effective on live television than his speaking style might lead one to expect. He displayed the "intimate conversational style" that Kathleen Jamieson argues is essential to effective communication through the medium.[37] In the single debate of the gubernatorial campaign, he was very skillful in projecting his personality. He was described as relaxed, unshakable, forceful, and appearing to relish the chance to mix it up. His sincerity was obvious, and he also demonstrated an ability to think on his feet and to turn a graceful phrase. This was demonstrated most tellingly in a single exchange, when Chiles turned toward Martinez and said: "We've got a week to go. Why should we keep up this 30-second barrage [with television ads]? Why don't you and I just go around and just talk to people about these issues? " Martinez weakly sought to deflect the question, only to have it hammered home by Chiles later: "Crackers don't like a dog that won't fight." [38] Fifty-two percent of the viewers who called in to the host television station thought that Chiles had won the debate.[39]

During the legislative session and in the battle waged over government reform that began in earnest after the session, Chiles also demonstrated willingness to appeal over the heads of legislators in pursuit of his goals. During the session one episode was particularly dramatic. This was his effort to pressure the leadership of the legislature on one of the major themes of his administration, rightsizing government.

One element of this theme was that the existing career service system did not provide the flexibility needed in a rapidly changing state and economy. Pay was determined on seniority rather than performance, the job classification scheme was inequitable, and when there were layoffs, senior workers were able to keep their jobs while more productive junior employees were sacrificed. Chiles promoted a variety of solutions to this problem, but, in the face of a strong reaction from state employees and general opposition to change from the legislature, was unable until nearly the last day of the session to get legislation moving that would address his concern.

Two days before the required adjournment of the legislature, House and Senate leaders met with the governor to present their "final" legislative package. Since Florida sunshine laws are very stringent, this and the meetings described below were attended by Florida reporters. The list provided to Chiles did not include action regarding the personnel system. Chiles insisted that some provisions be included regarding this matter. The leadership returned to their respective bodies and on the following morning brought to Chiles a proposal to study the problem. Chiles was clearly upset. With reporters crowding around taking notes, Chiles said, "You can fool the fans, but you can't fool the players, and I'm a player." He then seized the opportunity to lecture publicly those present—including the leadership and the state senator who represented many state employees and who most strongly opposed the legislation—about his commitment to change in the system and to articulate a rationale for such a change. Suitably impressed by this public defense of the proposal, the House and Senate leadership backed down and agreed to allow a bill "sunsetting" the existing personnel system to come to a vote. It passed easily. Thus, over the course of the next year, the Florida career service system will be reviewed for purposes of making the changes Chiles sees as important to his agenda of revamping state government.

In his efforts to convince the legislature of the necessity of beginning government reorganization during the special session called to balance the budget, the governor has also tried to use public opinion to his benefit. He has used three mechanisms in this effort. The first was the "no new taxes" budget described earlier. Released to the media, this budget was designed to show Floridians, in a dramatic way, the situation the state faced. The second was a "special message" sent to citizens throughout the state asking them to convince their legislators that Chiles had a "sensible plan that needs their stamp of approval." Paid for by the Polk County Democratic Executive Committee, this message was mailed to 40,000 households throughout Florida. Chiles followed this up with an "economic summit" to which fifty of the state's most important business executives were invited and at which he made a pitch for his plan.

Thus, both during and after the legislative session Chiles has kept his vision for Florida state government squarely in the public eye and has refused temptations to be pulled in other directions. Many observers think he has done "an excruciatingly good job of what the executive ought to do—get our attention, explain the problem and coax change. Chiles climbed into the bully pulpit last January and hasn't stepped down since. (Even if sometimes we wanted to get the hook for relief.)" [40]

The Resources of Leadership

Lawton Chiles assumed office with a sizable store of political capital. A brief discussion will illuminate the nature of his holdings. We then turn to an analysis of the extent to which they were utilized in his pursuit of his objectives. We look first at his legislative support.

Legislative Support

When Chiles came to power, the Florida House of Representatives had seventy-three Democrats and forty-seven Republicans, and the Republicans wielded only minimal influence within the body. (Since that time, the Democrats have gained one convert from the Republican party.) Further, the Speaker of the House, T. K. Wetherell, a smart, tough-minded former Florida State University football player with a Ph.D. in education, exerted substantial control over his colleagues and shared much of the philosophy of the Chiles administration. In addition, Bo Johnson, the Speaker-designate (in Florida, the presiding officers of both the Senate and the House serve only one term), had once been a member of Chiles's Senate staff. This combination of circumstances was clearly advantageous to Chiles. While there were disagreements between the governor and the House of Representatives, the governor had supporters in the body who wanted to make him look good and who provided him a mechanism through which he could easily pursue his policy agenda.

The state Senate was a more difficult environment. To begin with, interparty competition was much more intense in the body; the Democratic edge was only twenty-three to seventeen. (As the result of a special election in July 1991, the numbers are now twenty-two to eighteen.) Further, it was not until the final days before the Senate's organizing session that there was assurance that the person who had been elected president-designate in the previous session would be elected Senate president. For weeks before the session, a conservative Democrat and former Senate president claimed to have the support of the seventeen Republicans and five "renegade" conservative Democrats, enough to elect him and to put the Republicans in control of the body. In the end, Chiles put heavy pressure on the Democrats involved; the three Republicans who are Hispanic announced (in exchange for two subcommittee chairs on the Senate Reapportionment Committee) their support for the president-designate; and she was elected. Nevertheless, four Republicans were awarded committee chairs and the renegades exacted pledges of conservatism on taxes, the size of state government, and various growth and environmental issues affecting their districts. The result was a body somewhat less congenial to the Chiles administration than the House. It was not, however, a hostile environment and was clearly more responsive to a Democratic than a Republican governor. Indeed, if, as Paul Light says, overall party support is the "gold standard" of political capital, Lawton Chiles was rich.[41]

Public Approval and Electoral Margin

Chiles added some personal political capital to the existing legislative support by winning decisive victories in both the primary and the general election. His general election margin of 14 percent reflected support in every section of the state. He won fifty-two of the sixty-seven counties in Florida and lost none, even in the heavily Republican gold coast, by overwhelming margins. Some observers attribute the success of the Democrats in fighting off a well-financed Republican challenge in the state Senate to Chiles's popularity, and others say that Chiles's success turned what would have been normal victories into landslides. Thus Chiles seems to have created the possibility of future influence with the legislature—that is, he has left the impression that he can help individual legislators with their constituents.

Despite the margin of his electoral victory and his substantial success in the first legislative session, Chiles's public popularity has

Table 6-2 Performance Ratings of Lawton Chiles and Robert Martinez During the First Year of Their Terms

	Excellent/ Good	Fair/ Poor	Don't know/ Undecided
January-March			
Martinez [a]	23%	27%	48%
Martinez [b]	31	17	52
Chiles [b]	39	27	34
April-June			
Martinez [c]	43	45	12
Chiles [b]	50	24	26
July-September			
Martinez [b]	12	53	35
Martinez [d]	24	65	11
Chiles [e]	58	33	9
October-December			
Martinez [c]	32	65	3
Chiles [c]	33	63	4
Chiles [c]	23	76	1

[a] Florida Annual Policy Survey, Florida State University

[b] *New York Times* Poll

[c] Mason-Dixon Poll

[d] Hamilton and Staff

[e] Florida League of Cities

suffered. Table 6-2 displays the results of polls taken at different times by different organizations. Each poll asked respondents, in slightly different ways, to rate Chiles's performance in office. For comparative purposes, results of similar polls taken during the previous administration are also provided. In the first four polls, citizens were more approving of Chiles than his predecessor at comparable periods in his administration. He also gained steadily in esteem. The fifth poll, taken in October, at the height of publicity about impending budget cuts, saw the governor lose 25 points in his positive ratings. And the sixth, taken after three more months of bad economic news, saw an additional 10 percent decline. As is usual in these circumstances, the budget crisis and the state of the economy took a heavy toll. Chiles is now less "popular" than his predecessor was at a comparable time.

Other disturbing signs were evident in the May poll. This poll indicated that respondents didn't think that Chiles had done much to achieve his primary goals, ending waste, fraud, and abuse in state government. Sixty-one percent of the respondents in this poll said government efficiency was the same under Chiles as under his predecessor. Sixty percent said that state government was no more honest under Chiles. And only a slight majority (52 percent) said that

Florida's government was less wasteful than it had been when Chiles took office.

The latest numbers put Chiles in an unaccustomed position vis à vis the Florida electorate. In his last year in the U.S. Senate, 65 percent of Floridians rated Chiles's performance as excellent or good.[42] Further, the explanations offered for some of the low ratings both in Florida and by other research on gubernatorial popularity provides no comfort. Research in Minnesota and in California has found that gubernatorial popularity is more strongly correlated with the condition of the national economy than with any other factor.[43] The vice president of the company that conducted the May poll on Chiles also attributed the governor's standing to economic factors. Saying that he had seen similar results with incoming governors in other states, he "attributed the low numbers to tight state budgets and the recession." [44] In October and in December, this same analyst attributed much of the decline to forces beyond Chiles's control.[45] There is certainly very little that Chiles can do to change the nature of the national economy, and neither budget cuts nor tax increases are likely to help his popularity ratings. This situation is particularly troubling in light of the argument that "the absence of public approval eventually undercuts potential for success." [46]

Professional Reputation

Richard Neustadt argues that professional reputation is one of the key variables in presidential power. "Out of what others think of him emerge his opportunities for influence with them." [47] If this is true and reputation among other political figures is indeed a political resource, then, once again, Lawton Chiles is rich. Professional politicians, both in Washington and in Florida, have enormous respect for his abilities. A survey of top-level U.S. Senate staffers conducted in the spring of 1987 ranked him fourteenth in the Senate in terms of "respect in the congressional community." [48] And political professionals in Florida refer to him as an "icon." While some minor political gaffes made during the early days of his administration seem to have had some impact on his professional reputation, he is clearly accorded a great deal of respect among professional politicians in Florida. The Republican leader in the Senate called him "bigger than life" at the time of his gubernatorial election. And, even during the controversy that raged in September and October over how best to handle the budget crisis, several longtime participants in the Florida political process remained optimistic because of Chiles's reputation for leadership. The attorney general said, "This is vintage Lawton Chiles. At the appropriate time, it will come out that Lawton is leading and has been leading." And the state comptroller argued, "He's a smart politician. He probably can get what he wants." [49]

Some scholars and staff assistants to various presidents discount the relationship between reputation and executive performance. "As one Nixon assistant argued, 'The mistakes you make will always follow you, but they aren't that important in the long run. We made some mistakes on welfare reform, but I doubt that they affected the revenue sharing bills.' " [50] Nevertheless, the respect accorded Chiles by his peers can't hurt.

Leadership Opportunity:
The Political and Economic Situation

Like all governors, Lawton Chiles accepted the mantle of leadership at a particular time and faced a particular constellation of political and economic circumstances. Also like other governors, his primary task as a political leader is to develop a strategy of government congruent with these circumstances. By focusing exclusively on the political skills that Chiles demonstrated during his first few months in office, we ignore the hypothesis that there are situational constraints that affect gubernatorial action. "There may be bounds to what even the most skillful [governor] can accomplish under some circumstances—indeed, under normal circumstances." [51] On the other hand, "positive" environments make gubernatorial leadership easier and help governors maximize their political skills.

The Political Environment

The political environment into which Chiles was initially thrust seems perfectly suited to a centrist. Ideologically, only 16 percent of Floridians consider themselves liberals, with the remainder split almost evenly between conservatives (43 percent) and middle-of-the-roaders (40 percent).[52] Further, more people in the state now identify themselves as independents than as either Democrats or Republicans.[53] The following brief outline of developments in Florida politics in the last twenty-five years will provide some texture to this simplified picture.

The dominant political power in Florida until well into the 1960s was conservative Democrats. It found its expression in the legislature in the "Pork Chop Gang." This coalition overrepresented the northernmost counties of the state at the expense of the south, which had been the site of most of the astonishing growth that occurred in Florida during the post-World War II years. The Pork Chop Gang's control over the legislature was broken when the U.S. Supreme Court ordered reapportionment in 1968; the overwhelming Democratic dominance had been destroyed in the elections of 1966 and 1968. In these years, Richard Nixon won the state's electoral votes, and the Republicans elected their first governor, captured their first U.S. Senate seat, and picked up forty-one seats in the legislature. The forces involved here, the tremendous demographic changes, the shift of power to the southern part of the state, and the rise in strength of the Republican party converged to introduce more competition into state politics— competition between the two parties, between various areas of the state, and between various social and demographic groups (for example, older people and younger people).

Despite the gains made by the Republicans in the state, their status generally has waned in the past few years. As recently as 1986, they elected the governor and two constitutional officers and improved their numbers in both the House and the Senate. In 1989, they had an eleven-to-eight edge over the Democrats in Congress. In that same year they also held a 42 percent to 33 percent edge in partisan identification. Since 1988, they have lost the governorship, lost a congressional seat that they had gained when an incumbent Democrat changed parties at the urging of Lee Atwater, lost two seats in the House (one in an election and one to a party switch of an incumbent Republican), registered no gain in the State Senate despite a well-financed effort, and suffered a loss of 10 percentage points in partisan identification.[54] While still a force in the state, the party seems less likely to continue the kind of growth that has characterized its recent past and should not expect to attain majority status in the state. Chiles's insistence that cuts be made in the state's budget before any efforts are made to alter the tax structure may contribute to the party's problems by undermining what has been an effective Republican campaign strategy—to attack the Democrats as big-spending liberals—and thereby reduce even further the party's chances of gaining ground in state politics. On the other hand, some observers feel that the state is entering a period of dealignment rather than realignment and that neither party will "gain a consistent and enduring advantage over the other." [55]

Thus the long-term trends in Florida politics seem congenial to Lawton Chiles. Demographic and political changes have forced on the state a broader set of policy alternatives than existed in the recent past, but have not yet brought about no-win options. His party is in the majority and has rid itself of some of the conservatism that made him uncomfortable as a member of the state legislature. At the same time, the Republican party and other forces are not pushing Chiles to do something that would make him truly uncomfortable.

Unanticipated Events

Other, more immediate political events that were to have a tremendous impact on Chiles's performance vis à vis the state legislature were also being played out as he took office. These were the completion of two investigations of malfeasance on the part of state legislators: one of a member of the House of Representatives for sexual harassment of a female staff member, the other for failure on the part of state legislators (House and Senate) to disclose gifts from lobbyists. Both of these investigations received dramatic, even salacious, attention from the media. They reinforced Chiles's call for higher ethical standards in government and put great pressure on legislators to accede to new regulations. Indeed, some of the campaign reform and ethics legislation that Chiles supported was, at the time he took office, already under consideration in the House and had widespread, if begrudging, support there. In fact, one element of Chiles's ethics proposal was enacted in a special legislative session prior to his inauguration and was signed into law by Governor Martinez during the transition period. In the regular session after Chiles was inaugurated, additions were made to this proposal that accomplished virtually all of Chiles's goals regarding ethics. Thus, the investigations were critical to Chiles's success in this area. (In the previous legislative session, before the emergence of the scandals, ethics rules akin to those proposed by Chiles had been suggested by Governor Martinez and had earned him boos from the chamber.)

The Economic Situation

The state's economic and financial situation, which was terrible and is getting worse, played into Chiles's hands initially. After years of growth that had fueled increasing revenues, Florida began to face in the mid-1980s the effects of slower growth and a revenue stream heavily dependent on the sales taxes that accompany tourism (travel-related industry accounts for 20 percent of the state's retail sales tax). First the rate of increase in total state personal income changed from 101 percent over the years 1976 to 1981 to 45.8 percent during the years 1982 to 1987.[56] Beginning in 1985, school enrollment and prison populations began to grow faster than the general population. At almost the same time, per unit costs of many services went up faster than inflation, outstripping gains in revenue. Then the recession began to make matters much worse. Chiles's predecessor had been forced to cut the 1989 fiscal year budget by $254 million only five months after it was adopted. This had come after Martinez, a self-proclaimed fiscal conservative, had signed off on more than $6 billion in tax increases since 1987. These actions were not enough, and Martinez was preparing to ask for another cut in spending when he was defeated. He permitted Chiles to make these cuts during the transition period, and Chiles asked state agencies to find additional ways to cut their budgets.

Further, state economists were predicting a $1.3 billion shortfall in the 1991-1992 fiscal year.

Circumstances such as these would have been daunting for most new governors, as they were for Chiles. There was clearly no money for new services, and many observers felt that existing services had been cut to dangerously low levels. Chiles, however, tried to turn the circumstances to his advantage. The situation provided him the lever he needed to get an agenda oriented to making government smaller and more productive. He acknowledged the value of the economic situation in public comments, saying that he would be better able to get the attention of state agency heads in these circumstances than when times were good. In the transition period he asked state agencies to reduce their budgets by 5 percent and emphasized his "smaller but smarter" theme by rejecting across-the-board reductions and insisting that agency heads identify their programs with the lowest priority for complete elimination. Further, when, in October of 1991, the state faced lower than anticipated tax revenues and Chiles was forced to ask for an additional 6 percent cut from agency budgets, he also responded with reference to his rightsizing emphasis, saying, "We need to make the government more productive and efficient before we start adding more money into a system that's broken." Even when the rapidly deteriorating budget situation forced him into actions that he would have preferred to avoid, Chiles continued to use the crisis as a lever to accomplish the longer term goals of substantial governmental and tax reform. Thus, a situation that many elected officials would have found intolerable has been used as a catalyst.

Leadership Strategy

At its most general level, the political strategy adopted by Lawton Chiles has been somewhat unorthodox. To a large extent he has sought to reach beyond the "usual" politics of representation and of appeal to specific groups. In so doing he has rejected, implicitly at least, the bargaining model of leadership that dominates much of strategic political thinking. Instead of appeals to specific interests with promises of specific, programmatic rewards, he has sought the achievement of the "common good," with the expectation that all citizens will benefit and that all will support him. His policy aspirations are idealistic, and a central theme of his governorship is that "normal" legislative, bureaucratic, and interest group politics has had disastrous results for the state.

Chiles has combined the appeal to the public interest with the message that a time of new problems has arrived in Florida, that fresh definitions of the public's interest are required, and that the old ways of doing business are no longer adequate. In addition to his efforts to reinvent government, both Chiles and the lieutenant governor have consistently brought into question *the* article of faith in Florida, that continued growth is the basis of prosperity. Thus, his goals go beyond consolidation of past gains. He is trying to identify the parameters of a new political, economic, and social era in Florida.

Finally, the substantive focus of the Chiles strategy has been narrow, having two main themes: the need to restore faith and trust in state government and the need to rightsize government. He has stuck to these themes, even in the face of charges that he has exercised "stealth leadership."

Chiles's efforts to implement his strategy are characterized by a decision-making process that he dominates. He is the integrating force within the administration, he gathers information from a variety of sources, and he insinuates his priorities into the actions of the government.

Conclusion

The central question in the appraisal of a governor's effectiveness is whether he or she has matched his or her "style of policy leadership to the historical context of opportunities and constraints." [57] For the moment, Lawton Chiles seems to have done so. An experienced political figure who possesses substantial skill, Chiles came into an extremely favorable political environment and faced an economic situation that, in a perverse way, enhanced his goals. He adopted a strategy that appears congruent with his initial policy goals, and his accomplishments have been substantial when measured against his stated objectives. Will this happy scenario continue? Two facts about the future raise serious questions.

First, as indicated above, the single most difficult problem facing the state of Florida was finessed during most of the first year of Lawton Chiles's tenure in office. This is the problem of raising adequate revenue to meet the service and infrastructure demands of the nation's fourth largest state. While Chiles acknowledged the problem in his inaugural speech—"I know we need tax reform"—he declared that he would not seek new taxes until "we have earned your confidence by being more efficient, effective and accountable." He repeated this claim in September and again in October, when it became apparent that cuts would have to be made in the fiscal 1991-1992 budget. The only poll yet taken on this issue indicated that Chiles has yet to earn this confidence. Nevertheless, because of the state of the economy in Florida, he will be forced to face the issue directly in the next legislative session. The October proposals for cuts in the 1991 budget had some of Chiles's strongest supporters angry with him for his resistance to immediate efforts at tax reform, and they will be pushing him for action on this front. And, as usual, Republicans are lying in the grass, waiting to bite whoever suggests the need for additional resources. Thus this issue will be the major test of the Chiles administration. As the first legislative session ended, one prominent state senator stated publicly that Chiles should have already attacked the issue when, as the senator put it, the governor's "influence is greatest."

The issue of taxes appears to be one that will stretch the organizing capacity of Chiles's current political strategy. That is, it is difficult to conceptualize tax reform as being in the public interest when it has such obvious redistributive effects. Therefore, Chiles's appeal to all Floridians may have to be modified. One question is whether he can engineer agreement within the citizenry, and in the legislature, on what segments of the population, if any, should bear additional tax burdens. (Chiles's options are constrained because of a constitutional prohibition against a personal income tax and because of almost violent negative feelings about such a tax.) A second, and more profound, question is whether a man who throughout his political life has been guided by a conception of politics that sees all Floridians as the equal beneficiaries of government action can now visualize a different strategy.

Second, very few of the reforms Chiles initiated to reinvent government in Florida have been fully implemented. Civil service reform, decentralizing public education, improving corrections, addressing human services needs, and launching initiatives to involve the private sector and to make state government more productive are in the early stages of development. Other proposals will require legislative action and are likely to get bound up with tax reform and reapportionment, the two major issues to be faced in the next legislative session. Whether any of these proposals will get off the ground and how they will be received is yet to be known. Certainly the reaction to them, both in the government and among the voters, will affect Chiles's standing and his strategy for the remainder of his term.

Notes

I would like to thank Michael L. Hollers, a student in the department of political science at Florida State University, for his assistance with this chapter.

1. *Miami Herald,* April 13, 1990, 12.
2. Ibid., December 13, 1990, 4C.

3. Inaugural speech, January 8, 1991.
4. State of the State address, March 5, 1991.
5. Hilda M. Lynch, "Lawton Chiles," in *Citizens Look at Congress* (New York: Grossman, 1972).
6. Neal Pierce, "Florida Seeks to Redesign the Way It Runs Itself," *St. Petersburg Times,* June 6, 1991.
7. *Tallahassee Democrat,* October 10, 1991, 1.
8. Ibid., October 18, 1991, 4A.
9. Ibid., October 30, 1991, 7A.
10. Michael Barone and Grant Ujifusa, *The Almanac of American Politics* (Washington, D.C.: *National Journal,* 1980), 273.
11. Barone and Ujifusa, *Almanac of American Politics* (1982), 209.
12. *Tampa Tribune,* December 11, 1990, 1.
13. Alan Ehrenhalt, *Politics in America* (Washington, D.C.: Congressional Quarterly Press, 1986), 293.
14. Lynch, "Lawton Chiles," 5.
15. Reg Murphy and Hal Gulliver, *The Southern Strategy* (New York: Scribner's, 1971), 153.
16. Barone and Ujifusa, *Almanac of American Politics* (1986).
17. Barone and Ujifusa, *Almanac of American Politics* (1991).
18. Ehrenhalt, *Politics in America* (1986).
19. Dave Bruns, "Chiles, Like Others, Will Make His Own Mark," *Tallahassee Democrat,* July 14, 1991, 1C
20. Richard Chackerian and Frank Sherwood, "Organizing the Chiles-MacKay Administration," *Governing Florida* 1 (November 2, 1991): 6.
21. Ibid., 7.
22. Bruns, "Chiles, Like Others."
23. *Miami Herald,* November 10, 1990, 4C.
24. Chackerian and Sherwood, "Organizing the Chiles-Mackay Administration," 7.
25. Ibid.
26. *Orlando Sentinel,* November 8, 1990, 1.
27. Tim Golden, "Florida Governor Aims to Reinvent State," *New York Times,* August 11, 1991, 10.
28. *Tallahassee Democrat,* October 30, 1991, 1.
29. Richard Neustadt, *Presidential Power* (New York: Wiley, 1960), 10.
30. *Miami Herald,* October 7, 1990.
31. Barone and Ujifusa, *Almanac of American Politics* (1986).
32. Ehrenhalt, *Politics in America* (1986).
33. Jeffrey Tulis, *The Rhetorical Presidency* (Princeton: Princeton University Press, 1987), 10.
34. *St. Petersburg Times,* November 8, 1991, 1.
35. Tulis, *Rhetorical Presidency,* 4.
36. *Tampa Tribune,* November 1, 1991, 15A.
37. Kathleen Jamieson, *Eloquence in an Electronic Age* (New York: Oxford University Press, 1988).

38. *St. Petersburg Times,* October 31, 1990, 1.
39. *Tallahassee Democrat,* October 31, 1990, 1.
40. Ibid.
41. Paul Light, *The President's Agenda* (Baltimore: Johns Hopkins University Press, 1982), 27.
42. Survey Research Center, Florida State University, *Florida Annual Policy Survey,* 1987.
43. Robert E. Crew, Jr., and David Moon, "Gubernatorial Popularity in Minnesota: A Preliminary Model" (Paper presented at the Midwest Political Science Convention, Chicago, 1985); Robert E. Crew, Jr., and Gregory Weiher, "Gubernatorial Popularity in California" (Paper presented at the Southern Political Science Convention, Atlanta, 1990).
44. *Tampa Tribune,* May 17, 1991, 1.
45. *Tallahassee Democrat,* October 18, 1991, 4A, and December 11, 1991, 5A.
46. Light, *President's Agenda,* 28.
47. Neustadt, *Presidential Power,* 60.
48. John R. Hibbing and Sue Thomas, "The Modern U.S. Senate: What Is Accorded Respect?" *Journal of Politics* 52 (November 1, 1990).
49. *Tallahassee Democrat,* October 11, 1991, 6A.
50. Light, *President's Agenda,* 29.
51. Tulis, *Rhetorical Presidency,* 146.
52. *Florida Annual Policy Survey,* 1991.
53. Ibid.
54. Ibid., 1990, 1991.
55. Stephen Craig, "Politics and Elections," in *Government and Politics in Florida,* ed. Robert Huckshorn (Gainsville: University of Florida Press, 1991), 102
56. U.S. Department of Commerce, *State Personal Income,* 1982, 1989.
57. Erwin Hargrove, *Jimmy Carter as President* (Baton Rouge: Louisiana State University Press, 1988), 162.

7. ILLINOIS: JIM EDGAR, THE NEW GOVERNOR FROM THE OLD PARTY

Samuel K. Gove

On January 14, 1991, Illinois got its first new governor in fourteen years, when Republican Jim Edgar succeeded fellow Republican Jim Thompson. This was the first time in sixty-two years that one governor succeeded another of the same party. Beyond their shared party, the men had little else in common. Thompson is a Chicagoan; Edgar, who comes from east central Illinois, was the first downstater in thirty years. Thompson is a lawyer; Edgar, who is not, was the first nonlawyer governor in thirty years. Thompson had had no previous state government experience; Edgar had spent his entire career in state government and state politics.

There are also significant differences of style and personality. Thompson is open and gregarious; Edgar is reserved and private. Thompson enjoys travel and an active social life; Edgar is a family- and church-oriented person. There were other differences as well that would affect the governorship and state government. Even so, Edgar had to prove in the primary and fall campaigns and in the first months of his administration that he was not a Thompson clone.

The Illinois Governor's Office

The office Jim Edgar sought is one of the strongest in the country—at least with regard to constitutional powers. The governor has strong appointment powers (although they have been limited to an unknown extent by a recent U.S. Supreme Court ruling, *Rutan et al. v. Republican Party*).[1] The governor has unlimited tenure, subject only to voter approval. The governor has power to reorganize the executive branch subject to legislative disapproval. The governor has strong budget-making power that is supplemented by veto powers. And these veto powers under the 1970 constitution give Illinois governors considerably more influence than most others. Along with the usual veto and line-item veto powers, the governor can reduce appropriation bills and also has the controversial amendatory veto power.

But with all these powers, Illinois governors still have to perform in the real world of Illinois politics. Illinois is a partisan state, and politically divided government has been the rule in recent history. The Republican Thompson had to work with Democratic majorities in both houses of the legislature for all but two of the fourteen years of his tenure. Most of the other statewide executive-branch offices were held by Democrats. Also, the governor of Illinois has to interact with the mayor of Chicago and accommodate the political power of the Democratic party in Cook County.

Complicating the administration, especially for a downstater like Jim Edgar, is the growing power of the Chicago metropolitan area. The Democratic legislative leaders both come from Cook County; the Republican leaders are from suburban DuPage County. During the Thompson administration the state built the controversial State of Illinois Center in Chicago's loop—not in the capital, Springfield. This building centralized in Chicago much of the executive and legislative business. Thompson even decided to house his family in Chicago, virtually abandoning the executive mansion in Springfield.

Edgar's Background

As stated, Jim Edgar was a very different man from his predecessor. Edgar was born in Oklahoma in 1946 but grew up in Charleston in central Illinois, the home of Eastern Illinois University (EIU). He attended EIU, where he was student body president, and graduated in 1968. He became the first elected Illinois governor who was a product of the state's public higher education system.[2]

After graduation he became a legislative staff intern in Springfield, where he worked with a strong and progressive political leader, Sen. W. Russell Arrington. He stayed on the legislative staff after his internship until he ran unsuccessfully for the Illinois House of Representatives in 1974. He ran again in 1976 and was elected. (In 1974-1976 he was on the staff of the National Conference of State Legislators in Denver.) He was reelected in 1978. Jim Edgar was the first governor with legislative experience to be elected in sixty-six years.

Governor Thompson selected Edgar as his director of legislative relations in 1979. Edgar's next move was to the office of secretary of state, an important office with some 4,000 employees. The former secretary, Alan Dixon, was elected to the U.S. Senate in 1980, and Governor Thompson appointed Edgar to fill the vacancy.

The secretary of state is a visible position, as the office administers driver's licenses and automobile registration. The secretary is the state librarian as well as the custodian of the state capitol complex in Springfield.

In the secretary's office Edgar selected his public issues carefully, sticking to those that affected his office. He campaigned statewide against drunk driving; he is a teetotaler. As state librarian he campaigned against adult illiteracy. He established the Illinois Literacy Council, which promoted volunteer tutoring programs around the state. He also was successful in getting a mandatory auto insurance law through the General Assembly—an effort that had been unsuccessful for some seventeen years.

After his appointment as secretary in 1980, he ran statewide for election in 1982 and won by 233,656 votes. He ran for reelection in 1986 and won by 1,574,079, the largest plurality of any statewide candidate in Illinois history. He received some nationwide visibility and was named in May 1986 by *U.S. News and World Report* as one of the thirty "rising stars in American politics." *Illinois Issues* featured an interview with Edgar in July 1985.[3] Jim Edgar has the reputation of being a good family man. He and Brenda Smith were married while he was an undergraduate at EIU. They have two children. News stories tell of close family relations. In the 1985 *Illinois Issues* interview, Edgar was asked whether he was interested in running for the U.S. Senate. He answered: "Brenda thinks it would be a mistake. She has some reservations about me running for governor, but the thought of running for U.S. Senate at this point makes the gubernatorial race make a lot more sense to her."[4]

In the summer of 1989 Jim Thompson, in a surprise announcement, said he was not going to run for a fifth term as governor. The jockeying for a replacement began in political circles. Attorney General Neil Hartigan was frequently mentioned as a Democratic candidate, although he had disappointed some Democratic leaders in 1986 by announcing for governor and then withdrawing to let Adlai E. Stevenson get the nomination. Hartigan got the nomination this time. The Democrats did have primary contests for state comptroller and state treasurer, but the candidates at the top of the ticket, governor, lieutenant governor, and secretary of state, had no opposition.

Jim Edgar announced that he was going to run for governor on August 8, 1989, in a quick trip to the state's TV media centers. Lt. Gov. George Ryan, who some felt would run for governor, was selected as the Republican candidate for secretary of state, the position Edgar was leaving. The party leaders put together a balanced statewide slate that included a woman for comptroller. Only Edgar was challenged in the March primary. Edgar was endorsed by President George Bush and Republican party chairman Lee Atwater. Such a primary endorsement broke precedent, but Edgar had been an early Bush supporter.

Steve Baer, thirty years old and executive director of the conservative United Republican Fund, entered the race late on December 15 on a platform of low taxes and antiabortion policies. In declaring his challenge he said, "We aim to present the Republican voters of Illinois with a real choice between the mainstream conservative values of the Republican national platform and the special interest liberalism that dominates the powers-that-be in Springfield today." [5]

Baer was particularly critical of Edgar's earlier support for making permanent the "temporary" increase in the income tax approved by the legislature and Governor Thompson at the 1988 spring legislative session. The mover of the temporary tax increase was the powerful Democratic Speaker, Michael Madigan of Chicago. Edgar's position on the permanent tax provision was to be a big issue in both the primary and the general campaigns.

At his candidacy announcement, Baer supported a proposed "tax accountability" amendment to the state constitution that would require a three-fifths majority vote by the legislature to raise taxes; he advocated property tax relief; and he vowed to cut what he termed a "bloated" state budget. There were other provisions in the amendment.[6] The proposal had been initiated by the Tax Accountability Committee in July 1989.

Both Edgar and the Democrat Hartigan had supported the amendment and signed petitions to get the initiative on the ballot. (Illinois has a limited initiative that permits changes only to the legislative article of the state constitution.) The proposal was challenged in the state courts and was eventually taken to the Illinois Supreme Court by the Chicago Bar Association. That court ruled the issue off the ballot in August 1990 because it would "violate the intent so clearly expressed in the convention committee reports and debates to limit constitutional amendments by initiative to structural and procedural subjects of the legislative article and to prohibit the incorporation into such amendments of substantive matters." [7]

The primary campaign highlighted the fiscal issues of the state, and Jim Edgar responded in February 1990 in an address to the City Club of Chicago. He announced his platform to control spending. The provisions included:

1. Moving from an annual state budget to a biennial budget.
2. Requiring a three-fifths vote of the legislature to override gubernatorial vetoes of excessive spending.
3. Making sure that there would be no more state employees under the governor's jurisdiction on the day his term expired than on the day he took office.
4. Creating a management council—including experts from the private sector—to report to the governor on whether

standards for accountability to taxpayers have been established and met.

5. Promising to veto any new program that did not include a sunset provision and the means to pay for the program using available resources.

The primary campaign was relatively quiet, although Steve Baer did get attention in certain parts of the state, especially the collar counties around Chicago. The primary was on March 20 and had a low turnout (33 percent of the registered voters), as has been the case in other recent primaries. The Democrats turned out 1,123,972 voters, compared with the Republicans' 805,381.

The Republican results were surprising by the strength of Steve Baer's total vote, 34 percent. Edgar had 63 percent of the vote. Edgar had expected to have a much larger margin. (There was a third candidate on the ballot who received 4 percent.) Edgar carried all but five counties statewide. The defectors to Baer were small downstate counties that were thought to have been influenced by Baer's antiabortion stand.

A side effect of the antitax, antispending movement occurred in DuPage County, where the longtime president of the county board was defeated, as was a Republican party legislative veteran. But Edgar beat Baer 2-1 in DuPage. Edgar also did well, for a Republican, in Chicago and Cook County.

The campaign did not seem to leave any sharp divisions in the Republican ranks. It did, however, force Edgar to use campaign funds that he had intended to use in the fall campaign.

After the March primary, the campaign slowed down. The campaign staffs were organized and began preparing position papers. Edgar had constitutional amendments introduced in the spring legislative session for his fiscal issues—biennial budgets and three-fifths vote to override a governor's reduction veto. These were heard in legislative committees, but were easily defeated by the Democratic majority.

As the campaign seriously got under way in the fall, public opinion polls showed Edgar with a good lead over Democrat Neil Hartigan. Both candidates had spent the summer making mandatory appearances at state and county fairs. Both candidates prepared position papers on the main issues of the day. But the issue that dominated and came up regularly was Edgar's position on making the temporary income tax surcharge permanent. Hartigan would not commit himself on the issue. Because Hartigan did not support the surcharge for local governments, newspaper stories said this put him in conflict with Mayor Richard M. Daley.

Hartigan attacked the Thompson administration in debates and elsewhere, for waste in government in the "277 boards and commissions." He said he could run government by eliminating the waste and not raising taxes. He also criticized Thompson for his numerous tax increases. Repeatedly he tied Edgar with Thompson.

Edgar stuck by his guns on the permanent tax increase and received some support from unusual places, such as the Illinois Education Association. A group made up of University of Illinois faculty members endorsed Edgar; that was against custom—most were Democrats. He received support from most of the newspapers in the state, including the *Chicago Tribune.*

Although Edgar supported the surcharge—which he considered continuing at the current level of taxation—he opposed any new taxes consistently. He also continued support for the principles of the Tax Accountability amendment, including a three-fifths vote on any measure that would increase revenue. He also made a cap on property tax increases a major part of his fiscal program. He gave little specific attention to the fiscal disaster that was on the horizon. However, the candidates were not too far apart on the fiscal issues—with the income tax surcharge as the main exception.

The campaign followed the usual pattern, with the candidates aiming their appearances at the TV media centers. There were the usual League of Women Voters debates. The press tried to differentiate the candidates on tax and other issues. *Illinois Issues* devoted four articles to the candidates' positions on taxes and finances, welfare, health care and mental health, economic development, and education. (Hartigan did not participate in the last article because "at the time of the interview the campaign had not yet released its education position paper.")

Near the end of the campaign, polls showed that Edgar's margin was slipping rapidly. Some polls showed Edgar ahead (*Tribune*), and others had Hartigan in the lead (*Sun Times*)—although the polls were taken at different times. In the other visible statewide race, for U.S. senator, incumbent Paul Simon (D) had a substantial lead over Rep. Lynn Martin (R). The races for governor and senator were independent and did not seem to influence each other.

Around the state some local issues had an impact on the campaign. Tavern owners in southern Illinois organized an anti-Edgar campaign because of his strong position against drunk driving. Neil Hartigan had problems in Democratic ranks for some of his earlier political moves, especially in Chicago, where he had been perceived to be against black candidates for mayor in earlier campaigns.

Another factor in black disaffection with the Democrats was that blacks had tried to get a slate of Harold Washington Party candidates for Cook County offices on the November ballot. The Democratic leaders tried in the courts to keep the slate off the ballot. The Illinois Supreme Court argued that the Washington Party had not met the statutory number of signatures on the petitions. The U.S. Supreme Court reversed this decision, and at the last moment the party was placed on the ballots. Many blacks were unhappy with the Democratic leaders, including Hartigan.[8]

Although tax and fiscal matters received the most attention in the campaign, Edgar made education his top priority. It paid off to the extent that the education community gave him strong support, especially when viewed in terms of teachers' traditional support for Democratic candidates.

After the long campaign, on election day (November 6) the voters elected Jim Edgar as governor and his running mate, Bob Kustra, as lieutenant governor by a slim margin of 83,909 out of 3,420,720 votes cast. There was a modest statewide turnout of 56.7 percent of the registered voters. The results for the gubernatorial candidates were 50.7 percent for Edgar, 48.2 percent for Hartigan. This compared to the 65 percent to 35 percent win by Paul Simon in his successful reelection bid for senator.

Edgar won about half of the counties in the state. He did not do as well in the collar counties as Thompson had in 1986. His losing margin in Cook County was 110,000, but this was offset by his winning margin in DuPage: 81,000. For a Republican he made inroads in the black community, although the black turnout was very low. He did well in the education-oriented Champaign and McLean counties. But Edgar did not do well in southern Illinois. This area, which has suffered economically, went for Hartigan. The central Illinois bell-wether county, Moultrie, went for Edgar by 57 votes, 2,441 to 2,384.

In the other races, the Democrats continued their control of both houses of the legislature. In the executive branch, the Republicans held on to the office of secretary of state, while the Democrats continued to hold the offices of attorney general, comptroller, and state treasurer. Elected to the board of trustees of the University of Illinois were two Democrats and one Republican. Divided partisan government was to continue in Illinois.

Transition

After the election and a vacation, Governor-elect Edgar attended the new governors' conference organized by the National Governors Association. Edgar then organized his transition team of some forty-five citizens—a rather large number. The members represented ethnic, business, labor, and other groups. They also came from all parts of the state. There were several minority and female members. Most members of the team or their organizations had supported Edgar in the campaign—although one member had openly supported Steve Baer in the primary.

Members of the transition team were asked to recruit qualified people to serve in the administration. They were asked to look for savings in the agencies of state government, given the precarious fiscal condition of the state.

The leadership of the transition team was unusual. There were four co-chairs—Stanley O. Ikenberry, president of the University of Illinois; Nancy Jefferson, a leader in the Chicago black community; Bob Kustra, lieutenant governor-elect; and William Weiss, chairman and CEO of Ameritech. The full forty-five members met as a group four times during the process. The governor-elect presided at these meetings and was an active participant. The transition team was not a paper organization, as has been the case in some states.

Also attending some of the meetings as honorary chair was former governor William G. Stratton (1953-1961), Edgar's model as a hands-on governor. Edgar also mentioned the late governor Richard B. Ogilvie (1969-1973) as a model of a progressive, idea-oriented governor.

Most of the work of the transition team was done in small committees called review teams. There were eight such groups, with functional charges such as education, economic development, and public safety. The review teams were given the transition papers prepared by each agency under its jurisdiction, and met with agency heads and relevant interest groups. The committees met frequently, and it was at these meetings that much of the transition work was accomplished. As the review teams completed their reports, each with the governor after he had been inaugurated.

The staff director of the transition team was Governor Thompson's director of policy, Paula Wolff. Each of the eight committees' staff usually consisted of one person from the secretary of state's office and one from the staff of Governor Thompson.

The final transition report was made to Edgar, now governor, on January 28, 1991, at the executive mansion in Springfield. The report had eight themes:

Fiscal control
Educational excellence
Economic development
Revision of the health care system
Controlling substance abuse

Environmental sensitivity
Control of the state's personnel system
Fairness in distribution of resources and lack of discrimination

During the transition period Jim Edgar was inaugurated the thirty-sixth governor of Illinois. In an impressive ceremony with a strong patriotic theme at the Convention Center in Springfield, the new governor was sworn in and delivered his inaugural address. Much attention was given to the outgoing governor, Jim Thompson, whose fourteen-year term was by far the longest in Illinois history. Long, enthusiastic applause and standing ovations were given to the outgoing governor. Edgar's speech was delivered in his direct, no nonsense style—a contrast to the flamboyant style of his predecessor.

After the inaugural ball, Governor Edgar had to turn to putting his administration together with appointments to key departments.

Appointments

During the transition, Governor-elect Edgar told the transition team he would not reappoint any of Governor Thompson's cabinet members. This obviously was another effort to distance his administration from Thompson's. In reality he did appoint some Thompson agency heads, but to different agencies.

Edgar's first appointment was his press secretary, who had been with him in the secretary of state's office. His duties were to include serving as a policy adviser. Edgar's chief of staff was a young lawyer from private practice who had experience in state government. His chief counsel had been counsel to the transition team. His chief of government operations (a woman) had been a department director in the Thompson administration. For the critical post of budget director, he chose the first woman to hold this office; she had been on his staff in the secretary of state's office.

Edgar appointed eight executive assistants. Each of them was assigned a series of agencies in a broadly defined functional area—for example, public safety, which included such agencies as corrections, police, and fire marshal. No suggestions were made that these assistants form an alternative cabinet—but they obviously had better access to the governor than most agency or department heads. Most of the executive assistants had had experience in state government. Edgar reduced the size of the governor's staff from Thompson's 180 to 140 but increased the salaries of the executive assistants.

In his cabinet (which consists of agency heads) he selected a diverse group, including ten women. He selected several blacks and one Asian. The term *cabinet* in Illinois is not clearly defined, but in the

Edgar administration it included heads of forty-four agencies—departments, boards, commissions, offices, and authorities.

Edgar's appointments to his cabinet all came from Illinois, with one exception. That was the director of the Environmental Protection Agency, who came from the federal EPA in Washington. She had, however, an Illinois background. None of Thompson's major department heads was reappointed to the same agency, although the acting director of the Department of Public Health was appointed director. Some of the appointments received strong public support; none was publicly criticized—except by interest groups.

One of the surprising appointments was the president of the Taxpayers' Federation of Illinois as director of revenue. This appointment received editorial plaudits. One controversial appointment was a woman to the "old boy" office of director of agriculture. That appointment is still controversial.[9] Edgar was commended for his appointment of a career employee to head the Department of Transportation. His appointee as director of conservation was unusual for having been trained in the biological sciences. Two of the appointees were sitting legislators who had just won reelection in November. Another was a legislator who had been defeated in the November election.

During the campaign, one of the agencies and programs that was criticized as being wasteful and of questionable effectiveness was the economic development programs run by the state Department of Commerce and Community Affairs (DCCA). Governor Thompson had supported this agency when budget increases were the order of the day. He had selected young people from his cadre to administer the department. He had established foreign offices in some thirteen cities around the world—and he had made many trips to these and other places abroad. DCCA was Thompson's baby, but near the end of his term, several critical reports about the agency came from legislative agencies and others. Both Hartigan and Edgar vowed to cut DCCA's budgets and programs and to appoint a businessman to run the agency. Edgar's director had experience in the private sector in management consulting.

Overall, Edgar's appointments were sound but not flashy. They came from Illinois, with most having state government experience. Most were not outsiders, and they were not there to rock the boat other than on fiscal matters. Among them were many more women and members of racial minorities than before.

The Gubernatorial Messages:
State of the State and Budget

Governor Jim Edgar delivered his State of the State address to a joint legislative session on February 13.[10] It was his first substantive public statement since taking office. He said his administration would be marked by openness, cooperation, and involvement, a theme he had used in his inaugural speech. The speech provided a checklist that could be used as a scorecard later.

His top priority was education, especially early childhood education programs. By 1996, he wanted every child entering kindergarten ready to learn. He had other recommendations. In an unusual move, he said Lt. Gov. Bob Kustra would be his point man on Chicago school reform and other education efforts; Kustra had taught at universities for many years. Specifically, Kustra was to work with the state Board of Education, the Board of Higher Education, and the Community College Board to make sure all were on the same path toward making sure that students get the best possible education to prepare them for tomorrow's jobs.

Edgar had another assignment for his lieutenant governor: to coordinate efforts to combat drug abuse. He resisted creating an office of "drug czar," which would have been perceived as a new office and an increase in bureaucracy. He said he would convene a first ever Governors' Conference on Substance Abuse within the next six months. By October he had done so.

Edgar also said he would convene a Governor's Conference on Housing to set an agenda for the 1990s and that he would create a task force on water resources and land use priorities. And, following other governors' leads, he gave his wife, Brenda, an assignment. She was to head a committee to review the state's adoption system—"to ease adoption red tape."

He did follow through quickly on some of his initiatives. He issued an executive order on February 15, as he said he would, to expand recycling efforts in state facilities and increase the purchase of recycled materials. Also, in September he created the Human Resource Advisory Council, as recommended by the privately organized Commission on the Future of Public Service, a "little Volcker Commission." That commission found the state's personnel system hopelessly cumbersome and outdated. The system discourages "the best and the brightest" from entering the state's work force. He made no reference to the U.S. Supreme Court's *Rutan* decision, the Illinois case involving former governor Thompson, in which the court declared patronage unconstitutional.

He made some mention of the dire condition of state finances, but without specifics. He did say, "There are those who believe all the tough budget talk is a ploy to gather support for the extension of the income tax surcharge." He said this is no ploy, and the budget situation is bleak, even if the surcharge is extended.

Edgar told the legislators he was going to call a special session "later today" to carry out his campaign promise to cap property taxes. The special session ran concurrently with the regular session to focus attention on a specific issue, here property tax relief. The special session did meet throughout the regular session, but no legislation was passed. The property tax legislation was adopted in the regular session as part of the "summit" negotiations at the end of the session.

The governor did not propose any of the sort of wide-ranging reorganizations that are often found in a new governor's first State of the State address. There were some reform proposals, including the moving back of the early primary date from March to September, which had been proposed by the Senate president. (It did not pass.) He did discuss redistricting and proposed "that we launch a bipartisan effort to remove that stalemate and draw fair congressional and legislative maps that accurately reflect the population shifts in our state."

The State of the State address made reference to the state's fiscal condition in general. The budget message, delivered March 6, gave specifics. Governor Edgar opened this message saying the state had been on a "spending binge." And he uttered here a widely quoted phrase: "It is time that we tear up our credit cards and put a screeching halt to the spending spree." For specifics there were $627 million in old bills that needed to be paid—there was a shortfall of more than $500 million. The shortfall was caused by excessive spending during the previous two years.

The governor continued to make education his top priority. The budget increased funding for child abuse programs. The budget "preserves an emphasis on programs that stress early medical screening and diagnostic treatment, prenatal care and the prevention and treatment of alcohol and substance abuse."

The budget had many cuts, with the controversial DCCA being hit hard: $170 million cut. That department's programs that encourage existing businesses to expand were emphasized over incentives for new business.

The budget provided that some 4,400 state jobs were to be eliminated and 1,400 employees were to be laid off. Edgar resisted making across-the-board cuts but was selective, as illustrated by the DCCA budget.

The budget was built on four principles, the governor said:

1. The surcharge must be made permanent.
2. The cash balances must be increased.
3. There must be a fundamental change in state spending.
4. "And lastly, state government will make the necessary

cuts, no matter how painful, to stay with our current level of taxation."

And the governor included two campaign pledges in his message—biennial budgets and the three-fifths vote to override reduction vetoes. Both would have required a constitutional amendment and were not passed.

The Legislative Session

The struggle over the budget and the income surcharge dominated the media coverage after the governor's budget message. The governor stuck to his campaign promise to make the surcharge permanent. He recommended that education receive half of the increase, but he also recommended that state government receive part of the local government half of the temporary 1988 surcharge. During the session the majority Democrats took various positions on the surcharge, primarily that it should be continued temporarily for two years. This meant it would come up again in 1993; 1994 is the reelection year for the governor. The Democratic president of the Senate early on took the position that the surcharge should be made permanent. Most of the controversy was on the House side. There were public protests and rallies by state employees and welfare recipients at the state capitol in June.

As in the past, observers expected that the issue would go down to the wire but be resolved at the end of the session around June 30 by a summit meeting of the governor and the legislative leaders. June 30 came and went without a resolution, although there were many meetings of the leaders. A federal court intervened to provide that welfare recipients could receive their checks, but some 20,000 state workers went unpaid. The governor stood firm and, unlike his predecessor, worked closely with the two Republican leaders.

One issue was the property tax cap that the governor wanted for Cook and the collar counties. Both of the Democratic leaders came from Cook and did not want that county included in any agreement. School officials in Cook and the other counties fought the cap, as it would have the most adverse effect on them.

The stalemate between the governor and the Democratic leaders continued; their daily meetings continued to get headlines. Finally, on July 18, a compromise was reached; it was adopted by the legislature on July 19. This was the longest overtime spring session in Illinois history. The vote on legislation after July 1 requires a three-fifths vote, meaning that the governor's campaign pledge of a three-fifths vote on all revenue measures was kept.

The July 18 compromise provided for the education half of the income tax surcharge to be made permanent. On the local government half of the surcharge, the state and local government split evenly the proceeds for fiscal 1992. In fiscal 1993 the split will be 75 percent for local government and 25 percent for the state. That half of the surcharge remained temporary.

The compromise provided for a property tax cap in the collar counties, while Cook County was exempted. The caps limit the annual tax increases in local governments without home rule to 5 percent or the rate of inflation, whichever is lower. After the session, pressure was building up for a Cook County cap, especially from Democratic legislators in suburban Cook County.

Also part of the July 18 compromise were agreements on the level of appropriations for state agencies. Some agencies, such as DCCA, were sharply cut, as had been proposed in the campaign. Overall, education was declared a winner. Human service cuts were much less severe than proposed. The governor used his veto powers extensively on appropriation bills that did not satisfy the terms of the summit agreement. In his veto message he said, "These reductions carry out an agreement between the legislative leaders and the budget conferees to have the governor take administrative action to bring spending in line with available revenues."

The governor took several quick fix actions to help balance the budget. The biggest item was a new assessment program for hospitals and nursing homes. The proceeds from the assessment would be matched by federal Medicaid money.[11]

The general opinion of reporters and other observers was that the governor was a winner in the revenue, property tax, and budget agreements. Even the Speaker of the House had some complimentary things to say about the governor's performance.

Although fiscal matters received much attention during the session, redistricting was important to the legislators and other political leaders. The legislators had three tasks: congressional redistricting (Illinois lost two seats), legislative redistricting, and first-time districting for circuit courts in Cook County. The last task was accomplished, the others not, although much time and effort were devoted to them.

Throughout the three redistricting debates was the question of more districts for blacks and Hispanics. Republicans tried to embarrass Democrats in this regard. A legislative map was adopted by the Democrats in both houses, but it was vetoed by the governor. The governor said the Democratic map did not meet the standards of the Thirteenth and Fourteenth Amendments of the U.S. Constitution and the 1965 Federal Voting Rights Act. And "in addition, I find that the proposed map is not politically fair."

The legislative redistricting issue as provided in the Illinois Constitution was turned over to a bipartisan legislative redistricting commission. This commission was not able to agree on a map, thereby triggering a unique Illinois political device, a commission tie-breaker. Two names, one from each party, are selected by state supreme court justices and are placed in a hat or crystal bowl. One is selected by the secretary of state. In 1981, Secretary of State Edgar selected a Democratic name out of a hat; in 1991, Secretary of State Ryan selected a Republican name out of a bowl. The chances for the Republicans in the next decade look very good in the General Assembly, and might mean an end to (or lessening of) the divided government that Illinois has had for more than ten years.

On the congressional redistricting, the Democrats could not obtain agreement because of the controversy over black and Hispanic districts. The House did adopt a map, but the Senate could not come up with enough votes. The issue went into a federal court for resolution. The three-judge panel was composed of judges appointed by President Reagan. The Democrats were not happy with their prospects.

There were, of course, many other issues, including school reform and funding for a billion dollar expansion of McCormick Place in Chicago—measures that the governor approved. The governor used his veto powers, including the amendatory veto, on several bills. On bills that were labeled antibusiness (such as mandatory maternity leave) he vetoed the measure. He vetoed a comparable-worth bill thus irritating some feminists. These two vetoes earned him an antifeminist label in some circles. He countered that he was not, and he pointed out that he had supported the Equal Rights Amendment when he was in the legislature.

He approved some controversial issues such as a "right to die" bill. He also approved a bill requiring the National Collegiate Athletic Association (NCAA) to use due process when investigating alleged irregularities at Illinois public universities. He vetoed a bill that would prohibit universities from dropping Reserve Officer Training Corps (ROTC) programs, stating that this was a proper decision for the university itself. He signed a "no-knock" bill to let police enter an establishment without a warrant, a move that upset the American Civil Liberties Union.

Governor Edgar carried out one of his campaign pledges that was included in his State of the State message: he opposed state mandates for local governments. He vetoed several mandate bills on Local Government Day at the state fair. He said, "Local government costs have risen because of directions from state government. It is time to reverse that irresponsible trend for the sake of the taxpayer we all serve."

Other Gubernatorial Issues

During the early months of his administration Edgar took many stands that indicated that there was a new style and tone in the governor's office and in state government. This is illustrated by his actions at the state fair in August. The sedate governor did not go on the water slide as had Governor Thompson. Because Edgar disapproved of Willie Nelson's image, the entertainer did not perform as he had in the past. And to discourage drunkenness, there was only one beer tent at the fair instead of the customary several.

At the National Governors Association summer meeting in Seattle he did not seek national visibility like some of the other new governors. He did, however, take the lead in defending the hospital assessment of the Medicaid controversy.

The Edgars lived and entertained in the executive mansion in Springfield. Governor Edgar built a retreat in Williamsville, ten miles from Springfield, instead of in Wisconsin as Governor Thompson had done.

He had criticized the expansion of publicly approved gambling in the state, although he is a horse racing enthusiast and has made wagers at the track. He said he would not have approved the riverboat gambling that had been adopted the session before his election.

He did not take any trips abroad during the first six months of his administration, but he was quite busy as a new governor with serious legislative problems. But it is unlikely that he will travel as often as Thompson, whose junkets many observers considered excessive.

Edgar had to deal with the no-patronage *Rutan* decision. He issued detailed instructions to agencies under his control on how interviews for prospective employees were to be conducted.

The governor got involved in one unusual controversy and came out a winner. The governor is an ex-officio member of the board of trustees of the University of Illinois, but by custom does not attend meetings. The controversy was over the filling of the vacancy for the chancellorship for the Chicago campus of the University. Paula Wolff, policy director for Governor Thompson and staff director of Governor Edgar's transition team, sought the chancellor's position. She had academic credentials, but not those that the campus search committee sought. The committee voted not to interview her. Political leaders and newspapers took sides on the controversy. Former governor Thompson, Mayor Daley, and many others supported Paula Wolff. Governor Edgar supported Wolff initially but did not lobby for her. The *Chicago*

Tribune supported Wolff, while the *Chicago Sun Times* supported the established search procedures. The controversy became a major media issue in Chicago.

Because of pressure from outside, the search committee relented and interviewed Wolff, but it did not recommend her. It recommended that Acting Chancellor James Stukel be named chancellor. The crucial meeting for a decision by the board of trustees was Thursday, March 14, 1991, on the University's Urbana-Champaign campus.

The weekend before the meeting, Governor Edgar, a basketball fan, attended the state high school tournament and an Illinois-Indiana Big Ten Conference game on the Urbana campus. During the games he had several discussions with University President Ikenberry and the president of the board of trustees.

During the weekend the news media continued to give the controversy much attention. But on Monday, March 11, Governor Edgar, breaking precedent, announced that he would attend the Thursday meeting, and that he would vote for Stukel. The next day Paula Wolff withdrew as a candidate.

At the Thursday meeting, Governor Edgar arrived at the board meeting to a standing ovation from the predominantly faculty audience. Most TV stations in the state covered the meeting. After appropriate remarks from the governor and President Ikenberry, the roll of trustees was called and Stukel was elected chancellor.

In the eyes of many, Governor Edgar came out a winner for solving the controversy, and for supporting the academic community and the search process. On Tuesday a *Tribune* article said, "By helping to resolve the matter, Edgar would appear statesmanlike, and his intervention would lend credibility to Stukel and make it easier for him to lead a campus bitterly divided over the issue of a new chancellor." [12]

On an upbeat note, Governor Edgar was able to turn to other important matters, such as the state's budget crisis.

Conclusion

Within about six months in office Jim Edgar had set a new tone in state administration. He had distanced himself from Jim Thompson on many fronts. He was generally well thought of by the public and his fellow politicians. His stand on the budget in the prolonged legislative session won him good marks in the media.

Edgar's approval rating by the public in early September polls was favorable. He had a job approval rating of 65 percent and a favorable impression of 70 percent. For Illinois, his "honest" rating of 78 percent was very good. Despite big budget cuts, his "caring" rating was 74 percent.

Whether these ratings reflected a "honeymoon" period is debatable. He did keep his broad campaign promises: no new taxes were adopted, but the surcharge on the income tax was renewed in an end-of-the-session compromise. Property tax caps were adopted, but not in Cook County.

But despite these positives, Jim Edgar faces some real problems in the future. The fiscal crisis that he faced would continue for the foreseeable future. In late summer two bond rating houses—Standard and Poor's and Moody's—lowered the Illinois bond grades. An unfavorable ruling by the U.S. Department of Health and Human Services on the Medicaid assessments plan could wreak havoc with the state budget. Another year or two of no raises for public employees could cause serious morale problems. On the other hand, a more sympathetic legislature after redistricting, with more Republicans—even a majority—might help Edgar obtain agreement with his wishes on fiscal affairs.

Jim Edgar has proved to be a competent, no-nonsense governor. He has not sought national attention. He is a hands-on administrator who knows state government. He has surrounded himself with a capable, but not flashy, staff.

Jim Edgar is off to a good start despite the serious fiscal problems that face his state.

Notes

1. 110 U.S. 2729 (1990).
2. Gov. Sam Shapiro, a Democrat from Kankakee County, was a graduate of the University of Illinois. As lieutenant governor he succeeded to office when Gov. Otto Kerner was appointed a federal judge. Shapiro was defeated when he ran for governor in 1968.
3. Diane Ross, "Jim Edgar: Heir Apparent?" *Illinois Issues*, July 1985, 6-10. *Illinois Issues* is a public policy magazine published by Sangamon State University in cooperation with the University of Illinois.
4. *Illinois Issues*, July 1985, 10.
5. *Tribune* (Chicago), December 15, 1990.
6. Also included were provisions for a revenue committee in each house of the legislature (twenty-five members in the House; thirteen in the Senate). The amendment further provided that legislators could not serve on the revenue committees for more than four years. The revenue committees would be required to hold public hearings on revenue bills with at least two weeks' notice to the public.
7. *Illinois Issues*, October 1990, 28-29.
8. Charles N. Wheeler III, *Illinois Issues*, December 1990, 6-7.

9. The agriculture director was the subject of a cover story in *Illinois Issues,* July 1991, 10-12.
10. The constitution provides that the governor at the close of his term of office "shall report to the General Assembly on the condition of the state. . . ." Governor Thompson did not deliver a speech as had been the custom, but presented a book-length report on his administration with several positive personal references with pictures. He made some recommendations. He concluded, "I am confident Gov. Jim Edgar has the character and ability to continue an era of cooperation in a state often marked by divisions. May he always know when to lead and when to follow, when to listen to others, and especially, when to listen to his own heart."
11. Hospitals are assessed a fee by the state. The federal government matches the assessed fee, and the state receives all the monies. The program is expected to be phased out by the federal government in the near future. See Michael D. Klemens's insightful analysis in Illinois Tax Foundation, *Budget Reporter,* September 1991.
12. For a more detailed discussion of this case, see Samuel K. Gove, "A Wolff at the Door of Illinois Higher Education: A Case Study of Politics and Education," *Comparative State Politics* 12 (June 1991): 1-15.

8. MASSACHUSETTS: WILLIAM F. WELD AND THE END OF BUSINESS AS USUAL

Dennis Hale

The End

As all the world now knows, Michael Dukakis returned to Massachusetts after his failed 1988 presidential bid to find a state teetering on the brink of ruin: the Massachusetts "miracle" had run its course, and the state was being pulled into the wake of a regional recession that worsened considerably in the following years. More important, the mood of the electorate was even grimmer than the economic news. Governor Dukakis was widely perceived as having let the state down by failing to be "tough enough" or "liberal enough" (depending on which faction you belonged to) and for having embarrassed himself, and the Commonwealth, before the nation's voters. Legislative leaders were not on good speaking terms with one another or with the governor, an impasse that complicated the state's response to the fiscal crisis.

To make matters worse, the governor and his wife were both showing scars from the stress of the presidential campaign, and Mrs. Dukakis would soon succumb again to the alcoholism she had been struggling so long to overcome. The two years remaining in Governor Dukakis's third term looked as if they might be too awful to watch. Some seriously suggested that he resign; no one suggested that he run for a fourth term. "It's going to be ugly," one state legislator remarked. "There's going to be blood all over the place." Things were so bad, in fact, that it looked like it might actually be possible to elect a Republican governor, and even—though only the boldest dared think this out loud—that the GOP might pick up a few additional seats in the legislature, where Republicans were outnumbered 128-31 in the House and 31-9 in the Senate.

The Beginning?

Two years later: the recession has gotten worse, several Massachusetts cities are on the edge of bankruptcy, banks are failing everywhere, there are empty condos and "see-through" office buildings all over the state, and the unemployment rate has hit 9.6 percent. Drug gangs roam Boston's poorest black neighborhoods, killing each other and innocent bystanders almost at will. Scandals abound: many of the state's municipal court workers and judges are discovered to be working three-hour days while cases back up for years; questions are raised about the way the state treasurer has been investing the state's money; a state college president, one of Governor Dukakis's appointees, has been forced to resign in disgrace. The voters, in poll after poll, express almost unbelievable hostility toward the state's political establishment. And what is most astonishing of all, the party that has presided over virtually every nook and cranny of Massachusetts government for a generation (having held majorities in both houses of the legislature since 1959 and the governorship in twenty-two of the previous thirty-four years) has just come within 76,000 votes of winning *another* gubernatorial election and has held on to its majorities in both the House and the Senate.

The Rout of the Regulars

These two snapshots define the political situation in Massachusetts: the "ins" appear to be on the way out, but the "outs" have not quite made it in yet. Amidst the euphoria of their election night victories (Republicans also captured the state treasurer's office for the first time since 1948), only a few Republicans noted the paradoxical quality of the election returns, which were bringing a solid Democratic majority back to the House and a slim Democratic majority back to the Senate (so slim that it would be difficult for the Democrats to override the governor's vetoes, which were expected to be numerous). For the moment, it was enough that the Republicans had won the governor's race—it was their first such victory since 1970—even if they had to do it with a candidate who had been denied his party's nomination at its convention and who was denounced frequently by the party chairman.

Both party conventions, in fact, nominated losers. The endorsed Republican candidate in the primary was a little-known Republican member of the House, Steven Pierce; the Democratic endorsement went to a veteran officeholder, former attorney general Francis X. Belotti. Pierce was a new style conservative: against taxes, against government programs of all kinds, against abortion, for the "little guy." Belotti was a traditional liberal, with close ties to most of the liberal interest groups active in Massachusetts politics, from feminist organizations and organized labor to environmental groups and community housing activists. In the end, neither party's endorsement was worth very much.

Independents are allowed to vote in Massachusetts primaries, and given the hostility of the voters to politics as usual, the presence of a large number of nonpartisan voters in the primaries all but doomed the anointed candidates.[1] Pierce was defeated handily (60 percent to 40 percent) by William F. Weld, an "old money" Yankee who had resigned his position as assistant attorney general in 1988 to protest the ethical climate in Ed Meese's Justice Department. Pierce made much of the contrast between his own humble origins and Weld's patrician background, but this is apparently not a good strategy in a Republican primary in Massachusetts.

Belotti faced two opponents in the primary: Lt. Gov. Evelyn Murphy, a Dukakis protégé; and Boston University President John Silber, who was so unpopular at the Democratic state convention that he barely qualified for the primary ballot. Democratic party activists didn't like him, but the voters did; in a few weeks Silber was the front runner. A few days before the primary, Murphy dropped out, throwing her support to Belotti, and Silber took 51 percent of the vote in what was essentially a two-way race.

The Weld-Silber contest was one of the most interesting governor's races of 1990, as the extraordinary 75 percent voter turnout suggests. Each candidate, while running against the other, also ran against the central tendency (and the leadership) of his own party, which resulted in some confusing subversion of stereotypes. The Republican candidate gave speeches to gay rights organizations, pledged his unqualified support for abortion rights, and supported the distribution of condoms in the public schools—to the utter consternation of the Reaganite leadership of the state party.

The Democratic candidate, meanwhile, stepped on a different set of liberal toes every day of the campaign, providing the public with a steady stream of what came to be known as "Silber shockers." "Why are there so many Cambodians in Lowell? " he asked one day. "Is Massachusetts becoming a welfare magnet for Asians? " In a speech about health cost control, Silber noted that the old have a less compelling claim to expensive medical treatments than the young— "When you're ripe, it's time to go." Asked why a major anticrime speech was delivered from the steps of the State House instead of in the city's major black neighborhood, Silber went out of his way to offend: "Why should I give a speech about drug crime to an audience filled with drug addicts?" On slow days (which were few), reporters dug out the older controversies that have dogged Silber during his tenure as president of Boston University: his refusal to grant a charter to the campus gay rights organization; his decision to reimpose parietals in the student dorms; his reference to the English Department as a "damned matriarchy" and to its chairwoman as "Henry the Eighth with tits." [2]

Was this madness, or was there method as well?

Conventional wisdom, of course, says that candidates should not go out of their way to offend either the voters in general or organized interest groups in particular—but each time Silber said something outrageous, his numbers went up, which may explain why he ignored the advice of his more temperate advisers to simply shut up. Anecdotal evidence suggests that many voters admired Silber's "candor," and interviews with voters often turned up mixed signals. The day after the "ripeness" comment, for example, reporters visited several nursing homes and found many residents in full agreement with Silber's comments. Similarly, a black Boston resident interviewed after the "drug addict" remark observed that the neighborhood *was* filled with drug addicts. "You can't leave your house anymore. That's what the man was saying, and he's right."

Whatever their effect on the voters, Silber's unpredictable comments had the predictable effect of making it virtually impossible for liberal Democrats to vote for him—assuming that any had been tempted to do so in the first place, which is doubtful. (Silber made no secret of the fact that he had voted for both Reagan and Bush.) Was *this* the method to Silber's madness, to drive the liberals out of the Democratic party, or at least to put them in their place? If so, the strategy almost worked. Liberals voted for Weld, and Silber almost won without them.

Almost, but not quite. The combination of die-hard Republicans, moderate independents, and liberal Democrats was enough to give Weld a margin of 3.1 percentage points: 76,000 votes out of 2.5 million cast, and less than a majority of the total vote. ("Blanks" and minor candidates took 6 percent.)

The election returns leave no doubt about who elected William Weld, and it wasn't Republicans. In Cambridge, for example—a traditional stronghold of Democratic liberalism, which gave Dukakis 26,000 votes in 1982 (the last gubernatorial election in which Dukakis had a serious opponent) [3]—Weld got 18,000 votes to Silber's 14,000. In Newton and Brookline—also liberal strongholds—Weld received a combined total of 34,000 votes to Silber's 26,000; Dukakis had received 46,000 votes in these two communities in 1982. All over the state, the results were the same: Silber carried the cities and Weld carried the small towns and the affluent suburbs.

The grittier the place, the more likely it was to vote for Silber. Fall River, New Bedford, Boston, Chelsea, Revere, Worcester, Chicopee, Holyoke, Springfield, Lowell: the old, decaying, ethnic and industrial heartland of Massachusetts voted for Silber. The Democratic share of the two-party vote in these eleven cities was 59 percent. But as the precincts got tonier, the Weld vote went up. In Medford (per capita income in 1987: $13,675), Silber took 51.3 percent of the vote; in neighboring Winchester (per capita income in 1987: $23,019), Weld won with 57.9 percent of the vote. Both communities went for Dukakis in 1982.[4]

Tribal Warfare

In one sense, then, the 1990 gubernatorial election was a throwback to an earlier period in Massachusetts partisanship, when the most comfortable voters (even the reformers) voted Republican and the afflicted voted Democratic. Consistent with this pattern, Weld and Silber drew a fairly clear line between them on economic as well as on social issues. When he wasn't baiting liberals, Silber talked like a traditional Democrat, with one important exception: he would not support new taxes to balance the budget. The state government would have to live with its current revenue, but within those limits Silber argued for a redirection of resources (and public attention) toward the inner cities, the poor, and the public institutions that make a difference in the lives of middle- and lower-income families: public schools, especially. Two years earlier, Silber had pushed Boston University to seek a contractual arrangement with the struggling city of Chelsea to run its school system, promising to make the state's most deprived schools work. (He also promised to abolish the BU School of Education if the effort failed.) And unlike Weld, Silber campaigned hard against Question 3, a ballot initiative that would have rolled Massachusetts tax rates back to 1988 levels, requiring an immediate 25 percent reduction in the 1991 budget.[5] Weld strongly supported Question 3.

Adding to the traditional nature of this particular campaign was the victorious candidate himself. If you had to redesign the classic Massachusetts Republican for a more contemporary, upscale market, Bill Weld is what you would get. The descendant of a family that was prosperous at the turn of the nineteenth century, and prominent even before that, William Weld has trod a familiar path: prep school, Harvard, Harvard Law, Oxford, public service, with just the right touches of eccentricity (he likes the Grateful Dead) to fill out the picture. Because of what he is, Weld's candidacy inflamed all of the ancient tribal passions of Massachusetts politics, and when John Silber called him "an orange-headed WASP," only a few stuffy editors thought he had committed a genuine offense: offending racial minorities and the elderly is politically incorrect, but WASP-baiting has the sanction of custom.[6]

The Budget Battle: Round One

When Governor Weld took office in January 1990, he faced an unusually difficult situation. The unemployment rate was down a bit, but still very bad—8.5 percent—and the Federal Reserve Bank had just announced that the current recession was the worst in the state since 1946. The fiscal 1991 state budget, adopted in July by Governor Dukakis and a Democratic legislature, was still $850 million in the red—despite two consecutive years of billion dollar tax increases. Moreover, the gap between committed spending and incoming revenues was growing worse daily. Weld had stated very plainly, and repeatedly, his absolute opposition to new taxes.

The legislature, meanwhile, still overwhelmingly Democratic, was more or less firmly opposed to "severe" cutbacks in "essential services" and aid to local governments. But the state Senate, with sixteen Republicans (nine of them brand new), was no longer veto-proof. Under the circumstances, it was probably inevitable that the legislature would blink first.

Adding to the pressure on the legislature to do something about the budget mess was the bad news from Wall Street. Standard & Poors had dropped the state's bond rating to BBB, and had been threatening since September to drop it even further—to "junk bond" status—if the state could not come up with a plan to deal with the fiscal crisis.[7]

The people who would have to face this crisis were, for the most part, new to their jobs, though not to government. Besides Governor Weld and Lt. Gov. Paul Cellucci, there was the new Speaker of the House, former majority leader Charles Flaherty, a "lunch-bucket" Democrat from the blue-collar end of Cambridge—an experienced liberal politician who had for most of his career skillfully balanced the "draft beer" and "white wine" factions in Cambridge, which is no easy task. Flaherty was putting together a new leadership team; significantly, the chairman of the Ways and Means Committee, Thomas Finneran (D-Boston), would be new to his job.

In the Senate, William Bulger, of South Boston, who was definitely not new to his job, was reelected to his seventh term as president, after a gleeful but futile challenge from the Republicans. The message had been sent, however: the old days had passed, and Senator Bulger would have to play by different rules. By mid-January, the outlines of the coming year were all in place; all that remained was to fill in the details.

Governor Weld's inaugural address established the main theme, a Reaganesque assault on government. Government is the problem, not the solution. Government is too big, too clumsy, and too greedy; tax increases only feed its worst appetites and vices. The only way around the problem of government is to have less of it. In the inaugural address, and in the weeks and months to come, Weld offered a vision of a stripped down state government that would tailor its benefits first to its revenues and second to need. Instead of placating interest groups with "pilot programs" that quickly become entitlements, the government would encourage competition and entrepreneurship, even to the extent of turning the management of public programs and institutions over to private contractors. We will not abandon the safety net, he promised. But we *will* abandon nearly everything else. And there will be *no* new taxes, period.

What required immediate attention, however, was not the future but the present. The 1991 budget was still out of balance by $850 million. On January 31, Weld submitted his proposals for dealing with that deficit.

Governor Weld's first budget proposals, although they sent an immediate shock wave through the state's political establishment, were curiously tentative. Much of the $850 million was to be raised by selling a motley assortment of state assets: abandoned hospital buildings, vacant land, and the like. The rest was to come from cuts in nearly every human service program, cuts in the aid sent to local governments, an increase in the cost of state workers' health insurance premiums, and a ten-day unpaid furlough for all state employees at the end of the fiscal year.[8] Governor Weld insisted that he had kept his promise to balance the budget without inflicting pain and suffering on the truly needy. Responded Speaker Flaherty: "His definition of pain and suffering doesn't correspond to mine."[9]

Flaherty faced a restive Democratic majority as the new session got under way. The inclination of the rank and file was to send the whole package back to Weld and tell him to try again. The Speaker explained, patiently but firmly, that that would not do. The pressure from Wall Street, on one side, and the voters, on the other, was too intense. There was no alternative to the kind of cuts Weld was proposing, except for different cuts. "No program or policy will escape our scrutiny," he told the legislators, "We must recognize that all claims are not equal."[10]

By the end of February, as the House scrutinized the budget, still looking for painless cuts, Governor Weld began badgering the leadership to get moving. The Speaker had announced his opposition, for example, to the unpaid furlough for state workers, a powerful lobby in any state legislature. The governor accused him of caving in. "You can lead the House to order," he quipped, "but you can't make it think."[11]

And that is pretty much how it went, from January to May. The governor denounced the legislature—whose standing with the voters was even lower than usual, a full 17 points below the governor's—and the legislative leadership taunted the governor for being a rich, out-of-touch Yankee with no sympathy for ordinary folks.[12] The governor helped his critics with an ill-advised decision to give $20,000 raises to his cabinet secretaries. The Democrats pounced on this mistake and played it for all it was worth before the governor was finally forced to back down. Meanwhile, the deficit had reached nearly $1 billion and counting.

In May, aides to Speaker Flaherty and the governor persuaded their bosses to get together for a breakfast meeting and try to repair their relationship. According to *Boston Globe* reporter John Powers's account of this meeting, Flaherty told the governor that the House was prepared to work "with" him but not "for" him, and that it was time to "cut out the bullshit." Flaherty, on his part, promised to deliver a balanced budget, as long as the governor could promise to deliver the Republicans, many of whom were beginning to develop broader views on the question of what constituted an "essential" service. Weld, for his part, promised to stop baiting the legislature.[13]

Once the governor and the Speaker agreed to a more cooperative relationship, things began to move fairly smoothly. First, the governor's secretary of administration and finance, Peter Nessen, sat down with House Ways and Means Chairman Thomas Finneran to "agree on the numbers." The last two years of the Dukakis administration had been a circus of warring revenue estimates; Nessen and Finneran agreed to find a conservative number they could agree on, and to stick to it. They finally settled on a revenue estimate for 1992 of $8.3 billion; Weld's original budget for 1992 had assumed revenues of $9.2 billion. It would be necessary to find another $1 billion in cuts.[14]

Between May and July, the House and Senate leaders sold a bare-bones budget that ended 1991 without a deficit, to be followed by an even more skeletal budget for 1992. At no time in the recent past would these legislators have passed such a budget, let alone two such budgets in a row. (There had not been two consecutive years of declining budgets since 1960.) The leadership's argument, ever since the session began in January, was the same: Wall Street is fed up, the voters are fed up, and if we don't bite the bullet the state could end up in the hands of a receiver. During the entire session—from January through late summer—the corridors of the statehouse were filled with lobbyists pleading their various causes: public employee unions; AIDS victims; people in wheelchairs; schoolteachers; social workers; childrens' advocates; and advocates for the elderly, the blind, the poor, and the homeless. They camped out in front of the leadership's offices; they sat on the statehouse steps; they displayed rude signs accusing the Democrats of becoming Republicans.

None of it mattered. At an emotional Democratic caucus near the middle of May, Ways and Means Chairman Finneran read from

Churchill's *The Gathering Storm:* "Delight in smooth-sounding plati-
tudes, refusal to face unpleasant facts, desire for popularity and
electoral success irrespective of the vital interest of the state, utter
devotion to sentiment apart from reality. . . ." It was an apt description
of the Democratic party at the end of the Dukakis era, and by then
most of the members knew it. The leadership held firm, the governor
prodded, and by the end of June the deed was done. The 1991 budget
had been trimmed by $800 million, and the 1992 budget had been
trimmed by $1.8 billion. For his efforts, Finneran was served an
"eviction notice" by the Cambridge First Church [Homeless] Shelter.
All the members, especially those with the closest ties to liberals
(including the Speaker), received similar insults.[15]

Practically speaking, what did all this budget-cutting amount to?

- Approximately three hundred programs suffered some
  degree of cutting, including rent subsidies, public health
  (except for AIDS and prenatal care), welfare, higher
  education scholarships, the operating budgets of the state
  colleges and universities, the state's contribution to the
  Massachusetts Bay Transportation System, and public
  employee compensation. If the 1992 budget had continued
  all services, programs, and subsidies at 1991 levels, the
  budget would have been $15.6 billion; Weld's budget came
  in at $12.8 billion—an 18 percent reduction.

- Some of the cuts—a substantial portion of them—came in
  the previously sacred local aid fund, which had grown by
  leaps and bounds since Proposition 2½ was passed by the
  voters in 1980. This tax-limit initiative placed a 2.5 percent
  cap on the growth of annual property tax levies at the local
  level, forcing cities and towns to rely increasingly on aid
  from the state. During the flush times in the 1980s, the aid
  was generous; by 1988 the well had begun to run dry.
  Local aid was level-funded for the first time in 1989, and in
  1990 it decreased for the first time since 1981. The 1992
  local aid account was reduced by 12.6 percent, for a savings
  of $328 million.

- The contribution state employees make to their health
  insurance premiums would increase from 10 percent to 50
  percent, for a savings of $65 million. An additional $65
  million would come from the job furlough. For the fifth
  year in a row, state employees would receive no pay
  increases.

- State employment would be shrunk: it had already declined

by an estimated 11 percent since 1988, and it was slated to decline by another 9.7 percent in 1992.[16]

- General Relief—which serves about 38,000 people not served (in theory) by other welfare programs—was slated for a 50 percent reduction, for a savings of $47 million.

For all the furor over the final outcome, however, there was almost as much "smoke and mirrors" in the 1992 budget as in previous efforts. The governor did not get all that he asked for, and some of what he asked for he did not get at all. The cuts in General Relief, for example, were much less severe than he had proposed. Instead of eliminating seven of the ten categories of eligibility, the legislature eliminated only three. The proposed increase in state employee health insurance premiums was rejected outright.

Rather than prolong the budget battle, however—and risk entering the new fiscal year without a budget—Weld agreed to withhold some of his vetoes until September, when the legislature reconvened, and after the state had received the expected pat on the back from Wall Street. This proved to be a sensible strategy, at least in the short run: Weld's presentation in May to a group of New York investors was very favorably received. The official spin on the spring's events—the governor had cut the budget and refused to raise taxes—was just what Wall Street had been waiting to hear.[17] The state's bond rating remained at BBB, but at least it did not sink to junk bond status, as everyone had feared.

The Budget Battle: Round Two

Consequently, when the legislature reconvened in September, everyone was poised for the battle of the budget vetoes. What happened next, though somewhat anticlimactic, was nevertheless revealing.

The first battle was over how much to charge state employees for their health insurance. In rejecting Weld's proposal in June, the legislature opted for the status quo, in which the state picked up 90 percent of the cost of insurance premiums; Weld had proposed a 75 percent contribution from the state, a change that would have saved the state (according to the administration's calculations) $45 million a year. The practical effect of this change on state workers was relatively small: the average family of four would have seen its insurance premiums go up by about $19 per month, from $39 to $58. But state employees had gone without a pay raise for four years (and would get none this year), and had been forced to accept an unpaid ten-day furlough in June. The legislature was receptive to the argument that it would be unfair to ask for more sacrifice from those who had already paid so much. Either because of the fairness argument, or because state employees are well organized, Weld suffered his greatest defeat to date: his veto was overridden in the House by a vote of 130-21 and in the Senate by a vote of 31-0.[18] Said State Democratic Committee Chairman Steve Grossman:

> [There is a] new contentiousness after six months of deferring to the chief executive. Democrats in the legislature will articulate increasingly, with increasing levels of passion and clarity of vision, who they are and what they stand for as a fundamental alternative to the Republican administration.[19]

They got their chance one month later, when the governor's veto of the General Relief fund came before the legislature. General Relief recipients are apparently not as persuasive as state employees. The House managed to override the governor's veto, but the Senate proved more intractable: failing to muster enough votes, Senate President Bulger called for a compromise. After a lengthy debate, culminating in a twelve-hour bargaining session, legislative leaders and administration officials agreed on a measure that would cap General Relief spending at $168 million (a savings of $80 million) by eliminating 14,000 clients from the welfare rolls (out of 38,000 in 1991).[20] This was a smaller cut than the governor had proposed originally, but it was a significant reduction, and the governor's people claimed a modest victory, pointing to the provision in the bill that gives to the governor the authority to change benefits and eligibility criteria if welfare expenditures approach the $168 million cap. Liberal Democrats were more somber. Senate Ways and Means Chair Patricia McGovern, arguing that it could have been much worse, tried to be philosophical: "You take your victories where you can get them." [21]

As dramatic as these budget battles were, the fall ended with a whimper. In addition to budget questions, Weld submitted a complicated legislative agenda to the legislature, and the legislative leaders had some pet projects of their own to pursue. Weld submitted bills dealing with crime prevention (including a restoration of the death penalty), court reform (a response to the scandals of the previous year), pension reform, consolidation of state police forces, early retirement for state workers, state receivership for the bankrupt city of Chelsea, and the deregulation of abortion. He also promised a package of education reforms. By the end of the legislative session in December 1991, only two of these items—receivership for Chelsea, and pension reform—had been acted on.

There was one significant development during the fall, however, that may prove troublesome: state revenues began to go up, to the surprise of everyone, and the embarrassment of some. In early October, the secretary of administration and finance announced that tax revenues were ahead of projections, and that if this trend were to continue, the state would end the fiscal year with $830 million more than anticipated. Subtracting losses in federal Medicaid reimbursements and declines in other nontax revenues, the state could still be $430 million ahead.[22] In the early days of the budget debate, back in March, the legislature and the governor had "agreed to agree" on a set of conservative revenue estimates that now appear to be unrealistically low. If the earlier agreement breaks down, the legislature might try to reopen the budget question all over again, and the state would be back where it was in February.

A New Kind of Conservative?

Back in the spring, while the House wrestled with the budget, Speaker Flaherty tried to explain to a group of social service lobbyists what it was they were up against: "The problem isn't that the governor doesn't understand state programs; the problem is that he doesn't care. He just doesn't think these programs are necessary." [23] Certainly, no Massachusetts governor in modern times—and that includes Republicans like Frank Sargent—has been so willing to risk the perception (whatever the truth might be) that he simply doesn't care what happens to the poor, or to assert that the needy would do just fine without state assistance.

It is also clear that this attitude is not as widely shared among the voters as Weld's election might suggest. A Becker Institute poll taken in late October, for example, found that 41 percent of the voters had a "favorable" opinion of Weld, while 37 percent viewed him "unfavorably." This represented a 26-point slide in his favorability rating since early February, at the start of the budget battle, and a 15-point increase in his unfavorable rating. In the same poll, only 19 percent found the budget cuts "acceptable," while 35 percent objected to the cuts "strongly" and 40 percent objected "mildly." [24]

One obvious conclusion to be drawn from these responses is that the voters are not polarized into warring camps over the issue of public spending, so much as they are profoundly ambivalent about the Democratic party, the state legislature, and their joint stewardship of the state government.[25] They have rejected the Democratic party's promiscuous spending habits without at the same time embracing Governor Weld's Ayn Randish dream of a stripped-down, entrepreneurial state that "steers but doesn't row" (to borrow one of the governor's favorite metaphors). Silber was so popular among rank-and-file Democrats precisely because his hostility to the Democratic establishment was combined with a willingness to use government to solve problems that voters take very seriously: bad public schools, failed welfare policies, crime, and economic decline. A good bumper sticker slogan for Silber would have been: "He's mean, but he cares." Weld's would have been: "He doesn't care very much, but he's nice."

That niceness, however, is buttressed by enough steel to have forced the legislature into its first experience at budget cutting since the 1960s. An instructive contrast is provided by the state's last major fiscal crisis, in 1975-1976, during Michael Dukakis's first term as governor. Having given the voters a "lead pipe guarantee" of no new taxes, Governor Dukakis discovered a $350 million deficit left over from the administration of outgoing Republican Frank Sargent. Dukakis's first response was to propose a list of budget cuts, but the legislature—faced with the prospect of laying off state workers and cutting their favorite state programs—demanded a tax increase. After a brief struggle, Dukakis succumbed. For breaking his no-new-taxes promise (among other sins) Dukakis was defeated in the 1978 Democratic primary by a conservative antitax Democrat, Ed King.[26]

A New Kind of Liberal?

But there is another side to Weld, and it raises intriguing possibilities for his career in Massachusetts and beyond. Although he is conservative on economic questions, Weld is a liberal on matters of private conduct, opposing laws that would restrict abortion or exclude homosexuals from public life. He also has the outdoorsman's traditional concern for conservation, which places him on the liberal side, most of the time, when environmental policy is discussed. These qualities drew a significant contrast during the election between Weld and Silber, making it possible for liberals to vote Republican without feeling too guilty about it.

But Weld is more libertarian than liberal, more Ayn Rand than John Anderson. When he talks about government "leaving people alone," he also means that the government should not ban the sale of assault weapons or impose 55 m.p.h. speed limits on the Massachusetts Turnpike. When he talks about "limited government," he means turning public schools, libraries, hospitals, and prisons over to private management companies.[27] On the other hand, Weld likes to stress the obligations that citizens have toward the community, and he has recently offered several proposals designed to reinforce those obligations, including "scarlet letter" license plates for people convicted of drunk driving; a work requirement for welfare recipients; denying driver's licenses to teenagers who have not completed high school; and restoration of the death penalty. None of these schemes will make liberals happy.[28]

During the campaign, however, the Ayn Rand side of Weld's philosophy went relatively unnoticed: all that mattered was that he had come out solidly behind a "woman's right to choose." Another good sign for liberals was his appointment, during the transition, of an openly gay Republican to be an official liaison with the gay community.

However, once Weld's position on the budget became a fact rather than a position paper, the liberal disenchantment began, much to Speaker Flaherty's disgust. ("Didn't they listen to what he said? Did they think he didn't mean it?") Toward the end of his first year in office, therefore, Governor Weld reached out to the left, principally by upping the ante on abortion rights.

In early October, after the bruising and not entirely successful fights over his budget vetoes, Weld moved the abortion issue to center stage. In a speech in September, Weld proposed that abortion be deregulated completely in Massachusetts. This idea had first been introduced into the abortion debate by Lt. Gov. Evelyn Murphy, during the Democratic primary campaign, apparently as a way of distinguishing herself from her liberal opponent, Francis Belotti, who was also pro-choice. John Silber pointed out at the time that this policy would make it possible for a woman to have an abortion in the ninth month of her pregnancy, and asked how this would differ from infanticide. Governor Weld's proposal drew the same kind of response from Cardinal Bernard Law of Boston, who issued a scathing attack on what he termed the "enormous crime of abortion," concluding that Weld's proposal would make Massachusetts "the commonwealth of death for the innocent." Significantly, the cardinal linked the abortion proposals to the cutbacks in General Relief, denouncing both as signs of a callous disregard for human life.[29]

Whatever the merits of Weld's proposal, it had the effect of rallying liberal Democrats and women's groups once more to his side, however uncomfortable it might have made them feel.

Is this the kind of Republican candidate who could do well in a presidential campaign? Weld has a number of qualities that make him an obvious presidential possibility: he is young, smart, handsome, experienced, and independently wealthy. He speaks well and has a good sense of humor. He can handle pressure and is quick on his feet—he even survived Senator Bulger's notorious St. Patrick's Day breakfast in South Boston, where the Senate president roasts his friends and foes before an appreciative crowd of well-lubricated, mostly Irish Democrats.[30]

Massachusetts is changing, in much the same way that the country is changing. Suburban voters are more important than they once were, and they are registering and voting Republican, as are younger, first-time voters. Furthermore, there has been a perceptible shift in the loyalties of blue-collar families, who no longer see the Democratic party as speaking for them. In 1992, suburban voters will constitute a majority of the national electorate for the first time, and in Massachusetts, Democrats and independents are switching their party registration to Republican, although in fairly small numbers.[31] And the places that constituted the old reliable base of the Massachusetts Democratic party—the cities that voted for Silber in 1990—are a smaller proportion of the state's electorate now than they were in 1960: the state's central city population was 47 percent of the electorate thirty years ago; it is 39 percent today.

A younger, more suburban electorate might respond well to a socially moderate Republican who protects their private freedoms while refusing to raise taxes in support of "failed social programs." Even successful social programs will mean little to people who have left the city behind, who don't work or shop downtown, and who know the city only through lurid newspaper headlines and crime spots on the TV news. Of course, this analysis assumes what may not be true: that suburban voters will never themselves feel a need for help from the government. Surely, this is what Republicans are counting on—that the "opportunity society" will keep the wolf from the door, even in the suburbs, without the need for government programs.

But already there are unmistakable signs that social decay is spreading from the cities to the suburbs, and that moving out of the old neighborhood does not mean escaping the old problems: drugs, crime, bad schools, corrupt politics. On top of social breakdown there is economic collapse: more and more of the state's residents are experiencing their vulnerability to the recession, even those in the middle class.[32] Weld's budget cutting, significantly, does not touch only the poor. Recently, his administration eliminated Medicaid nursing home reimbursements for everyone with income greater than $14,000 per year—that is, everyone who is not poor. Younger couples with growing families and elderly parents will face a double squeeze: private school tuition and nursing home payments. As in the Depression, they may be forced to choose between their children and their parents.

And there is this further problem: so far the goal of "prosperity in one state" has eluded every governor who has pursued it. State economies rise and fall with the national economy, and the national economy is out of the hands of state politicians. But it *is* in the hands of Republicans, and if things are no better by 1994, every Republican governor will be in trouble, no matter how good his record at home.

Pro-choice, tax limits, and economic growth: is this the new winning combination?

Not if you ask Republican party activists in Massachusetts; their disenchantment with Weld's "social liberalism" has a long history. The people who "Reaganized" the state party back in the 1980s wanted the whole package: a pro-life and pro-family social policy *and* limits on public spending *and* a tax policy that would spur economic growth. In their eyes, Weld is an apostate, willing to sell his soul to the liberals in order to carry places like Cambridge and Newton. Steve Pierce was one of their own, and they have no real enthusiasm for Governor Weld even now, when he is at the height of his success.[33]

In an analysis published in the *Boston Globe* in October, former GOP state chairman Andrew Natsios took partial credit for Weld's victory by noting the organizational improvements brought to the party under his tenure and that of his successor, Ray Shamie: better fundraising, phone networks, candidate training sessions, recruitment of new registrants. He noted also that the party had been given a clearer ideological focus (that is, it had been Reaganized). But even with all of these improvements, the Republican party is still small in Massachusetts—registration is about 8 percent lower than it is nationally. And Weld and Cellucci, Natsios charged, have no plans to solve this problem. Instead, they have come up with a "simplistic" strategy of "fiscal conservatism and social liberalism." This strategy has no appeal, Natsios claims, to the "working class"—especially to young families worried about their economic future and who care relatively little about abortion, gay rights, and the environment. New voters are interested in "opportunity" and they will not register Republican unless the party holds out the prospect of hope, especially the hope that public education might once again be made an avenue of social advance. But, Natsios admits, "This program will cost money, a good deal of it, none of which should come from a tax increase." [34]

This is a curious analysis—even without the alchemy of more money without more taxes. It seems to be suggesting that Weld should have campaigned on Silber's platform—which was also based on the premise of no new taxes, but which promised, unlike Weld's, to redirect public spending toward important public programs, such as education. The sticking point is "social liberalism"—many of the people who voted for Weld did so precisely because of his stand on abortion, and they weren't all disaffected liberal Democrats from Cambridge and Brookline. Most of them were suburban Republicans and independents who wanted lower taxes and more private liberty. Like liberal Democrats from Cambridge, they may have been offended by Silber's lecturing about infanticide and the breakdown of the two-earner family—themes that had more appeal among blue-collar and lower-middle-class voters, and even, perhaps, among the poor.

Barring a major disaster, however, Weld can expect little serious trouble from the Reagan wing of the Republican party; the defeat of "real Republican" Steve Pierce is a difficult argument to answer. Ray Shamie was replaced as state chairman after the election by a Weld ally, so if Weld retains his support among independent voters and liberal Democrats, he should have little trouble winning a second term in 1994. There is even talk of a run against Sen. Edward Kennedy, who faces reelection in 1994. (There is talk also of John Silber running against Kennedy in the Democratic primary, which raises the tantalizing possibility of another Weld-Silber contest, this time for the U.S. Senate.)

The Party of Things as They Are

The real question is what kind of candidate the Democrats will nominate to run against Weld the next time around. There will be great pressure from the party's left wing to nominate a "real liberal," on the grounds that Silber's loss of liberal votes cost him the election in 1990—and anyone to the left of John Silber will automatically qualify as a "real liberal." On the other hand, there was a real liberal on the ticket in 1990—Frank Belotti—and he could not survive the voters' anger at the Democratic party establishment. There is little reason to think that a liberal candidate would do better in 1994.

Much will depend on how the Democratic legislative leadership behaves over the next two years—specifically, on whether the Democratic party can overcome the public's skepticism regarding the party's fiscal prudence and common sense. A good test is shaping up over the issue of public education. In October, Governor Weld held press conferences in two urban school districts, one in Worcester and one in Holyoke, in the company of Secretary of Education Lamar Alexander, in order to introduce his package of educational reforms, which are inspired by the Bush administration's America 2000 initiative.

It was a curious and lackluster performance, partly because it was held outside the state's major media market, and partly because of the substance of the package. Beginning with the premise that there would be no new money slotted for public elementary and secondary education, the package offered a potpourri of libertarian solutions for the public school crisis, including abolishing teacher tenure; adding another layer of tests to determine which schools were succeeding and which were failing; creating links between business and the schools, including the possibility of corporate funding for school programs; turning public schools over to private contractors; and expanding the state's new and extremely tentative "school choice" law, which allows students from one community to go to school in another—and which transfers state aid from the old school to the new one. These proposals were announced in an elementary school in the blue-collar community of Holyoke, where class sizes average forty, and where one-third of the faculty has been laid off because of local budget cuts and the reduction in state aid.[35] The disparity between the problem and the proposed solution was striking—especially since the governor's own children attend a private school.

Is the disparity wide enough to offer an opening to the Democrats? The legislature's Joint Committee on Education and the Arts, co-chaired by Rep. Mark Roosevelt (D-Boston) and Sen. Thomas Birmingham (D-Chelsea) is preparing its own set of proposals on public school reform, and once those proposals are on the table there may be a spirited debate. The debate should prove interesting, for two reasons. First, the business community has recently taken a great interest in what goes on in the schools, and the Business Roundtable has been closely watching the legislative hearings, while offering very little comment on the governor's proposals. Second, the problem presented by the decline of the public schools threatens to expose each political party's special weakness.

The Republican weakness is money: it is hard to imagine school reform without a larger investment in public education and without some form of income redistribution. Massachusetts now ranks forty-ninth among the states in the amount spent by state government on K-12 public schools. This means that public schools in Massachusetts are supported by the municipal property tax to a greater extent than in most states. The gap between what wealthy communities can spend and what poor communities can spend is large and growing larger, and it is now among the widest in the country. Brockton, for example, spent $4,171 per pupil in 1990, while the state's wealthiest town, Weston, spent $8,012.[36] The poorest twenty communities spend half of what the richest twenty communities spend, a fact that the governor alluded to in his press conference, even borrowing the term "savage inequalities" from education critic Jonathan Kozol.[37]

The Democrats' problem is structure: any serious effort to improve public schools will require changing the way schools are managed; the way teachers are hired, trained, and supervised; and the way money is spent. Why should teachers have to endure the standard school of education curriculum, where they are taught how to teach but don't learn any math, or science, or history? Why is it so hard to fire bad teachers? Why does every school have to have exactly the same curriculum, and why are there so many administrators? More money may be a necessary condition of improving the schools, but it is clearly not a sufficient condition: Boston spent $6,679 per pupil in 1990—ranking twentieth in the state—while Winchester, with a much better school system, spent only $5,561—ranking sixty-first in the state.[38] Admittedly, Boston has a more difficult task than Winchester, a middle-income suburb; but the Boston school system also suffers from managerial and political paralysis, and Winchester's does not. To improve the schools it is going to be necessary to do a lot of things differently, and that is the Democrats' weak spot. As the party of things as they are, the Democrats are going to have a difficult time telling their organized constituents (especially the teachers' unions) that things have got to change, and they will have a hard time getting the voters to cough up more money until they do.

It is the problem that David Stockman identified in the 1980s as the characteristic weakness of modern democratic governments: the inability to distinguish between strong clients with weak claims and weak clients with strong claims.[39] The Democratic legislature displayed this same weakness, it could be argued, when it chose to strike 14,000 people from the welfare rolls rather than ask state employees to pay $19 more per month for their health insurance.

The Party of Things as They Might Be

The Republican opportunity is clear, if its leaders can find the means to take advantage of it. How?

It seems very unlikely that any state government can survive for long if it cannot do anything for middle-class voters. State governments in some parts of the country have found the key to this problem in supporting a major occupational or demographic group: farmers in the Middle West; ranch and oil interests in the Southwest; the urban middle class in the East and on the West Coast. The means vary: road building, favorable regulation of natural gas and oil resources, low-cost tuition at decent public colleges and universities. But in Massachusetts this formula has not worked. The public universities have suffered from being in the shadow of the Ivy League—the University of Massachusetts is not the bargain that the California system has been for Californians. And the Massachusetts economy is not dominated by a single industry whose care and feeding helps keep the voters happy. (In fact, the opposite is the case: one of the state's major industries is health care; keeping doctors and hospital administrators happy does not translate into happy voters.) The high technology sector is an important part of the state's economy; but its leaders are divided, and they are distracted by the uncertainties of the computer business. High tech does not know what it wants from the state, and it is not certain that it wants anything except lower taxes.

As a result, the middle class feels the normal squeezing that all middle-income citizens experience during a recession, but they have not had the comfort of knowing that their state would be there to help them. Especially considering the high tax rates in Massachusetts, state government has offered very little to the voters who pay the bills.

Public schools, higher education, and health care: these are the services that mean the most to middle-income families. But there will be no way to pay for these things unless much of the money comes from existing revenue. That means cutting some programs completely, tightening up everywhere, and redrawing the balance between programs designed specifically for the poor and programs that are more generally available to the entire public.

This is, quite frankly, an unlikely scenario. But the only circumstance under which it might be possible would involve several major institutional and constitutional changes in state government.

- Something will have to be done about the archaic and appalling civil service laws in Massachusetts, which make it nearly impossible to run any agency or program with any degree of efficiency at all. Civil service rules are implicated in nearly every major public service failure, from law enforcement to public education to public health.
- The legislature will have to be persuaded to get out of the business of trying to micromanage state agencies.
- There are too many statewide elected officials. Massachusetts finds it necessary to elect the governor, lieutenant governor, secretary of state, state treasurer, state attorney general, and state inspector general; there are six different shops, each retailing its own version of state policy.
- The ten-year-old impasse over the municipal property tax will have to be resolved. Much of the recent fiscal crisis has been a consequence of the very rapid growth in state aid to local governments. In the past, Massachusetts gave too little to the towns and cities; until very recently, it had been giving too much. Meanwhile, the property tax cap passed in 1980 prevents communities from digging more deeply into their own pockets for their own local needs.
- Dealing with the problem of local government finance will mean dealing also with the Massachusetts tax system. It is unusually regressive, and the state courts have insisted that progressive rates require a constitutional amendment. Several have been attempted in modern times, and all have failed. (Another progressive income tax initiative may find

its way to the ballot in 1992.) But part of the anger of the middle class can be traced to the fact that middle-income voters bear a disproportionate share of the tax burden in a state where they receive very few services, and where they are now going to receive even fewer than before.

• Texas and Louisiana have oil and natural gas lobbies to deal with. Massachusetts has doctors and hospital administrators. They have two things in common: they make lots of money and they want to be left alone. No reform of the state's health care costs can proceed without taking on the health care lobby.

This is an ambitious agenda, easily proposed by an armchair critic of state government. Some of it has already found its way, however, into the Weld administration's public musings (civil service reform, for example); other elements—such as reform of public school management—have gotten farther than that. These are hopeful signs. But if Governor Weld truly means to spark a revolution in state government, he is going to need much more than a no-new-taxes pledge as fuel.

Notes

The author gratefully acknowledges the assistance of John Barry MacDonald, a senior political science major at Boston College, and Margaret Lutz, a Ph.D. candidate in the department's graduate program.

1. The primaries drew the highest turnout in modern times, in both parties: 82.7 percent for the Democrats and 111 percent for the Republicans—that is, more people voted in the Republican primary (457,000) than there are registered Republicans (412,000). The general election also drew an historic turnout: 75.4 percent, the highest in a nonpresidential year since 1970—which is, significantly, the last time the Republicans elected a governor. Public Document No. 43, *Massachusetts Elections Statistics: 1990* (Boston: Elections Division, Office of the Massachusetts Secretary of State, 1991).

2. Curtis Wilkie, "Siber's Odyssey in Pursuit of Truth," *Boston Globe,* February 11, 1990. 17.

3. In 1986, the first two Republican candidates had to withdraw after being tarnished by scandal; the third and last candidate was an inexperienced Greek-American businessman who ran a largely perfunctory campaign.

4. Public Document No. 43, *Massachusetts Elections Statistics: 1982, 1990* (Boston: Elections Division, Office of the Massachusetts Secretary of State, 1983, 1991); *Massachusetts Municipal Profiles: 1990-1991,* ed. Edith R. Hornor (Palo Alto, Calif.: Information Publications, 1991).

5. The ballot initiative was soundly defeated, 60 percent to 40 percent, in part because of the fear of what it would do to local school budgets, and in part because of the certainty that a new team, unaffiliated with the Dukakis administration, would be taking office in January, no matter who won the gubernatorial election. Had Question 3 passed, the deficit on January 1 would have been just under $3 billion, instead of $850 million.

6. John White points out that there is still an important religious/ethnic element in New England party identification, although both religion and ethnicity are less important than they were in the past. Catholics in Massachusetts are still more likely to be Democrats than Catholics nationally, and the same is true of ethnic identification: Irish, Italian, Polish, and French-Canadian voters are more Democratic in New England than they are in the country as a whole, and more Democratic than WASPs by about 20 percentage points. This pattern persists even though many of the old distinctions between Protestants and Catholics, and ethnics and Yankees—income, for example—have diminished or disappeared ("The Protestant-Catholic Divide in Southern New England: Policy Change and Party Response" [paper presented at the 1979 annual meeting of the Northeastern Political Science Association]). The abortion . debate, however, might bring new meaning to some of these old divisions.

7. John Powers, "Storming the Liberal Heartland," *Boston Globe,* October 6, 1991, 1.

8. In the end, the fiscal 1991 budget was balanced by a miracle: a parttime employee in the Department of Welfare discovered something everyone else had missed—the federal government owed the state $500 million in Medicaid reimbursements.

9. John Powers, "Storming the Liberal Heartland," 1.

10. Ibid.

11. Ibid.

12. There was wonderful symbolism in the fact that Weld and Flaherty both live in Cambridge; Flaherty is in fact the governor's representative in the House. Flaherty's home is in a blue-collar middle-class neighborhood of two- and three-family homes; several blocks away, the governor lives in a considerably grander place, in a neighborhood of Victorian and Georgian homes with spectacular gardens.

13. John Powers, "When the Budget Fight Stopped," *Boston Globe,* October 7, 1991, 1.

14. Ibid.

15. Ibid.

16. Peter J. Howe, "State Layoffs Easier Said Than Done," *Boston Globe,* April 28, 1991, 1. Massachusetts was the *only* state that actually managed to reduce its state work force in 1991. In spite of the decrease, total compensation costs increased by 0.6 percent, a sign of how significant health benefits and unemployment compensation have become.

17. Jolie Solomon and Peter Howe, "Wall Street Shows Faith in State Finances," *Boston Globe,* May 22, 1991, 1.

18. Frank Phillips, "Weld's Bid to Hike State Workers' Insurance Defeated," *Boston Globe,* September 5, 1991, 1.

19. Peter J. Howe, "Weld Set to Impound $65m in Health Insurance Funds," *Boston Globe,* September 6, 1991, 24.

20. Teresa M. Hanafin, "House OK's Substitute for General Relief," *Boston Globe,* October 10, 1991, 1; Teresa M. Hanafin, "Weld Version of Welfare Becomes Law," *Boston Globe,* October 11, 1991, 1.

21. Hanafin, "Weld Version of Welfare."

22. Peter J. Howe, "Revenue Forecast Is Clouded for State," *Boston Globe,* October 2, 1991, 25.

23. Powers, "When the Budget Fight Stopped."

24. Scott Lehigh, "Poll Shows Weld Losing Favorability," *Boston Globe,* October 26, 1991, 25.

25. This conclusion is consistent with an earlier poll, taken in 1989, which asked voters if they would pay higher taxes for a variety of public programs, including education, welfare, and the environment. Responses were overwhelmingly favorable (in the 60-80 percent range) when the higher taxes were hypothetically earmarked for these specific programs. When it was proposed that the additional tax revenue be given to the legislature to spend on these same programs, the response turned overwhelmingly negative (only 27 percent in favor). (M. E. Malone,"Poll: Bay State Voters Oppose General Tax Hike," *Boston Globe,* November 13, 1989, 1). A similar response has been reported by Gerry Chervinsky, "Massachusetts," *Public Perspective,* July/August 1990.

26. King's vote in 1978 resembled Silber's: that is, he carried the cities and lost most of the liberals. But there were some significant differences. For one thing, King's margin of victory in the state's thirty-nine cities was much higher than Silber's: 132,270 for King and only 66,752 for Silber. The 1978 primary turnout (67.1 percent) was much lower than in 1990 (82.7 percent), and King did slightly better than Silber in the general election among suburban voters and voters with higher incomes. In fact, a comparison of the two elections suggests that Silber's appeal was based on income to a much greater extent than King's. In 1978, the Democratic candidate averaged 62.1 percent of the vote in the state's eight poorest cities and 52.3 percent in the state's eight wealthiest cities. In 1990, the Democratic share barely changed in the poorest cities (61.2 percent) but dropped dramatically in the wealthiest cities (to 46.8 percent). Both elections pitted a conservative Democrat against a socially moderate but fiscally conservative Yankee Republican.

27. A New York investment company, in late October, offered to buy the Massachusetts Turnpike. The governor's press secretary denied that this proposal was being seriously considered.

28. They will make conservatives happy, however, which may be all that is required of them, since they were introduced in mid-November, almost certainly too late to be acted on before the end of the legislative session in December.

29. Patricia Nealon, "In Another Strike on Weld Moves, Cardinal Rips 'Crime' of Abortion," *Boston Globe,* September 23, 1991, 13.

30. For a description of Weld's St. Patrick's Day performance, see Richard Brookhiser's profile of Senator Bulger in "Dancing with the Girl That Brung Him," *New Yorker,* October 28, 1991, 44-85.

31. A survey conducted by the Republican State Committee found that "GOP voter registration has risen in 61 communities since last October, while Democratic registration dropped. . . . Republicans recorded a net gain of . . . 6.2 percent while Democratic voters dropped by . . . 3.1 percent." Teresa M. Hanafin, "Party Claims Converts Among Former Democrats," *Boston Globe,* September 23, 1991, 13. In Somerville, a working-class community (median household income in 1979; $14,401) on the outskirts of Boston, Republican registration increased by 7.9 percent between 1990 and 1991, while Democratic registration declined by 3.1 percent and independents declined by 9.9 percent.

32. It may be significant that one haven of the middle class—the Catholic Church's parochial school system—is also experiencing a budget crisis. The archdiocese was forced to close several parochial elementary and secondary schools this fall—not because of declining enrollments but because of budgetary constraints.

33. Steve Pierce received a minor appointment in the Weld administration, and then resigned to seek the congressional seat left vacant by the death of Rep. Silvio Conte, the lone Republican in the Massachusetts congressional delegation. Pierce won the nomination but lost to a former senator, Democrat John Olver.

34. Andrew Natsios, "How High Can GOP Go?" *Boston Globe,* October 20, 1991, A25.

35. Jonathan Kozol, "Widening the Gap," *Boston Globe,* November 3, 1991, A17.

36. Ibid.

37. Karla Baehr Deletis, "Spending Matters," *Boston Globe,* November 3, 1991, A17. Kozol has made a case for equalizing education spending in *Savage Inequalities: Children in America's Schools* (New York: Crown, 1991).

38. Kozol, "Widening the Gap," A20.

39. William Grieder, "The Education of David Stockman," *Atlantic,* December 1981, 27-40.

9. MICHIGAN: NO MORE BUSINESS AS USUAL WITH JOHN ENGLER

Carol S. Weissert

It was a clear, cold New Year's Day when Republican John Engler took the oath of office and became the forty-sixth governor of Michigan. To say that Engler's position on that 1991 inaugural platform was a surprise would be a gross understatement. Engler, the balding, pudgy, unphotogenic, and uncharismatic former Senate majority leader, was the underdog throughout the entire election, facing a two-term incumbent governor who was nothing if not slick and sure. "In our hearts of hearts, we never thought we would lose," said the campaign director of Engler's opponent, Democratic governor James Blanchard.[1]

The win was a narrow one; there was a margin of only 17,595 votes, or some 2.6 votes per precinct. For the first time in thirty-eight years, Michigan would be governed by a man who failed to get a majority vote. In a race where fewer than 45 percent of the registered voters went to the polls, Engler garnered 49.8 percent of the vote, Blanchard 49.1 percent.

Perhaps only Engler himself—as a professional politician elected to the legislature right out of college, he had never held another job—truly thought he would win. After all, he had been written off at several points in his career: each of the three times he had unseated legislative incumbents. His first upset was when he was only twenty-two years old and defeated a veteran Republican legislator following the blueprint he described in a political science term paper on how to win a legislative race. Following redistricting, he defeated another Republican incumbent in 1972; in 1978 he ousted a veteran state senator. In fact, he had not lost an election since 1967, when he ran for president of his dorm at Michigan State University.

John Engler served as Senate majority leader for eight years and was viewed by many as a consummate politician and political strategist. But he had never run for statewide office and was little known outside of Lansing and his rural central Michigan Senate district. His first task was to become widely known, and then liked, no small feat for a man who was a poor public speaker, who always looked a little rumpled and slightly overweight, and who is far more effective in small groups than before large audiences and more comfortable discussing political strategy than taping thirty-second television commercials.

But it was not simply his appearance that made him an unlikely victor. John Engler was a Republican who lacked significant business support, an ideological conservative in a state known as one of the nation's most generous to the poor and unemployed, and an antilabor voice in a state long dominated by labor interests. While Michigan has had twenty-six Republican governors, fourteen in this century, the recent mold—best characterized by George Romney and William Milliken, who served consecutively from 1963 to 1983—was a governor liberal in the social welfare arena who transcended the traditional business-labor split.

Unlike all his Republican and Democratic predecessors, Engler is not a consensus builder. Rather, as former Republican state senator William Sederberg put it, Engler's style is one of "polarization and dividing the public as opposed to bringing the public together. He has succeeded politically by drawing distinctions between him and his opponents." [2]

But the real story is not how he got elected (although that, too, is interesting), but rather who John Engler is and what his election means to Michigan. Those were the questions asked across the state that cold New Year's Day in 1991.

The Engler Agenda

Engler's platform was simple: to lower taxes, support funding for education, and make government more efficient. He reiterated these three points time and time again during the campaign, in the inaugural address, and in speeches in the early months of his term. He called for a smaller, less intrusive government that would be less costly and more accessible and for tax cuts and continued educational spending to create growth and opportunity. To launch what he has dubbed "the new state order," he called for budget cuts "to cure the overspending habits of state government." [3]

"I am determined to push forward with my agenda to invest in education, pass a job creation tax cut and have government live within its means," he said. "My plan [is] to bring jobs to Michigan ... [and] make our state the economic powerhouse of the Midwest again." [4] He said during the campaign, "We have been on a spending binge in Lansing and the fact that we have seen our state budget expand 68 percent above the rate of inflation is, to me, proof positive that there is plenty of room to find what amounts to a 6 percent cut [$1 billion]." [5]

On that cold morning in January, Engler told the citizens of his state in words sounding really Reaganesque that "we must restore the spirit of enterprise in Michigan. . . . We still have that same creative spirit. But sadly, because of government, it has been impaired. And, as a result, the capacity of citizens in Michigan today to achieve their dreams has been diminished." He called for government to reduce its "stranglehold" on individual initiatives, saying, "No bureaucratic decision as to who should be an economic winner or loser will ever substitute for the decisions made in the marketplace." [6] While known as a conservative, Engler surprised many with the strident far right tone of this inaugural speech. It was the first glimpse into what was ahead.

Thus, the politician who has never himself worked in the private sector outlined a vision for the state predicated on a revitalization of the economy by increasing the reliance on the private sector and reducing the tax burden. Unfortunately for the new governor, the state, like others in the early months of 1991, was not enjoying economic prosperity. While Michigan had made major advances in diversifying its economy in the 1970s and 1980s, disengaging itself from near-total reliance on the automobile industry, the break was far from complete and the state's economic fortunes were still closely tied to that of the domestic automobile industry. The long-term economic prospects of both were not rosy. The budget deficit on that New Year's Day was estimated as high as $1 billion. How could the new governor possibly cut taxes and still end the current fiscal year without a deficit?

The "Most Hated Man in the Capital"

Clearly it was not going to be easy—or popular. Eight short weeks into his term, Engler had become known as the "most hated man in the capital." Adjectives such as *mean-spirited, savage,* and *cold-hearted* were used to describe the early actions of the Engler administration. Hecklers and protesters were noticeable at his public appearances, and a movement to recall him garnered more than 300,000 signatures. What did he do to deserve this treatment? He spearheaded an effort to cut $800 million from the current year's budget by substantially cutting spending in state agencies, calling for a 9.2 percent across-the-board budget cut, freezing state hiring, cutting contracts, and "downsizing state government." While many of these cuts were first proposed by the Blanchard administration, the new governor endorsed (and took the political heat for) the reductions. In addition, cuts were proposed in

- Eligibility standards for Medicaid recipients and Medicaid payments to physicians

- Aid to Families with Dependent Children, general assistance, and state supplemental payments to the elderly and aged on Supplemental Security income
- Prisons and mental health facilities
- Foster care and adoption services
- Job training grants
- Migrant housing and veterans hospitals
- State support for arts

With these cuts, Engler infuriated Democrats and Republicans alike. The Democrats and advocates for programs benefiting the poor claimed he was hard-hearted and cruel. Republicans and advocates for spending for the arts felt his proposed elimination of state funding for the arts was excessive and misdirected.

True to his campaign promise, he did not propose raising taxes but endorsed a plan to cut them. He unveiled a 20 percent property tax cut proposal fifteen days after taking office and in his first budget message called for a 4 percent increase in education spending.

His problems with the Democrat-led house began early. (The Michigan Senate is controlled by the Republicans.) When he could not reach agreement on budget issues there, he took matters into his own hands, transferring money from the state's rainy day fund and attempting to use a little-known state administrative board to make eleven interfund transfers and to eliminate general assistance for able-bodied adults. The use of this obscure board enraged legislators and was on the political and judicial agenda for months. As of mid-September, a ruling on the use of the board to transfer money was still pending in the state Supreme Court and was the object of continuing legislative and executive branch negotiations on the fiscal 1992 budget.

Changes in the First Few Months

By May 15, state departments and agencies had laid off more than 2,000 permanent state workers; had instituted moratoria on out-of-state travel, and on the purchase of supplies, equipment, and contracting services; and state employees had been asked to take four unpaid furlough days in August and September to save $15 million. While some funding for Medicaid and other programs was restored in the fiscal 1991 budget, more cuts in positions and more unpaid furlough days were expected as the fiscal 1992 budget year commenced on October 1.

Welfare Spending

The dramatic cuts in Michigan's welfare programs during the first nine months of the Engler administration were inevitable, given that education was untouchable and taxes were off the table. Among the largest cuts were those made in the welfare program—particularly targeted was the state-funded general assistance program for able-bodied persons. Although Engler, through actions of the state administrative board, tried to eliminate the program, it survived through the current year but with reductions in spending of nearly 30 percent. However, with the advent of the new fiscal year on October 1, the program was eliminated, leaving more than 90,000 persons without state welfare cash assistance. Severe cuts were also proposed in a program providing emergency funds for utility bills and burial charges for the state's needy.

Although it was clearly a budget-saving measure, Engler claimed that the elimination of the general assistance program would have been a desired goal even in more prosperous times. "Our goal should not be to have the best welfare programs but the smallest welfare program in America with the most people at work," he said, noting that one out of nine Michigan residents receives welfare assistance.[7]

"We need to redefine our goals for the public assistance system in this state," he said. "I don't believe that our 30-year failed experiment can be continued without change."[8] We should not delude recipients into "believing that somebody called 'government' is going to look out for their every need."[9] However, others felt that the fiscal crisis gave Governor Engler solid footing to take an ideological position on social welfare cuts that he might not have been able to promote in more economically promising times. The attack on general assistance was unexpected; throughout his years in the legislature, Engler was not among those railing against the "welfare" state.

"I'm comfortable that the majority of people in Michigan believe that work is desirable over welfare and the incentives should be tilted toward working as opposed to not working," he said in June, even as he received criticism from protesters, newspapers, and Detroit's Mayor Coleman Young, who accused him of "courting disaster" with his crusade against welfare.[10]

Engler tried to make clear that he was committed to seeing that the truly needy are cared for but that those who can find a job do so. However, the general assistance program he has targeted for extinction also goes to women and children; young men make up less than 20 percent of the general assistance population.

For many, there is an apparent tradeoff between spending for the poor and spending for education. Of the two programs, education is clearly preferred by the Engler administration. "Everybody in Michigan benefits from education, so everybody's a winner," Engler said. "The debate over the size of a welfare check or the funding of a prison is a losing debate."[11]

Education

Education funding was exempt from the cuts proposed by the governor in the current fiscal year. And in the budget proposed for fiscal 1992, education (primary, secondary, and higher) received a 4 percent increase while most state agencies were slated for a 6 percent cut. In strongly supporting education spending, Engler is fulfilling a campaign promise to make education the "highest priority" of state government. "It means protecting and increasing state support for public schools," he said.[12] Engler believes that support for education is a good economic development tool to make Michigan more attractive to businesses as well as a primary means for "breaking the cycle of poverty."[13]

Engler wants to make education more effective, and he has called for bonuses to staffs in schools that produce improvements in achievement by all students; a teaching scholarship program to encourage top graduates to teach in public schools; the establishment of charter public schools which would allow teachers to set up their own schools and establish their own educational direction; changes in teacher certification requirements so that professionals would be allowed to teach; and requiring high schools to guarantee the competence of their graduates.

However, where the funding for such education innovations will come from is not clear. The proposals prompted Democrats to give Engler an "A" for rhetoric and an "F" for math. Engler also endorsed a legislative tax base sharing plan to address current inequities in spending between rich and poor school districts in the state. One educational reform outlined in the campaign—setting up schools of choice—was included as an option for local districts in the fiscal 1992 budget.

Property Tax Relief

Property tax relief was a major focus throughout the entire Engler campaign. "The people in this state want change," he said. "They look at their tax bill and say 'wait a minute.' We're paying the fourth highest property taxes in America . . . and not getting enough for it."[14]

In his fiscal 1992 budget, Engler called for a 5 percent property tax reduction in year one, a 10 percent cut in year two and a 5 percent cut in year three. However, the Democrats also sought to get political mileage from property tax relief, and furious interbranch and interparty negotiations and name calling ensued. What resulted was a law, a referendum set to go before the voters in 1992, and three competing initiatives.

1. Passed was a measure freezing 1992 property tax levies at 1991 levels.

2. Scheduled for the 1992 ballot is a proposed constitutional amendment limiting assessment increases for individual homes to the rate of inflation or 5 percent, whichever is lower.
3. The governor has launched an initiative campaign to insert a 30 percent property tax cut in the state constitution, accompanied by a 3 percent cap on assessments.
4. The Democrats are sponsoring an initiative drive calling for a constitutional amendment to erase $30,000 of a home's market value for school property tax purposes.
5. Another proposal spearheaded by a statewide taxpayers' group headed by Richard Headlee, a well-known tax-cut leader in the state, would cut the base of all property taxes by 20 percent.

Reorganization

Engler wasted no time in launching efforts to achieve another important goal: to streamline state government. "My objective in this effort is clear: to assure that state government is prudent, frugal and efficient and to structure the organization of state government accordingly." [15] One of Engler's first executive directives encouraged office directors to give serious consideration to organizational proposals that cross departmental lines and (1) eliminate functions that need not be performed; (2) transfer functions to the private sector if such functions can best be performed by that sector; and (3) produce more efficient and timely performance of functions either by simplifying and streamlining functions, reducing costs, or improving effectiveness, or by focusing on organization—integrating multiple or duplicative functions and improving communication.

Early in his term, Engler eliminated the Department of Licensing and Regulation and reorganized several offices, including the Office of Health and Medical Affairs, the Michigan Export Development Authority, the Office of Revenue and Tax Analysis, the Bureau of State Lottery, and the Office of Substance Abuse.

But he had more in mind than simply shifting responsibilities from office to office. The real objective, say top Engler officials, is to reduce the size and scope of government. That means a reduction in spending and in the work force.

"He's certainly shifted the center of debate to a question of *how* government will be downsized rather than *will* it be downsized," said Rep. Paul Hillegonds, a Republican.[16] Part of that downsizing, or "rightsizing" as Engler refers to it, includes major cuts in programs in the Departments of Social Services, Commerce, and Labor. For example, the Department of Social Services laid off 900 employees in 1991 and expects to lay off more in the coming fiscal year. The Department of Commerce, a favorite in the former administration, was targeted for major cuts in fiscal 1992. It will see general fund appropriations fall from $99 million in fiscal 1991 to an estimated $28 million in fiscal 1992. These reductions will translate into elimination or reduced funding of neighborhood initiatives programs, arson control efforts, local economic development programs, tourism efforts, rural economic development, and job training. The Departments of Mental Health and Public Health are also cutting back or eliminating programs.

Efforts are also under way to improve the management of state programs through better interagency coordination and "new thinking, not new spending." Cabinet-level appointees have generally received high marks on their skills, managerial experience, and willingness to cooperate even on issues involving traditional agency turf battles. The governor's chief of staff talks of a new management ethic where levels of "bureaucracy" are eliminated so that more money can go directly into "programs" rather than supporting the "process."

Other Campaign Promises

Some campaign promises were relatively easy to implement. For example, the new governor established regular public office hours and eliminated gubernatorial photos from state publications. By mid-June, he had already visited thirty-nine of Michigan's eighty-three counties in an effort to fulfill his pledge to visit every county in the state. He grounded the former governor's jetcopter and travels by Oldsmobile (although he did get stopped twice for speeding in his early months in office).

Other early accomplishments included settling a lawsuit where the state will return about $40 million a year to local governments (beginning in 1993) and reforming the single business tax , a move that will eliminate filing requirements for 18,000 small businesses and make permanent the capital acquisition deduction (a tax incentive that businesses argue keeps and creates jobs in Michigan).

He found it more difficult to keep some of his campaign promises:

1. He promised to get government off the backs of business. Cutting red tape was a standard theme: "We're trying to create an environment where we can be more competitive with other states as well as globally." [17]
2. He said in his first State of the State address that he would outlaw political action committees. Little progress has been made in that direction.

3. During the campaign he argued that the high cost of workers' compensation in the state has led to a cost differential that discourages employment and harms the ability of Michigan businesses to compete with businesses in other states.[18] A ten-point workers' compensation plan announced in August and designed to speed the resolution of cases was soon stalled in court.

Engler, like his peers in other states, has not looked to Washington to solve his problems. He did call for a federal constitutional amendment that would mandate Congress to fund programs and expenses passed on to states and localities (similar to Michigan's own constitutional amendment forcing the state to fund state-imposed mandates on local government), and he has, of course, met with the Republican president and members of the state's congressional delegation. But his primary focus has been on Lansing. There are "no answers in Washington," said one high-level state official, who describes Washington as being "irrelevant" to Michigan today.

The First Few Months in Perspective

"A year ago, Engler was an underdog candidate with low name recognition. Now he's at the center of a debate that could reshape state government for decades," said the *Detroit News* in an editorial on the governor's first five months in office.[19]

The question is whether this reshaping will, in fact, occur. Swept into office with the narrowest of margins, John Engler proceeded to put his mark on the structure and function of a state government known for its liberal social welfare program and professional state employment. Both areas were targets of Engler's efforts to make Michigan more competitive. Progress in the early months was stymied by the seriousness of the state's fiscal condition and has proceeded more slowly than Engler probably would have liked.

Clearly overshadowing the first few months of the Engler administration have been Michigan's economic difficulties. Although the state bounced back from a similar recession-induced fiscal crisis in 1983, the situation in 1991 seems particularly problematic for several reasons. The state is reeling from sustained high unemployment, the economic dislocations associated with the troubled domestic automobile industry, loss of population, and a lowered standard of living. The fact is that Michigan is no longer a wealthy state. During the 1980s, Michigan's per capita income was below or hovering around the national average, a marked departure from times when the state's average income was well above that of the rest of the nation. Unemployment rates are consistently high relative to other states, and the state is losing two congressional seats following the 1990 census. These economic and demographic woes have fueled a strong antitax climate that made any consideration of new taxes in 1991 impossible. Even if Blanchard had garnered the extra 18,000 votes and had regained his office, he probably would not have proposed new taxes—he would more likely have focused on reduced spending.

Michigan in 1991 is a "more conservative state, no question about it," said a top Engler official who has been active in Michigan politics throughout several Republican administrations. People want a change, says Dan Pero, the governor's chief of staff. They have grown "dissatisfied with the direction in which the state was going." Craig Ruff, president of Public Sector Consultants, a Lansing-based governmental consulting firm, agrees that Michigan has changed and that Engler reflects those changes. "He understands that the old political center has evaporated and there are more conservatives than liberals in this state." [20]

Yet the question arises whether the citizens, who elected Engler by fewer than 20,000 votes, actually do support the nature and extent of changes under way. Democrats charge that Engler has embarked on a right-wing agenda that Main Street Michigan residents find offensive. Early polling results seem to support the Democrats' contention.

A poll conducted in August found that 43 percent of respondents disapproved of Engler's job performance; 44 percent approved. Even more disappointing to Engler's supporters was the fact that 82 percent of the poll's respondents felt that the state was headed in the wrong direction.[21] While the poll results largely followed party lines—with three-fourths of Republicans approving of Engler's performance—one traditional Republican force, the business community, has also voiced some skepticism about the governor's first few months. A May 1991 survey of business leaders by the *Detroit News* found that only 7 percent gave Engler an "A" in improving Michigan's business environment. One-third of the respondents gave him one of the two lowest grades—"D" or "E." [22]

Some argue that these early polls are not good indicators of the governor's long-term political standing. For example, Democratic former governor James Blanchard, who assumed the governorship during the state's last major recession in 1983 and supported unpopular tax increases to balance the budget, had a lower public support margin six months after taking office (35 percent approving and 54 percent disapproving) and went on to win reelection handily three years later.

Engler himself seems pleased with his first few months, telling a group of Republicans in September that he has already achieved "significant and permanent change." [23] "Everyone should know that it's not business as usual anymore in Michigan." [24] Indeed, few would disagree with the governor's assessment. Governor Engler appears to be on his way to changing the way business is done in Michigan in both the policy and the political realms. While he has not succeeded in enacting all of his reform agenda, he has made inroads in downsizing state government, increasing education funding, reducing the property tax burden, and cutting the welfare rolls. Further, he guided the state through a major budget crisis without a tax increase and with education funding protected.

There is some irony in the Engler policy leadership evident in the early months of his term. In his years in the legislature, Engler was known to be more concerned with personal ambition than good public policy. Yet he is now leading on the policy front; apparently he is more concerned with changing state government than with his own political standing.

In the short term, the Engler administration has made its mark on the day-to-day political process of negotiation between the legislative and executive branches. Democratic House Speaker Lewis Dodak points his finger at Engler's "obstructionist" style, which demands capitulation, not cooperation, from the legislative branch.[25] The traditional Michigan politics of middle ground has been replaced by what has been characterized as the "politics of the middle finger." One veteran political reporter claims never to have seen such "political posturing" in the state before. Even Republicans acknowledge the new "politics of polarization." Engler was a controversial figure as a senator and as a candidate, and he continues to be controversial as governor, said his top aide.

Some feel that now that Engler has established his agenda and achieved some victories, he may pull back somewhat and become a more moderate force for change. Others see him continuing to push forward on the policy front and maintaining his career-long tendency for polarization rather than consensus building. One factor that may affect the governor's policy options may be the state's fragile economy. While he was able to use the budgetary problems to push for spending cuts in his first few months, if the recession continues to plague Michigan and its treasury, his hopes for major property tax reforms and education initiatives may be placed in jeopardy.

Clearly the next few months and years will be important ones for Engler and for Michigan. While Engler and his staff appear to have been surprised by the intensity of the verbal attacks by some opponents—and the often ascribed "mean-spiritedness" did, no doubt, affect his standing with the public—the public outcry against the governor has been fairly muted. On the day when 10,000 state employees began their four-day forced furlough (the remaining 15,000 could choose their own furlough period), the television stations in Detroit did not even cover the event. An effort to recall Engler garnered only around half of the signatures necessary to get the recall before the voters. And as the legislature went home for an August break, the talk was often as much about baseball pennant races as executive power.

Perhaps, appropriately, the last word should go to James Blanchard, the defeated incumbent governor. "John Engler will do just fine," he said shortly after conceding the race. "Nobody ever turns out to be as bad as you think they will be." [26]

Notes

1. Roger Martin, Nolan Finley, and the *Detroit News* Lansing Bureau (Charlie Cain, Mark Hornbeck, and Yolanda Woodlee), *The Journey of John Engler* (West Bloomfield, Mich.: Altwerger and Mandel, 1991), 93.
2. *Detroit News*, May 10, 1991.
3. Engler press release, January 16, 1991.
4. Engler press release, January 10, 1991.
5. *Detroit News*, February 28, 1990.
6. Engler inaugural address, January 1, 1991.
7. *Detroit News*, November 11, 1990.
8. *Detroit News*, February 28, 1990.
9. *Detroit News*, June 2, 1991.
10. Ibid.
11. *Ann Arbor News*, March 7, 1991.
12. Engler radio commentary on education, June 14, 1991.
13. *Detroit News*, November 11, 1990.
14. Ibid.
15. Executive Directive 1991-1993.
16. Martin et al., *Journey of John Engler*, 100.
17. *Detroit News*, December 24, 1990.
18. *Detroit News*, February 28, 1990.
19. *Detroit News*, May 10, 1991.
20. Martin et al., *Journey of John Engler*, 100.
21. *Ann Arbor News*, September 23, 1991.
22. *Detroit News*, May 26, 1991.
23. *Ann Arbor News*, September 23, 1991.
24. Engler press release, January 16, 1991.
25. *Detroit Free Press*, July 28, 1991.
26. Martin et al., *Journey of John Engler*, 100.

10. RHODE ISLAND: BRUCE SUNDLUN AND THE STATE'S CRISES

Elmer E. Cornwell, Jr.

On November 6, 1990, Bruce Sundlun rode to a stunning victory over incumbent Republican Gov. Edward DiPrete, who had experienced perhaps the most precipitous decline in popularity in the history of his office in Rhode Island. Sundlun's immediate "reward" for his triumph was the responsibility of dealing with the worst banking crisis in Rhode Island since the Great Depression.

In 1990 Sundlun made his third and this time successful try against incumbent DiPrete, who had first won office in 1984 in a major upset victory, with 60 percent of the vote. Two years later DiPrete's popularity was even higher and few Democrats had any stomach for the nomination. Bruce Sundlun, a wealthy businessman in his sixties who sought to cap his career with the governorship, made the only serious bid in 1986. The party accepted him, and his willingness to fund a race largely out of his own pocket, eagerly. The race was forlorn for the Democrats. DiPrete won with 64 percent of the vote this time.

In 1988, with DiPrete's image somewhat faded, Sundlun was willing to try again. He had no serious opposition. During this campaign there was a drumfire of revelations of questionable dealing, if not corruption, implicating the DiPrete administration. As a result, the governor held on to his office by a mere 6,600 votes. The next two years saw the further tarnishing of DiPrete's reputation for integrity (restoring integrity to government had been a major Republican promise in 1984), as the state slipped into an economic recession with its severe budget problems.

The corresponding rise in the potential value of the Democratic nomination for 1990 brought on a hot primary contest. The party endorsed Mayor Joseph Paolino of Providence, despite Sundlun's widely accepted claim on a third and more promising try. The results of the three-way primary contest once again demonstrated that the long-dominant Democratic party, indeed parties in general, had lost most of its grip on voters. Sundlun won with 40 percent; Mayor Frank Flaherty of Warwick, who had run a low-budget campaign, came in second with 32 percent; and the endorsed candidate ran a poor third with 27 percent.

The election itself was no contest. Sundlun breezed in with nearly three-quarters of the vote. This in itself was a striking demonstration of the fluidity of an electorate almost totally unrestrained by party loyalty. From 1986 to 1990, Bruce Sundlun's share of the vote, against the same opponent, rose from just over a third to nearly three-quarters. That this was a repudiation of the incumbent administration rather than a vote of confidence in the challenger seemed apparent, and that became clearer as the new administration tackled the state's monumental problems.

The Credit Union Crisis

A matter of hours after his January 1 swearing in, the new governor of Rhode Island went on statewide television to announce an executive order closing all forty-five credit unions and other banking institutions insured by the Rhode Island Share and Deposit Indemnity Corporation (RISDIC).[1] RISDIC, the evening before, had gone belly up when its board of directors concluded that it could no longer insure its member institutions. About one-quarter of all of the people of the state had accounts in one or another of the closed banking enterprises, and the chain of events set off by the failure promised to be a disaster.

Even without this horrendous crisis, Governor Sundlun's term would have begun in a far different atmosphere, and with far different prospects and possibilities, than those of his recent predecessors. In contrast to the relatively stable and prosperous economy that greeted J. Joseph Garrahy in 1976, Edward DiPrete in 1984, and even Phil Noel in 1972 (who took office facing a major Navy pullout), Sundlun was confronted by economic disintegration and incipient insolvency. Add to this the banking crisis, and the prospects must have seemed bleak indeed to his incoming administration.

The difference between 1991 and the normal scenario was almost total. Recent newly elected governors in Rhode Island had entered office following campaigns built around pledges to improve management in government, upgrade education, strengthen social services for needy groups, and in general move the state forward on a number of fronts. The governors assumed that they were inheriting a going concern, albeit one that offered challenges to be solved through imaginative ideas and skill. In other words, the normal goal of a new administration was to build a record in office of creative achievements to advance the welfare of the people and the well-being of disadvantaged groups.

The third Sundlun campaign had focused far more on the perceived need to root out wrongdoing, to correct abuses, and above all to deal with a rapidly worsening economy and state financial situation. New programs, new policy initiatives—especially if they cost any money—were conspicuously absent from the agenda. Nothing that was said during the campaign, however, could have prepared the people of the state—or, indeed the personnel of the new administration—for the disastrous situation and the need for immediate damage control that they faced on January 1.

At the top of the list was the credit union collapse. They had been closed on January 1 because by law no banking institution can operate unless covered by deposit insurance. Moreover, failure to close the credit unions would have resulted in a run when news of the RISDIC collapse became known. Panic would have ensued among the holders of the 300,000 accounts that totaled $1.7 billion, and the institutions would have been destroyed.[2]

The governor's executive order thus operated to conserve the assets of the institutions and allow time for remedial state action to be taken. From a legal standpoint, since RISDIC (despite its misleading name) was a private organization, the state had no obligation to do anything beyond closing the credit unions until they could remedy their lack of insurance. Quite aside from the legal situation, however, the Sundlun administration faced an immense political problem. Just as the federal government had had no political option save to deal with the savings and loan crisis, so the state had no choice but to deal with the fallout from the RISDIC collapse. The Sundlun people therefore acted with great urgency.

Coping with the Problem

For present purposes the technical details of the problem and the proposed solutions will be dealt with only insofar as necessary to make clear the political dimensions of the situation. In general, the governor had to respond to the conviction Americans have had since the 1930s that government can and must protect them against financial crises. In this case thousands of account holders had had all of their money frozen. At the same time, many of the credit unions had become depositors' bank of choice and had served more than one generation of many families. Thus, large numbers of depositors had emotional as well as financial ties to these institutions.

It quickly became apparent that many of the credit unions were in parlous financial shape, if not actually insolvent. Like savings and loan institutions around the country that were in trouble, these institutions had made too many bad real estate and similar loans, and they were reaping the consequences of other ill-considered and reckless banking practices as well. Hence the obvious solution to the problem—that is, to obtain federal insurance under the National Credit Union Administration to replace RISDIC—was an option for only a few.

All of this meant that the state must produce a plan that would (1) return depositors' money to them as soon as practicable, (2) enable as many credit unions as possible to secure federal insurance, (3) where necessary arrange mergers or buyouts that would enable credit unions to reopen, and (4) figure out how to fund the depositor payback using as little taxpayer money as possible—the state was already facing a severe budget deficit.

All in all, it was a no-win situation for the governor and for the overwhelmingly Democratic General Assembly. The administration's plan called for state takeover of the uninsurable credit unions and for payment of depositors using a combination of the proceeds from liquidation of the institutions' assets and an estimated $150 to $300 million in state money.[3] The legislation was first introduced in early January and passed after difficult negotiations between the governor and the Assembly, and many changes, about a month later.[4]

By midyear, most victims of the crisis had yet to see more than token payments on their deposits, and seemingly endless negotiations had not resulted in visible progress toward opening closed institutions through mergers or acquisitions. Nine months after the initial executive order, none of the planned takeovers by the state agency established for that purpose had been completed. Frustration among the depositors escalated during the late summer. Demonstrations were staged, which in some cases reached near-riot proportions. Cries were being heard for a special session of the Assembly to deal with the situation.[5]

It became increasingly obvious that there was less money available for paybacks to depositors than had been anticipated. The governor did, however, promise that all the money that was available would be put into the hands of its owners by the middle of October.[6] It was apparently hoped that this initial disbursement of funds would relieve some of the political pressure, although subsequent paybacks might be delayed. The bulk of the accounts were small ones, and many would be extinguished by this first payment.

The initial support that the governor had won by his decisive opening moves in this drama had long since given place to exasperation and cynicism in the minds of many. His businessman's approach had not produced results. In a June opinion survey, it was found that only a third of the respondents felt that the governor's handling of the crisis was excellent or good, while 63 percent replied that it was fair or poor.[7]

The Current Budget Deficit

Though delayed by its preoccupation with the banking closure, the administration also had to confront the state's urgent budget problems. The dropoff of anticipated revenues to support the 1991 budget had reached $160 million by the beginning of January, and ranked as either the highest or the second highest in relation to planned spending among the twenty-five states with a similar problem.[8] On January 9, in his State of the State speech, Governor Sundlun promised a proposal for revision of the current budget as soon as possible. Announcing that the deficit had been newly calculated at $200 million, he painted in general terms a grim picture of the tax increases and spending cuts that would be necessary.[9]

On February 1 he submitted his revisions.[10] They included a 20 percent income tax increase, 5 percent more on the gasoline tax, and a surcharge on the corporate income tax. He also proposed millions in program reductions, including an especially painful cut in local aid and cuts in government personnel. Some savings were to come from closing down state government for ten working days by the end of the fiscal year. Hardest hit by the cuts would be aid to cities and towns for education. The rationale for this was that painful as such reductions would be, cuts for social services for the poor and disadvantaged would be less justified.

The immediate practical problem the state confronted was the constitutional requirement that it have a balanced budget. Thus, the governor called for quick action on his proposals in order to maximize the impact of both the revenue increases and the spending cuts in the months remaining before the June 30 end of the fiscal year. The package included other devices to help ensure the mandated end-of-year balance, such as the deferral of a $42 million state payment into its employee pension fund. Speaker Joseph DeAngelis summed up the general reaction to the revised financial program when he said, "This budget is going to hurt, that's for sure." [11]

The governor blamed the state's money problems on his predecessor: "We're paying for DiPrete's mismanagement, pure and simple." [12] Of course, the sagging economy was the immediate culprit, but it is also true that in the happy years of rising revenue (despite some tax cuts), which the prior administration had enjoyed, spending had climbed steeply. The successive DiPrete budgets during his first two terms grew steadily, by a margin well in excess of the annual expenditure increases during the administration of Democrat Garrahy from 1977 to 1985. The comparison of the DiPrete levels of spending with the rigid austerity of the new Sundlun administration caused some wags to say that DiPrete had been the best Democratic governor the state had had, and Sundlun was the best Republican!

On February 14, after a long and at times impassioned debate, and after a number of efforts to soften the blow by amendments, the House passed the revised budget in much the same form the governor had submitted it. An effort to blunt the impact of the cut in school aid was turned back by a 46-40 vote.[13] The majority leader summed up the feelings of many when he said that the Democrats were being obliged to vote in effect to demolish many of the programs the party had put in place over the years, but there was no other choice. The Senate took far less time to grant its reluctant approval.

Armed with this new austere spending plan and the new revenue it promised, the Sundlun administration struggled to meet the constitutional mandate. The plan to shut down state government for ten scattered days was eventually replaced with a system of pay deferrals of 10 percent. Major state worker unions resisted this approach, but they gave in when the governor carried out his threat to make enough personnel cuts to achieve the same dollar result. Many state workers were let go, but the savings realized were reduced by delays occasioned by union members exercising their right to "bump" those with less seniority. In the end, the administration achieved a year-end technical balance of the books through a number of complex accounting maneuvers.

Politically, the administration emerged from this process having made few friends and a number of enemies—among state employees, taxpayers, and beneficiaries of programs that had been slashed. As the opening of school approached in September 1991, for example, a determined group of welfare mothers insisted on a meeting with the governor at which they demanded restoration of a $500,000 fund intended to help with the purchase of back-to-school clothes for children of the poor. The governor expressed sympathy but said that if he had half a million dollars, there were two or three even more pressing needs for which he would have spent it.

Providence Journal statehouse reporter Scott MacKay summed up the first phase of the new administration's tenure: "In ten crisis filled weeks in office, Governor Sundlun has shown a steely decisiveness and willingness to take tough stands carrying political risks. . . . [He] has cut programs, raised taxes to deal with a whopping state deficit, and battled with state employee unions, laying off workers." MacKay quoted Speaker DeAngelis: "We have just come out of 10 of the worst weeks in Rhode Island history. . . . The Governor has shown he is decisive and that he's a quick study. And once he's made a decision it's very, very difficult to move him from it."[14]

For many observers, these qualities of Sundlun were a timely asset, given the state's daunting problems. The public, apparently, was not so sure. An opinion survey taken in mid-January found the governor's popularity at 75 percent (those who felt he was doing a good or excellent job). However, a Brown University poll taken late in

February revealed an approval rate of 54 percent, down substantially in not much more than a month.[15] Even these figures do not reflect the full impact of the tax increases and draconian spending cuts made in the current 1991 budget, which the Assembly approved in mid-February. In any event, only the first round in the budget battle had been won, if that is the correct word for it.

The Fiscal 1992 Budget

On April 9, the governor transmitted to the General Assembly his 1992 budget.[16] Normally the first spending plan submitted by a new administration is the one that will take effect six months after it comes into office. Sundlun, as noted, had to virtually rewrite the budget in place on inauguration day before he could tackle the first of his own budget submissions. His own first budget was thus nearly six weeks late.

In preparing the 1992 budget the Sundlun administration faced a continuation of its problems. Revenue was still falling, the recession was still deepening, and there was no way of predicting when or whether there would be an improvement in the economy that might ease the budget crunch. As the *Providence Journal* headline put it, the budget "Slashes school aid, holds taxes, hikes fees." [17]

Again education was targeted for major cuts, in part, no doubt, for the reasons the governor had given when he made the 1991 cuts, and in part because it is, next to human services, the largest expenditure. Specifically the state's education contribution was to be cut 18.5 percent or $55 million.[18] Further state personnel reductions and savings through furlough days and layoffs were proposed, as were a large number of cuts affecting almost every program of state government.

The clearest concern came to be focused, both in the legislature and among outside interests, on the education rollbacks. Representatives and senators came under intense pressure from teachers' union groups and from their home communities to do something to mitigate them. The cities and towns faced either major layoffs in teaching staffs and program eliminations, or huge real estate tax increases, or both. The governor was adamant that he would not propose another state tax increase and that he would veto any put before him. Hence any relief for education and the local communities had to be found through rearrangements within the budget itself or through some truly ingenious ideas for new revenue.

A new revenue source did become part of a compromise package crafted between the governor and the General Assembly leadership in late May. After a long period of negotiation, in which the legislators took as their goal the restoration of $25 million of the $55 million the governor insisted on cutting, an intricate plan was devised. A key to it was $3.9 million in new revenue to be derived from the introduction of off-track betting (OTB) on out-of-state horse races simulcast at Rhode Island's existing dog track and jai alai fronton.[19] This idea aroused groups in the state opposed to any further legalized gambling, particularly since it was proposed that the legal requirement of a referendum for any new gambling authority was to be waived in this case.

The negotiators managed to find other sums here and there with which to complete the funding of their partial restoration of money for education and for the smaller upward adjustments the Assembly wanted in other programs. In short, the legislators managed to sweeten a little the bitter budgetary pill that they and the governor agreed the state must swallow in order to get through the twelve months beginning in July of 1991 without a deficit.

This basic compromise package ensured that the Sundlun budget would pass in substantially the same form in which it had been proposed. However, there was a last-minute glitch that had to be ironed out before the leadership felt confident it could secure enactment. The problem was not itself major, but it illustrated well the kinds of cross-pressures the members were feeling as they struggled to solve the state's fiscal problems without any more political pain for themselves than was absolutely necessary.

At the 1990 general election the voters of the state had been asked, as the law required, whether they approved of a plan to build an OTB facility in Pawtucket. As one of the older industrial cities of the state, with little chance of broadening its tax base, Pawtucket has faced increasing financial problems. Off-track betting was seized on as a way of generating some new tax revenue. The voters of the state thought otherwise, and the referendum question was voted down.

Pawtucket city officials faced financial problems in 1991 that were, if anything, more difficult than before, and they were understandably annoyed that the Assembly would now propose OTB as a revenue raiser for the state, without the referendum that had killed their plan. The Pawtucket House delegation accordingly backed a move by one of its members for an amendment to the budget requiring a referendum. Pawtucket was, however, prepared to make a deal. If it were to be given authority for a deferral in 1991-1992 of its $2.9 million annual payment into the state teachers' retirement fund, it would withdraw the referendum amendment.

This issue had bubbled up during floor consideration of the budget in the House on May 31, and it was being furiously negotiated behind the scenes while the debate droned on. Eventually the governor gave his reluctant agreement, the Senate leadership agreed, and the deal was made. The city of Woonsocket, which suffers from the same kinds of financial problems, for similar reasons as Pawtucket, gained the right to make a similar deferral, and the referendum amendment was not offered under Pawtucket's auspices. It was moved by a Republican representative later and soundly defeated.[20]

Overall there was little doubt that the budget would pass as presented by the governor and with the changes agreed to between the governor and the legislative leaders. This did not mean, however, that the process would be brief or painless. As the *Providence Journal* reported: "Final action came at about 4 a.m., after a tortuous debate and seemingly endless attempts by representatives to change the spending package for the fiscal year that begins July 1." [21] Fifty or more amendments had been prepared, and many, though by no means all of them, were offered during the debate. The few that had leadership approval passed; the rest were tabled or defeated.

A group of liberal Democrats offered one amendment that would have placed a 9.5 percent surcharge on incomes of $250,000 or more and would have produced some $15 million the proponents wanted for school aid. This was defeated, as was another hotly debated effort to change the formula for the distribution of school aid in favor of the smaller communities and at the expense of the cities. These and other amendments were pushed largely to enable individuals or groups of representatives to show constituents and the beneficiaries of badly cut programs that they were doing their best.[22]

From the point of view of the budget process as a whole, and particularly from the governor's point of view, the key to final enactment was the fact that, as the *Providence Journal* put it: "On the budget, DeAngelis' leadership team held sway again." [23] The tradition of a strong party leadership in the General Assembly has been subjected to a rising chorus of criticism from a group of dissident members, and from outside groups, in the last few years. The alleged failure of the legislature to provide proper regulation of the credit unions in the past has been blamed on the ability of the leadership to call the shots on legislation and thus to block needed reforms.

On the other hand, the ability of the Democratic leadership to negotiate an agreement with the governor on the budget, then to deliver the votes to get it passed, was of great importance to the administration and, indeed, to the state. The contrast with what happened in neighboring Connecticut, where the legislative leadership was once equally strong, is stark and significant (see Chapter 5). There a governor elected as an independent had to deal with party leaders with whom he had no partisan ties, and who, in return, had difficulty marshaling their own followers. The result was months of acrimonious deadlock over the 1991-1992 budget. Governor Sundlun was able to count on a legislature that could act decisively once the leaders had committed themselves to a spending plan that they had carefully sold to their followers while negotiating with the executive.

Other Legislative Action

Most of the rest of the work of the session paled in the face of the credit union and budget problems. There was little time or money left for legislative initiatives in other areas. There were some important achievements, however. Compulsory auto insurance, which had come unsuccessfully before every General Assembly for years, finally won passage in both houses. This had not been a particular goal of the governor's, but he supported it. A major updating of the state's zoning legislation had been passed by the House during the 1990 session but had not gotten through the Senate. It was brought up again, and this time became law.[24]

Sundlun-proposed reorganizations of the Departments of Corrections and of Children and Their Families were enacted. The area in which the governor pressed for legislation with less success was that of ethics in government. He had campaigned both in 1986 and 1988 promising to root out corruption and favoritism, accusing the DiPrete administration of serious lapses in these areas. When the credit union crisis engulfed the state, there was a flood of revelations of highly questionable, if not illegal, activity by the officials both of RISDIC and of many of the banking institutions. There were demands for explanations of why state regulators and the General Assembly had not taken steps in the past that would have prevented the collapse. There were charges of cronyism and favoritism involving legislators and the credit unions to explain the lack of regulatory reform.

Another scandal that preoccupied the press and the radio talk shows had to do with the disclosure of special deals on state pensions enacted in recent years by the Assembly for favored individuals. In short, the public perception was of a state government rife with corruption, addicted to special insider deals, and disdainful of the public interest. To all appearances the long-term trend in the loss of citizens' confidence in public officials—which dates from the era of Vietnam and Watergate—was taking a leap in Rhode Island toward total disaffection and cynicism. The political implications of all of this for elected officials generally, especially Assembly members—and indeed for the governor—hardly need to be emphasized.

Governor Sundlun responded by placing the improvement of ethical standards in government at the top of his list of priorities, right after the credit union and budget crises. He introduced legislation to tighten up the regulation of campaign spending, which did not make it through a tangle of legislative maneuvers. Some other ethics bills fared better: one streamlining the procedures of the Ethics Commission, another prohibiting officials from representing themselves before agencies on which they serve, and a number aimed at ending abuses in the state pension system. In the last category was a bill making state pension records public, something the governor had already achieved through a lawsuit he had initiated.[25]

A Volatile Public Reacts

In the months following the end of the legislative session in early June, public dissatisfaction with state government, far from having been allayed, became more vocal and more bitter. The lack of visible progress in returning money to credit union depositors was the chief cause. However, the prevailing feeling seemed to be that everything the government did was wrong, if not corrupt, and that all incumbents were somehow to blame. Despite the governor's efforts to deal with the state's monumental problems and to improve the ethical climate, he became the chief target for the hostility. Even if there had been resources for new policy initiatives to offset his problems on the debit side, these would probably have been submerged in the rising tide of criticism and denunciation.

The credit union crisis and other revelations hardly explain in themselves the depth and extent of the reaction. The roots lie, rather, in the kind of polity that has developed in recent decades: more and more people have become the recipients of public benefits and entitlements, which have given rise to a complex network of at times competing and contradictory policies. The whole concept of entitlement, broadly defined, has thus grown to vast proportions. It has really come to mean an overarching responsibility on the part of government to right every wrong, solve every problem, guarantee every advantage and comfort, and assume responsibility for every disequilibrium that might disturb the citizenry. The public has become hypersensitive to disturbances of any kind, and assumes that government is at fault. To the detached observer, the credit union depositors might be seen as investors who made a bad decision. They, however, insist that the state is wholly to blame and must fix it promptly at whatever cost.

Whether the public is justified in making these kinds of assumptions and indulging in these kinds of reactions, is not the point. The point is that a public imbued with such attitudes makes for highly volatile politics and a cumbersome political system. This volatility is in part the result of the enormous range and variety of expectations current public policy fosters. Again, the point is not whether these expectations should have been fostered by policy makers. They are there. And public officials must tread the minefield they have laid.

The Decline of Parties

The volatility is also the result of major changes in the infrastructure of politics. Political parties have very nearly disappeared as objects of loyalty or mechanisms for structuring the attitudes and responses of citizens in the political sphere. Few Rhode Island Democrats today would say of Governor Sundlun, "I don't agree with things he is doing, but he is my party's governor and I shall support him." Few indeed voted for him because of his party label. Rather they voted for him because of perceptions of him as an individual, or because he was not Ed DiPrete. And the perceptions of both candidates were formed not by extrapolation from their party affiliations but as a result of the images created for them by their consultants and TV marketers.

Elections have become freewheeling, partyless, popularity contests. As a result, even a candidate who wins with nearly three-quarters of the vote has no really solid base to depend on. Rather he must try to keep his balance on the shifting sands of public mood and short-term expectations. In times of prosperity, when a governor can fulfill promises and expectations, all may be well. In periods of stress and threatened deprivation, his support will quickly turn into disenchantment and hostility.

In short, the evidence is abundant that the current Rhode Island political system owes far less operationally to the role of political parties than it did in the past. The citizenry, despite some residual traditional party leanings, are far more likely to perceive themselves as political independents. They place immediate policy concerns and perceptions of candidate image and performance far above party loyalty in their hierarchy of cues to behavior. Examples of this from recent elections and the 1990 Democratic primary have been cited earlier.

Among activists and officeholders, party solidarity is also considerably less compelling than it once was. All of Rhode Island's statewide officers elected in 1990 were Democrats. Yet the governor and the general treasurer fought openly about the banking crisis; the lieutenant governor has not hesitated to take positions at variance with those of the governor; and the attorney general also has felt free to play a lone hand when it seemed advantageous, endorsing none of the candidates for the Democratic gubernatorial nomination in the primary. Only the secretary of state, long a firm Sundlun backer, has remained consistently and publicly loyal.

The dealings of the majority of the General Assembly Democrats, and particularly their leaders, with Governor Sundlun have been interesting to observe. Throughout the DiPrete administration a new approach to the state budget prevailed: a negotiated package, supported by both the governor and most of the Democrats, was enacted each year. The budget interface between the two branches was typically more cordial and consensual than it had been in the last years of Democratic governor Garrahy's term. This was true in part because DiPrete proposed generous and expansive budgets, and rising revenues made possible the funding of Assembly initiatives as well. Though the relationship with Governor Sundlun was formed in a different economic climate, it would be difficult to find evidence that shared party affiliation between the executive and the legislative leadership made agreement easier to achieve. There is reason to suspect that some Democratic legislators secretly wished at times that DiPrete were still there! Sundlun's rather abrupt businessman's style was a factor in the relationship.

Conclusion

Clearly the first nine months of the administration of Gov. Bruce Sundlun, following his inauguration in January 1991, were shaped uniquely by the potentially disastrous situations he faced at the moment he took the oath. The two major ones, the credit union crisis and the budget crisis, confronted him with no-win situations. In dealing with them, the best he could do was to minimize the political damage to himself. At the same time, he had few policy options to offset the powerful negatives with positive achievements. He was, in short, uniquely vulnerable in policy terms, and there was little he could do about it.

His vulnerability was exacerbated by the shallowness and unreliability of his political base. As noted, by the end of the legislative session in June, much of his electoral support had eroded. A new survey conducted for the *Providence Journal* in September, following the wave of depositor demonstrations that had begun in August, showed that the Sundlun administration was in serious trouble with the public.[26] Only a third of the respondents felt that the job the governor was doing was excellent (7 percent) or good (26 percent). Thirty-seven percent said only fair and 28 percent said poor, for a total of 65 percent. The corresponding percentages, when the sample was asked about how well the governor was handling the credit union crisis, were 26 percent excellent plus good, 31 percent fair, and 40 percent poor.[27] A Taubman Center (Brown University) poll released October 1 found 36 percent approving Sundlun's performance, 54 percent disapproving, and 10 percent not answering; these results confirmed the *Journal* poll findings.[28]

To have fallen so far in nine months does not augur well for the future of the Sundlun administration or for his chances of reelection in 1992. Yet miracles can happen in politics. A major effort to tighten the state ethics code might capture public interest and ameliorate the widespread citizen outrage. On October 7, the Ethics Task Force appointed by the governor issued its report amid promises by Sundlun that he would "push, and push hard" to secure implementation of its major recommendations.[29] Early signs suggest a likely confrontation with the General Assembly on several key points.[30] The governor may therefore have to put his relationship with the Democratic leadership on the line in his effort to win back public support.

It may turn out that a governor who can do little but engage in damage control will find himself cast in the role of a political sacrifice. It may be left to his successor to reap the benefits of that sacrifice and revive the ability of the system to move forward. This may in turn depend on when the confidence of the public in the good faith of its political leadership revives. The long-term downward slide of citizen trust in government is grounds for doubt that this will happen soon.

Notes

1. See *Providence Journal,* January 2, 1991.
2. Ibid.
3. *Providence Journal,* January 7, 1991.
4. See *Providence Journal,* January 26 and February 8 and 9, 1991.
5. The *Providence Journal* reported extensively on these demonstrations. An example was reported on September 23, 1991. A crowd of two to three thousand had rallied at the statehouse on Sunday, September 22, demanding among other things that Governor Sundlun resign.
6. *Providence Journal,* September 12, 1991.
7. Taubman Center, Brown University, *Public Opinion Report* 4 (Issue 2, June 1991).
8. "R.I. Deficit Among the Worst," *Providence Journal,* January 9, 1991.
9. *Providence Journal,* January 10, 1991. The text of the governor's State of the State address was issued as a press release.
10. *Providence Journal,* February 1, 1991.
11. Ibid.
12. Ibid.
13. *Providence Journal,* February 15, 1991.
14. "Sundlun Holds His Course on a Sea of Troubles," *Providence Journal,* March 14, 1991.
15. Poll cited; ibid.
16. *Providence Journal,* April 10, 1991.

17. Ibid.
18. Ibid.; see also *Providence Journal,* May 25, 1991.
19. *Providence Journal,* May 25, 1991.
20. *Providence Journal,* June 1 and 2, 1991.
21. *Providence Journal,* June 2, 1991.
22. Ibid.
23. Ibid.
24. *Providence Journal,* June 14, 1991.
25. *In re State Employees' Union,* Providence Superior Court, March 7, 1991.
26. The survey results were reported in three successive daily editions of the *Providence Journal,* September 17, 18, and 19, 1991.
27. *Providence Journal,* September 18, 1991.
28. Taubman Center, Brown University, press release, October 1, 1991.
29. *Providence Journal,* October 8, 1991.
30. A few days earlier the *Journal* headlined a story, "Tougher Rules on Ethics Kindle Political Fire Storm," which reported legislators' reactions to Ethics Commission moves to adopt new ethics provisions (*Providence Journal,* October 5, 1991).

11. TEXAS: ANN RICHARDS, TAKING ON THE CHALLENGE

Richard Murray and Gregory R. Weiher

When Ann Richards took the oath of office as Texas's forty-fifth governor on January 15, 1991, she had perhaps the bleakest political prospects of all the nation's new governors. The state faced grim fiscal problems with estimates of a budget deficit of $4 to $6 billion for the coming biennium. Other states faced similar shortfalls, but Richards was squeezed between a series of court orders mandating more spending for public schools, prisons, and mental health facilities and a jerry-rigged, inadequate tax system more akin to a Rube Goldberg contraption than an efficient revenue machine. The obvious, and possibly only, way out was to junk inequitable levies like the franchise tax and enact an income tax. But opposition to a personal income tax is an article of faith for a large majority of Texas voters, and for most of the political leadership. Richards would find it especially difficult to support an income tax after repeatedly saying during her 1990 campaign that she saw no need for one in Texas.

The governor's new problems were compounded by another unfortunate circumstance: although voters hold the chief executive accountable for state government, the Texas constitution and statutes give little power to the office. All other major state officials are elected independently of the governor, including a lieutenant governor who has great power in the state Senate. Governors are largely shut out of the budget process, and they have very limited directive powers over a decentralized state bureaucracy. Richards was able to make appointments to the boards of most state agencies, but this power is diluted by the necessity for Senate approval, the staggered terms of appointees (it takes years to put a majority in place), and the lack of removal power.

In Joseph Schlesinger's 1971 ratings, the Texas governor was the least powerful in the nation. By 1983, after the term of office was increased from two to four years, Thad Beyle moved Texas up to forty-ninth among the fifty states, a status it continued to hold in 1990.[1]

Since Texas governors have few formal powers, real influence depends almost entirely on their political standing, style, and ability to persuade. Richards appeared to be in bad shape on this front when she assumed office. Her accession came after a long, expensive, and nasty campaign that disturbed even voters inured to hardball, Lone Star state politics. Richards emerged from the fifteen-month, $50 million marathon with her personal reputation sullied, her once-reputed political skills in question, and her vision of a "New Texas" undefined. Richards won despite an "unfavorable" rating from 51 percent of the voters (only 37 percent gave her positive marks).[2] Many voters turned to Richards not because she was their first choice, but because she was the last chance to head off the Republican nominee, Clayton Williams.

Polls also showed that a majority of voters were concerned about her refusal to discuss past drug use, and many held her to blame for the decidedly negative tone of the Democratic primary and general election. Indicative of the difficulties confronting Richards was the lingering hostility between the new governor and a former governor, Mark White. White had been blasted out of the March 1990 Democratic primary by a Richards ad that accused him of "lining his pockets" by getting legal business from his public agency appointees after he left office in January 1987. White accused Richards of "Nazi-like" tactics reminiscent of Heinrich Himmler, pointedly withheld his endorsement in the general election, and did not attend the inauguration.

Across the partisan fence, many Texas Republicans remained resentful of Richards's putdown of George Bush in her keynote speech at the 1988 Democratic presidential convention. ("Poor George. He just can't help it. He was born with a silver foot in his mouth.")

In general terms, Richards was a Democrat taking office in a state more and more inclined to elect Republicans. She was widely viewed as a liberal in a state where according to polls self-described liberals numbered about 15 percent, whereas 45 percent labeled themselves conservatives. And she was Texas's first independently elected female governor,[3] and an avowed feminist, in a state noted for its good ole boy politics.

Taken together, the signs suggested Ann Richards was very likely to continue the recent Texas pattern of one-term, failed governors. However, after a year her prospects are much improved. Her popularity is up, her press notices have been almost universally positive, and even her most severe critics concede that she has mastered the rhetorical and public relations aspects of governance. Richards came out of the long, difficult legislative session in 1991 with her personal reputation largely restored, her political skills widely praised, and most of the programs and policies she promoted passed into law. She signed a $2.4 billion tax bill—but no income tax—and seems to have suffered little damage. Indeed, her early approval rating, 55 percent, is the highest in recent history for a Texas governor.[4] One would have to go back to John Connally's 1965 legislative session to find comparable success.

Ann Richards's experience seems an exception to the executive political capital model developed by Paul Light in *The President's Agenda.* Light sees elected executives beginning their term with a limited store of political capital that is rather quickly expended.[5] Executives thus have a narrow window of opportunity to exercise effective leadership. But Richards, in the early going, has been accumulating, not spending, political capital. The windows of opportunity appear to be opening, not closing, as she moves through her term.

What accounts for Richards's early success under very difficult circumstances? Are her political achievements superficial, or are they substantive? Will she be one of the rare Texas governors like John Connally and Allan Shivers who were effective chief executives despite the weak powers of the office? Or will she join her immediate predecessors Preston Smith, Dolph Briscoe, Jr., Mark White, and William P. Clements, Jr., in being voted out of office after a short tenure? We consider these questions in turn.

Sources of Early Achievements

In retrospect, one can identify a number of factors easily overlooked in January 1991 that augured well for the new governor of Texas. First among these was Richards's extensive political experience. Being a professional politician may not help one get elected these days, but it often comes in handy once in office. Richards began her political career volunteering in liberal Democratic campaigns in Dallas in the 1960s, managed campaigns in the early 1970s, and unseated a veteran Travis County (Austin) commissioner in 1976. Six years later she defeated the state treasurer, becoming the first woman elected to statewide office since Miriam "Ma" Ferguson stood in for "Pa" Ferguson (who was barred from running) in the 1932 governor's election. Holding elective office for fourteen years in the state's capital gave Richards an inside perspective on state government, politicians, and issues that is often lacking in new chief executives. She knew the script, the plot, and the players from her first day in office.

Richards used her years in politics to build a strong political base from two quite different sources. One was rooted in the emerging women's movement in Texas. Richards was a co-founder of Leadership Texas, which, over the past two decades, has introduced thousands of women to the paths of power in government, business, and the professions. Richards built an impressive network of women friends and allies across the entire state that cut across party and ideological lines.

Richards also forged strong ties with key leaders of the Tory Democratic establishment in Texas, including Lt. Gov. Bill Hobby and

U.S. Senator Lloyd Bentsen. Hobby, the most dominant figure in state government during his record eighteen-year tenure (1973-1991) served as a mentor to Richards from the early 1970s and was a co-chair of her 1990 campaign. And most of Bentsen's Texas team was behind Richards in the Democratic gubernatorial primary.

This broad base of support, stretching from radical feminists and gays on the left to conservative business leaders in Dallas and Houston, was essential to Richards's survival in a Democratic primary where she was politically mugged by Attorney General Jim Mattox. From beginning to end, Mattox hammered Richards with hard questions about her lifestyle, her acknowledged status as a recovering alcoholic, and her refusal to discuss past drug use. The fight took a toll on Richards personally, and it eroded her sizable primary lead. But in the end, her base support held and she led Mattox into a runoff with 39.3 percent to 37.0 percent. With former governor White out of the race, Mattox's rough tactics backfired and Richards pulled away to win 57 percent of the vote.

Nor did Richards's base support erode in the April-September period, when published polls showed her trailing her Republican opponent, wealthy businessman Clayton Williams, by margins of 10 to 15 points.

Richards's campaign was widely viewed as a failure (the 1992 *Almanac of American Politics* characterized it as "dismal and sometimes scurrilous"),[6] but it was not without its achievements. Richards raised a surprising $13 million—as much as the heavily favored Williams (he spent $21 million, but that included $8 million he "lent" his campaign). After an admittedly rocky primary campaign, Richards reorganized her staff in midsummer and ran a nearly flawless end game against Williams. Conventional wisdom was that Clayton Williams lost the race by a series of blunders starting with the comments, "The weather is like rape—all you can do is relax and enjoy it," and ending with his unprompted disclosure that he paid no federal income tax in 1986. One can readily argue that Richards won the race, however, by not cracking under extreme pressure, by raising the funds needed to get her message across, and by most skillfully exploiting her opponent's missteps (such as refusing to shake her hand at a joint appearance in October).

Retrospectively, the long and bitter campaign made questions about Richards's past old news and not likely to draw much attention once she took office. When asked about the tough race's impact on her, Richards noted: "I'm much stronger now. Perhaps that's the beauty of the process. You have to be pretty tough to be in this job." [7]

Richards rose to prominence partly because of an endearing, homey style that goes down well with most Texans. She is that rare politician who is genuinely funny, and she can make jokes at her own expense as easily as George Bush's. Like Ronald Reagan, Richards has a Teflon quality. One longtime observer of state politics says, "Ann Richards' greatest asset is she knows how to make people like her—even Republicans." [8]

The new governor is also an extremely hard working, focused politician. Clearly, she loves the challenges of the political arena, with all its ups and downs. Her activist style is well-suited to an office with so few formal powers.

Many people think of Ann Richards as a liberal feminist, but her political style is nothing like that of Bella Abzug or Gloria Steinem. Throughout her political career, Richards has been a consensus builder. She maintains friendly personal relations with opponents, Republicans, and members of opposing factions. As a policy maker, she wants all affected persons and groups interested in an issue to be heard, and she seeks to negotiate compromises that have broad support. If consensus cannot be achieved, she tends to delay decisions until it can. Again, this meshes well in an office where one must lead by persuasion, not command.

Finally, the new governor came to office with a well-honed ability to play against type. As a reputed "big-spending liberal," she espoused fiscal conservatism in the state treasurer job. A career politician, she trashes government and bureaucrats like a conservative Republican. "The reason people distrust government is that they think government wastes. I don't blame them. They're not getting their money's worth." [9]

Richards has counseled elimination of government waste before any consideration of new taxes. When Lt. Gov. Bob Bullock came out strongly for a state income tax at the beginning of the regular session, Richards demurred. She has consistently resisted appeals, aside from the lottery proposal, to seek out new revenues. She discouraged any idea of reaching budgetary solutions prior to the publication of the Texas Performance Review, the result of a study of ways to make state government more efficient. This posture is more reminiscent of the Grace Commission than of traditional Texas populism.

Most observers take Richards's budget-and-taxing posture as evidence of her determination to build a consensus behind her leadership that she can ride into a second term. She was expected to pursue a liberal agenda. She has resisted the temptation to do so, knowing that she might win a few symbolic victories, but at the expense of alienating most of the state's voters. She has chosen to be governor rather than leader of the liberal wing of the Texas Democratic party.

The 1991 Legislative Record

The Texas legislature required a regular 140-day meeting and three special sessions to address the myriad problems facing the state in

1991. These January to August meetings provided an immediate test of the new governor's talents.

Most scorecards show that Richards did very well. The issues she took public positions on—ethics reform, overhauling insurance regulation, strengthening the powers of the executive branch, passing a state lottery, tightening procedures for disposing of hazardous wastes—passed in some form. The governor played a limited role in securing these results, although she could claim credit for the outcomes. In general, her legislative style was to stake out a popular early position, stand back to let lawmakers do the heavy lifting in developing specific programs, and then reenter the process at the final stages to negotiate compromises.

In the few instances where she took positions that were politically unpopular, as in supporting a statewide property tax to fund public education, the governor quickly backed off.

Richards's pragmatic, compromising style drew fire from both sides of the political divide. Old line liberals like Ronnie Dugger, publisher of the *Texas Observer*, were dismayed that *their* governor would strike bargains so far short of what they felt Texas needed. On the critical tax issue, Dugger complained: "Where, in the Texas tax debate, is fairness? Where is the *graduated* personal income tax? Where, oh where, oh where, is the leadership of Gov. Ann Richards? 'A New Texas,' indeed. . . . This is abdication of leadership." [10]

Conservatives like Jack Raines, a Houston lawyer and unsuccessful Republican gubernatorial candidate, would "give her an 'A' on rhetoric and an 'F' on matters of substance. She was unable to provide the leadership with a Democratic House and a Democratic Senate. She opted for taxes instead of savings." [11]

Despite such complaints, the 1991 legislative results strengthened Richards's political position. The governor got credit from consumer activists for delivering on insurance reform. Her ethics bill was weakened but new rules were passed and an oversight commission was put in place. The result is not overly stringent, but it should prevent a reprise of poultry magnate Bo Pilgrim's performance during the last legislative session: he handed out $10,000 checks on the floor of the Senate to influence lawmakers on a pending workers' compensation bill.

Environmental laws were reworked, and arguably strengthened. Most important, Richards was able to sign a tax bill without the massive tax increases predicted in January. The personal income tax bear had again been kept from the door. The revenue measures approved—a lottery (subject to voters' approval), a corporate income tax, higher gasoline taxes, additional fees—engendered little public opposition.

Of major long-term significance was governmental restructuring giving the executive more power. The governor will now appoint the commissioner of education, there is a new czar of health and human services, and a new highway commission. Richards gained control of the Texas Department of Commerce, the Texas Department of Housing and Community Affairs, and the Film and Arts Commission. Richards argued for these reforms, with the support of State Comptroller John Sharp, in order to reduce service costs and stave off an income tax. Wary legislators, each trying to outdo the other in antitax rhetoric, acquiesced in structural changes that will significantly alter the state's political terrain for some time to come.

Gubernatorial Appointments in the New Texas

The area where Ann Richards most clearly shaped her "New Texas" was gubernatorial appointments. Even before taking office, she sent a powerful signal that things were going to be different by announcing that Lena Guerrero, a rising young Austin legislator, was her choice for a vacant Railroad Commission seat. Putting an Hispanic woman on the powerful three-person panel that regulates the oil and gas industry was definitely a break with the old way of doing things in Texas.

Similarly, Richards used her initial appointments to the University of Texas and Texas A & M University regent boards, the most coveted appointive posts in state government, to put key representatives of her supportive coalition in place. The UT spots went to an older Jewish man who had funded liberal causes for decades, to the most prominent black minister in Dallas, and to an East Texas writer/publisher who is the daughter-in-law of timber baron Arthur Temple. The A & M board got another male donor to Democratic campaigns, a prominent white female rancher, and the widow of the late congressman Mickey Leland.

By the end of the legislative sessions in August, 411 of Richards's appointees had been confirmed by the state Senate. They included 192 women, 77 blacks, and 98 Hispanics. In general, the governor has been able to minimize opposition to her choices by picking individuals with considerable ability (Guerrero is already a hit with Texas oilmen). And she has selected enough white men to allay fears that she would practice reverse discrimination once in office.

Concluding Assessments

Evaluating a new governor after she has served less than a quarter of a term is obviously a perilous task. In the case of Ann Richards, however, some things seem much clearer at the end of 1991 than when she took office.

Richards has clearly exceeded public and insider expectations. She immediately seized the initiative in state government and remained at the center of the stage. She has pushed the powers of a weak office to their limits. In the first months of her administration, for example, she rallied public opinion to force the resignations of two Clements appointees on the state insurance board, thus overcoming her lack of removal power.

Her critics may well be right in charging that regarding many of the things Richards claims credit for, like ethics reform, she (1) provided little actual leadership in pushing through the legislation and (2) ended up accepting a watered-down compromise that will not produce great substantive change. Nevertheless, and certainly in comparison with recent governors, she has a number of significant accomplishments. If she did not lead the legislature, she assuredly worked with leaders and key members in fashioning an impressive legislative output. The changes in government structure give the chief executive more power than any governor has had since the modern constitution was passed in 1876. Her appointive record is the most impressive in Texas history, combining competency and diversity.

And Richards has displayed a deft political touch. She has maintained ties with her base supporters while reaching out to others. For example, cognizant of the damage done by her comments about George Bush at the Democratic convention, Governor Richards has been exceptionally careful to treat her fellow Texan in the White House with studied deference (though during the gubernatorial campaign she pointed out, referring to Bush's claiming both Texas and Maine as home, that someone who lives in the Houstonian Hotel is called a tourist, not a Texan).

Richards has also learned from the mistakes of her predecessors. When Mark White assumed the governorship in 1983, he did nothing to discourage the idea that he was a serious prospect for the vice presidential spot on the Democratic ticket in 1984 or 1988. Richards, who can legitimately claim to be the most prominent elected female Democrat in the country, has been very careful to discourage any talk of a national role. She rarely leaves the state, and she has made it clear that she expects to seek reelection as governor in 1994.

Despite her early successes, relatively high public standing, and sure political instincts, Ann Richards is far from being a shoo-in for a second term. The great threat to her administration remains the budget/tax squeeze. In 1991, the governor and legislature finessed the difficult budget choices by a combination of clever accounting moves, some modest cutbacks, and a patchwork of tax and fee measures that caused little pain. Unfortunately, the system remains fundamentally flawed. The state's revenues continue to grow at a slower rate than the economy and population, which means that another large deficit is looming in 1993. There will be much less wiggle room then than was available to Richards and the legislature in 1991. The governor will most likely have to either sign off on deep and painful cuts in popular state services or bite the bullet and go for an income tax. Whichever choice she makes, her reelection prospects could well be sharply diminished when she does.

In the meantime, however, as journalist Paul Burka notes, "For the first time in goodness knows when, Texas has a real governor." And this governor, despite all the problems and challenges facing Texas, sounds believable when she says, "I'm having the time of my life." [12]

Notes

The authors wish to acknowledge the cooperation of Professor James A. Dyer, senior study director of the Public Policy Resources Laboratory of Texas A & M University. Professor Dyer generously provided gubernatorial approval figures produced by the Texas Poll, which is administered under his direction through the Public Policy Resources Laboratory.

1. Joseph Schlesinger, "The Politics of the Executive," in *Politics in the American States,* 2d ed., ed. Herbert Jacobs and Kenneth Vines (Boston: Little Brown, 1971); Thad Beyle, "Governors," in *Politics in the American States,* 4th ed., ed. Virginia Gray, Herbert Jacob, and Kenneth Vines (Boston: Little Brown, 1983); and Thad Beyle, "Governors," in *Politics in the American States* 5th ed., ed. Virginia Gray, Kenneth Vines, and Robert Albritton (Glenview, Ill.: Scott Foresman, 1990).
2. Data from a survey by the Center for Public Policy, University of Houston, October 28-30, 1990.
3. Miriam A. "Ma" Ferguson served two terms (1925-1927 and 1933-1935) as governor of Texas. She was, however, a "stand-in" candidate for her husband, James E. Ferguson, a former governor who had been impeached and was ineligible to seek another term. "Pa" Ferguson dominated the executive office in both terms.
4. R. G. Ratcliffe, "High Marks for the Governor," *Houston Chronicle,* August 5, 1991. The Texas Poll began asking Texans if they approved of the governor's performance in 1984. In addition to approving of Richards's performance in office, a majority of those surveyed felt her to be "a smart, caring, strong leader who is willing to do what is right, even if unpopular." Texans described themselves as feeling "personally warm" toward Governor Richards. Even among the Republicans polled, Richards received a 47 percent approval rating. By October, Richards's approval rating had declined to 48.5 percent (52.3 percent of those having an

option), a not unexpected manifestation of the honeymoon effect.

5. Paul C. Light, *The President's Agenda: Domestic Policy Choice from Kennedy to Carter* (Baltimore: Johns Hopkins University Press, 1983).
6. Michael Barone and Grant Ujifusa, *Almanac of American Politics, 1992* (Washington, D.C.: National Journal, 1991), 1174.
7. Quoted in Paul Burka, "Ann of a Hundred Days," *Texas Monthly,* May 1991, 128.
8. Ibid., 134.
9. Ibid., 130.
10. Ronnie Dugger, "The Fairness Question," *Texas Observer,* July 12, 1991, 4.
11. Quoted in R. G. Ratcliffe, "Richards Taps Away from National Role," *Houston Chronicle,* September 8, 1991, 5d.
12. Burka, "Ann of a Hundred Days," 128.

12. VIRGINIA: L. DOUGLAS WILDER, GOVERNING AND CAMPAIGNING

Thomas R. Morris

L. Douglas Wilder won by a razor-thin margin in 1989 to become the nation's first elected black governor. Wilder's race and the prominence of the abortion issue in his campaign attracted national attention to Virginia, one of only two states electing a governor in the year following the presidential election. Voter turnout was at a record level for the gubernatorial contest in Virginia, making Wilder's victory even more remarkable in a state with a predominantly white electorate. Given the record turnout, Wilder had to win 21 percent more votes (155,701) than the Democratic gubernatorial winner four years earlier in order to ensure victory. Even then, his winning margin of 6,741 votes out of 1,789,078 cast (less than .5 percent) was the closest Virginia governor's race in this century.[1] His victory was a poignant reminder of the progress being made in overcoming racial barriers. While race undoubtedly continues to be an issue in Virginia, Wilder's victory means that race is not always the determining factor in the outcome of elections.

Black well wishers far outnumbered whites as throngs of citizens crowded into Virginia's Capitol Square to witness Doug Wilder's inauguration. The intense pride felt by black citizens was expressed again and again. Retired U.S. Supreme Court Justice Lewis F. Powell, Jr., was on hand to administer the oath to Wilder; after doing so, he leaned toward the microphone and spoke for the vast majority of Virginians by proclaiming, "It's a great day for Virginia!" The size and excitement of the crowd coupled with the historic significance of the moment served notice that there would be a unique, inspirational dimension to the Wilder governorship not associated with previous governors in the modern era. Every day he served as governor of Virginia was destined to be an inspiration for all those who had historically been denied an equal opportunity to participate in the political process.

Proclaiming himself in his inaugural address to be "a son of Virginia," Wilder, a grandson of slaves who grew up in Richmond's segregated Church Hill neighborhood, stood on a platform constructed on the northside of the capitol to become the sixty-sixth governor of Virginia. Twenty months to the day after his inauguration, Governor Wilder announced on the steps of the south portico of that same state capitol that he was running for president of the United States. Addressing a lunchtime crowd of about one thousand, he identified with the "hallowed tradition" of Virginians who had paid the price "to make freedom ring from Valley Forge to Stone Mountain. It was Thomas Jefferson who *risked* everything," Wilder said, "to write the music . . . and . . . George Mason, who *sacrificed* everything by refusing to sing until *all* Americans could be included in the chorus." Wilder's announcement that he could not "stand on the sidelines" did not come as a surprise. Barely two months into his administration, it became clear that he had his sights set on the national Democratic ticket. Governor Wilder frequently spoke at out-of-state meetings, began to address national issues, and traveled to Iowa and New Hampshire. Revealing his national ambitions so quickly guaranteed that his actions as governor would be evaluated in light of his unannounced presidential bid; that campaign, which was made official on September 13, 1991, cast a long shadow over Wilder's first twenty months as governor of Virginia.

Shortly after his election as governor, Wilder shaved off the mustache he had worn in one style or another throughout most of his political career. The new look did not, however, signal a new Doug Wilder. His service as governor thus far has been consistent with his political style over the years. He remains the ever-charming campaigner, instantly putting people at ease when they meet him. Engaging in political intrigue and challenging establishment political figures are still his trademarks. Governor Wilder continues to be unpredictable in his political relationships; he plays political hardball with blacks and whites, friends and foes alike.

The Campaigns

In the three major political contests of a twenty-year political career in Virginia, Doug Wilder always announced his candidacy early and reached out to white voters to claim victory. In 1969, Wilder, a successful Richmond lawyer, announced his intention to seek the state Senate seat of J. Sargeant Reynolds several months before Reynolds was elected lieutenant governor. He said he would be a candidate with or without the City Democratic Committee's endorsement, prompting Reynolds to persuade the committee not to choose between Wilder and a conservative Democrat. Recognizing the need to attract white voters, Wilder opened his campaign headquarters in the white section of downtown Richmond, much to the consternation of some leaders in the

Crusade for Voters, a black, Richmond-based political organization. In the citywide contest against two white conservatives—one Democrat and one Republican—Wilder won with slightly less than 50 percent of the vote. Estimated to have received 18 percent of the white vote in a city with a black majority, but a substantial white registration edge, Wilder acknowledged on election night that he "received a gratifying number of white votes" and benefited from the decision of some whites not to vote. He said he "look[ed] forward to the time when all men can run as candidates on their qualifications, and not as a 'Negro' candidate or a 'white' candidate." [2]

Wilder was the first black to sit in the state Senate of Virginia since Reconstruction. As a result of the state Senate's decision to elect all senators from single-member districts following the 1970 census, Wilder was ensconced in a politically safe, 71 percent black district where he ran without opposition and served until he was elected lieutenant governor in 1985. First ignored by the other senators, Wilder gradually became a respected political insider among the overwhelmingly Democratic Senate, eventually serving as a chair of three major committees. Senator Wilder was generally perceived as a liberal with a civil rights agenda throughout most of the 1970s, but he abandoned his opposition to the death penalty and began to advocate stricter law-and-order positions in the 1980s as he looked toward a statewide campaign.[3] As he had done in his first Senate race, Wilder announced his candidacy for lieutenant governor early—a full eleven months before the Democratic convention. Efforts were made to find an alternative to Wilder among the Democrats, but it was a testimony to his political brinksmanship and power of the black vote in the Democratic coalition that he was nominated by the statewide convention without opposition.

Wilder's election as lieutenant governor in the second major political race of his career established him as the highest ranking elected black official in the country at that time. While his Democratic running mates for governor and attorney general were winning easily with 55 and 61 percent of the vote, respectively, Wilder received 51.8 percent of the total vote and 44 percent of the white vote against an unimpressive Republican state senator.[4] With more legislative experience than the previous five lieutenant governors combined, Wilder emphasized his experience and political moderation while pursuing a "deracial" political strategy designed to avoid racial polarization and underscore the nonthreatening nature of his campaign.

Like his white predecessors, Wilder used his four years in the largely ceremonial post of lieutenant governor to expand his contacts around the state. His determination to run for governor undoubtedly influenced the Democratic attorney general to announce well in advance of the 1989 Democratic convention that she would seek reelection, thereby clearing the way for Wilder once again to be nominated for statewide office without opposition. Given these advantages, it is difficult to imagine a minority candidate better positioned to win the governorship. His campaign was well financed, and he ran as the successor to two popular Democratic administrations. Despite these advantages he was vulnerable to the charge that he was a liberal masquerading in conservative slogans. Moreover, he trailed in all major polls until the third week in September, when he began to run television advertisements emphasizing the libertarian underpinnings of his pro-choice position on abortion. Without the abortion issue to paralyze the campaign and blunt the attacks of his pro-life Republican opponent, Wilder most likely would have lost the election.

Except for abortion, the Wilder gubernatorial campaign was short on issues distinguishing him from his opponent. Both he and his Republican opponent, Marshall Coleman, were on record opposing new taxes. Wilder almost failed to get the endorsement of the environmental coalition because of his campaign's failure to return issue questionnaires, but environmental leaders relented and permitted the Democratic candidate to state his positions verbally.[5] Wilder appeared to be willing to allow the contest to become a choice between two personalities with Virginia's opportunity to make history again hanging in the balance. The charismatic Wilder had the advantage here, especially in light of the adverse reaction to the negative advertising used by Coleman in his party's primary and in the general election. Late in the campaign, Wilder lost ground when the Republican campaign released a tape purporting to show that Wilder was soft in his support of the right-to-work law, a traditional litmus test issue for holding state office in Virginia. Coleman, a moderate on race issues, also scored points with his attacks against the press, especially the *Washington Post,* for its unfair coverage of the two campaigns.[6]

Wilder's winning margin came largely from Northern Virginia and Hampton Roads, the fastest growing regions of the state with the largest nonnative populations. So dramatic is the population shift within Virginia that he was able to win by carrying only twenty-two of forty-one cities and twenty-two of ninety-five counties. More secure with his white support than he had been four years earlier, Wilder also more aggressively sought to mobilize the black vote, emphasizing low-visibility Sunday appearances in black churches. With the overall turnout rate for a Virginia gubernatorial election at a historic high of 39.7 percent, there was not much room for slippage among the components of his biracial coalition. He received 41 percent of the white vote and benefited from a turnout rate among black registered voters that was estimated to be 8 percentage points higher than the figure for white voters; in 1985 the black rate had only been marginally higher than the white rate, almost 1 percentage point.[7]

The Virginia Democratic Party

Following the disintegration of the Byrd Organization in the 1960s, the state Democratic party was plagued by factionalism and declining participation in its statewide primary. Republicans held the governor's post throughout the 1970s, won a U.S. Senate seat, elected the first GOP lieutenant governor and attorney general of the century, and held nine of the ten congressional seats following the 1980 elections. Lt. Gov. Chuck Robb, the lone Democrat to win statewide office in 1977, was the catalyst attracting conservative and moderate Democrats back to the party, making it "socially acceptable" for many citizens to be a Virginia Democrat again. With State Senator Wilder, the state's leading black politician, vouching for Robb's civil rights credentials, the Democratic party assembled an impressive biracial coalition that swept all three statewide offices on three occasions— 1981, 1985, and 1989.

The Robb administration (1982-1986), labeled the "reserved governorship" by one author, served as a transition from Republican administrations and a precursor of a widening role for state government in Virginia.[8] If a classification of presidents as carrying out responsibilities of preparation, achievement, or consolidation in the cycle of politics and policy is applied to Virginia governors, Chuck Robb can be called a governor of preparation.[9] Cautious by nature and hampered by the recession of 1982 during his first year in office, Governor Robb targeted new education spending as a state governmental priority and prepared the way for his successor, Gerald Baliles (1986-1990), to be a governor of achievement. Buoyed by rapidly increasing state revenues due to an above average growth in personal incomes, Governor Baliles stressed initiatives in economic development, education, environmental protection, human resources, and infrastructure. With respect to the last, Baliles called a special session of the legislature in his first year in office to approve a package of tax increases to finance a bold $12 billion, ten-year initiative on transportation improvements.

Governors Robb and Baliles were both helpful in advancing Wilder to the governorship. Even though Wilder's closest political confidant had publicly complained that Robb took too much credit for Wilder's 1985 victory and despite Wilder's boasting privately that he did not need Robb's endorsement, Robb agreed to make a television ad for Wilder in the 1989 race that all observers agreed was extremely beneficial to the candidate.[10] Meanwhile, over a year in advance of the

1989 Democratic convention, Governor Baliles anointed Wilder as the nominee-to-be and spoke of Virginia's opportunity to make history in the 1989 elections. Moreover, the economic prosperity in the 1980s, which made possible a doubling of the state budget, allowed Wilder to portray himself as a part of the Robb-Baliles Democratic legacy in Virginia.

Late in October of the 1989 gubernatorial race, Coleman spent several days trying to draw attention to what he predicted was an impending financial crisis for the state. Although largely unsuccessful in his efforts, it became apparent soon after the election that Coleman had been correct. A substantial downturn in state revenues assured that Wilder was destined to preside over the third stage in the cycle of politics and policy as the governor of consolidation. Wilder's fate was to rationalize and scale back advances of the Robb-Baliles years without necessarily rejecting them. As it turned out, Wilder appeared to go out of his way to eliminate the pet projects of his immediate predecessor. When Baliles's final appointments to boards and commissions had not been approved due to the oversight of a legislative committee, Wilder replaced some of them.

There was always tension between Wilder and his two Democratic predecessors. As a state senator, Wilder threatened to run as an independent when Robb and other party leaders agreed on Owen Pickett, a conservative state legislator, to run in 1982 for the U.S. Senate seat being vacated by Harry F. Byrd, Jr. Seizing upon the prospective candidate's positive references to the conservative Byrd philosophy of government, Wilder played a major role in prompting Pickett to abandon his candidacy and in the process, established himself as a maverick politician to be feared within inner party circles. As lieutenant governor, Wilder served on the commission recommending Baliles's transportation package to the legislature, only to disassociate himself from the .5 percent increase in the sales tax after it had been adopted by the legislature. He also took issue with Governor Baliles's proposals favoring contact visits for prisoners on death row.

When later questioned about his political ambitions as governor, Wilder portrayed himself as one who defies conventional political wisdom: "I was apostate as far as my own administration was concerned. . . . I said these things [opposing Baliles's initiatives] 'publicly.' I was not a team player." [11] Once out of office Baliles conceded that Wilder "tends to practice the politics of confrontation rather than consensus. Ultimately you're going to be defined in terms of building your support, by whether you build bridges to people or whether you burn them. And there's been a lot of bridge burning going on." [12] As for his relationship with Robb, the long-simmering feud between the two burst into national view when it was discovered that Robb's staff had possessed an illegally taped telephone conversation of Lieutenant Governor Wilder and one of his supporters.

The Budget Crisis

Governor Wilder inherited the worst state fiscal crisis the Old Dominion had seen in decades, a revenue shortfall that eventually exceeded $2 billion. One of the last actions by outgoing Governor Baliles was to reduce agency spending by 1 to 5 percent, limit teacher salary increases, and reclaim lottery profits designated for construction projects to ensure that the proposed 1990-1992 biennial budget of $26 billion would be balanced as required by the Virginia Constitution. Governor Wilder responded a few days later in an address to the state legislature reminiscent of the pronouncements by Virginia governors during the "pay-as-you-go" Byrd era. Even though he quoted Dr. Martin Luther King, Jr., and John F. Kennedy, he rejected new taxes as a solution, backed away from a campaign statement supporting general obligation bonds to build more roads, saying it was not "the appropriate time," and called for a $200 million emergency reserve fund, the largest in the state's history, as a hedge against a further worsening of the state's fiscal situation. Furthermore, as an indication of his resolve, Wilder indicated he would not recommend a repeal of the state sales tax on nonprescription drugs, a reform he had long supported. [13]

Other than his proposal for a $200 million reserve fund, Wilder's legislative agenda in the 1990 session was extremely limited. Two actions highlighted the governor's determination to enact the reserve fund as part of the 1990-1992 budget. [14] Early in the session, he reached beyond the closed circle of senior lawmakers to include legislators with less seniority in the traditional briefing sessions. This move permitted him to outflank a longtime rival who headed the Senate Finance Committee. When opposition to his reserve fund began to develop midway through the session, Wilder also made an unprecedented appearance before the legislature's money committees to refocus public attention on the only major initiative of his new administration.

Toward the end of the session, the governor demonstrated his flexibility in responding to legislative developments. When a consensus emerged to take back approximately $116 million of a generous pension relief measure that gubernatorial candidate Wilder had pushed for a year earlier, the governor agreed. Moreover, despite his earlier pledge, he took advantage of a legislative opening in the House of Delegates to enact repeal of the sales tax on nonprescription drugs at a cost of $30 million a year, effective July 1, 1992, the beginning of the next biennium. Finally, Governor Wilder left no doubt that the goals of the Baliles transportation program would not be met in the stated ten-year time frame due to increased costs and declining federal grants.

As the revenue forecasts worsened, Governor Wilder resorted to the unprecedented step in Virginia of delivering a prime-time televised address to the citizens of the Commonwealth on August 16, 1990. The tone of his twenty-six-minute address was somber and the call was for "shared sacrifices" in the state's tight financial times.[15] He reiterated his pledge not to seek a tax increase or reduce direct aid payments to the poor or medically needy. Governor Wilder proposed to leave "our fiscal safety net"—the $200 million reserve—intact, but called for reduced state agency budgets, cancellation of a scheduled 2 percent salary increase for state employees and college faculty members, reductions in state aid to public schools totaling more than $150 million, incentives for early retirements by state workers, and elimination of state funds to private museums and attractions. To underscore further the gravity of the situation, Governor Wilder recommended the elimination of certain symbolically significant bodies—the Department of Volunteerism, the Council on the Status of Women, and the Council of Indians—and the absorption of their critical activities by other organizations. Finally, the proposals included the elimination of the Norfolk-based Department of World Trade, one of the creations of the Baliles administration's global trade initiatives, and the integration of its responsibilities into an existing state agency.

Governor Wilder's use of the enormous discretionary budgetary powers of the state's chief executive set the stage for a contentious 1991 legislative session with the state Senate over budget amendments. Complaining they were not sufficiently briefed on budgetary developments and questioning the governor's authority to take such actions as, for example, abolishing the Department of World Trade, the Senate leaders moved to limit the chief executive's sweeping budget powers and proposed to use some of the reserve funds to reduce cuts in local school aid. Wilder defiantly defended "the fiscal discipline" he imposed and boldly declared: "If I accomplish anything during my term, I want to restore the public's confidence in government." [16] The session ended with the governor getting most of what he wanted on the budget, but the Senate rejected fifty-nine of Wilder's eighty-six amendments to the budget bill and affirmed limited restrictions on his sweeping fiscal powers, especially with respect to making unilateral budget cuts.[17]

The Wilder administration, like previous administrations in similar circumstances, resorted to accounting measures and transferred funds to close up to one-half of the revenue gap. At the same time, more than $1 billion in real budget cuts without new taxes and massive layoffs tended to insulate Democrats from charges of being a tax-and-spend party. Consequently, state Republicans have found it difficult to get to the political right of Wilder on fiscal policy, or law-enforcement issues, for that matter. Wilder's stated goal of restoring public confidence in state government, on the other hand, was hampered by much publicized feuding with other Democrats and accounts of in-state helicopter flights for undisclosed purposes at taxpayers' expense.

Unlike his counterparts in other fiscally strapped states, Wilder appears to enjoy the politics of budget cutting. When asked by a *Playboy* interviewer if the economic conditions made it "a horrible time to be governor," Wilder quipped, "No, I love it! It's the perfect time to be governor. You can take the scalpel out and cut where you need to cut. Ignore the pain. People will grumble and gripe, but they know it has to be done. So then, when the economy turns around, that unneeded fat is gone forever." [18] Lean times also permit Wilder to practice what one observer has called the "push-and-shove" style of legislative politics that has characterized his political career.[19]

Other Administration Actions

Two events explain volumes about Wilder's record during the first twenty-two months of his administration.[20] Almost eleven months after taking office, Wilder unveiled his "basic vision for the future" of the state in a booklet outlining his "Agenda for Virginia." Few details were offered and little action has been forthcoming. Encompassing a long list of ideas for human services, law enforcement, and the environment, Wilder's proposals, by his own admission, would not involve spending much state money. In the month prior to the announcement of his presidential candidacy, Governor Wilder presided over a highly unusual open meeting of his cabinet. Conceding that he "would like to be more substantively perceived," the governor attempted to counter the widespread view that he was inattentive to Virginia issues and the management of state government.

Despite a few limited initiatives, style and symbolism have triumphed over substance in the first half of the Wilder administration. In a highly publicized commencement speech at historically black Norfolk State University, Governor Wilder called on state agencies and boards to divest themselves of South African-linked stocks. When guidelines were announced four months later, it turned out divestiture had no timetable and could be avoided if it resulted in a loss of investment earnings.[21] In a pattern that may not be surprising in a consolidationist period, the Wilder administration has primarily reacted to events. When efforts were announced prior to the 1990 session to revise the 1988 landmark Chesapeake Bay Preservation Act because of costly and burdensome regulations, Wilder earned praise from environmental groups by opposing any changes. Nevertheless, his administration has thus far been distinguished not by its accomplishments but rather by what it has not done—raise taxes or change Virginia's permissive abortion laws.

Prior to the U.S. Supreme Court's decision in *Webster v. Reproductive Health Services,* announced on July 3, 1989, Wilder's position on abortion was largely undeveloped; when pressed, he said, "I support the law of the land." [22] The high court's decision galvanized the abortion rights movement and provided Wilder with a critical issue to use against his pro-life opponent. Wilder quickly firmed up his position—he favored Virginia's pro-choice legislation with the one exception that he supported parental consent for those under age eighteen. Once in office, Governor Wilder refused to advocate any changes in the state's abortion law, saying simply he would "consider" any consent or notification legislation that came to his desk.[23] The governor's noncommittal stance in public and work behind the scenes has been pivotal in the legislature's failure to enact any new limits on abortion.

During the campaign, Wilder's Republican opponent used television ads to exploit public doubts about Wilder's conversion on the death penalty. As a state senator, Wilder had opposed the death penalty in the 1970s on the grounds it was discriminatory against blacks, but by the 1980s, Wilder voted to support the death penalty. In his first address to the state legislature, Governor Wilder recommended the expansion of the capital punishment statute to include certain drug-related killings, and over the course of his first twenty months in office, he rejected clemency pleas by four death-row inmates. In a fifth case, which attracted national and even international requests for clemency, Governor Wilder became the first Virginia governor to stop an execution since they were resumed in the state in 1982.[24] Joseph M. Giarratano, Jr.'s sentence was commuted, making him eligible for parole in thirteen years. Governor Wilder refused to call for a new trial, leaving that decision to Attorney General Mary Sue Terry, who quickly reaffirmed the earlier decision of her office that there were not grounds for a second trial.

Governor Wilder moved early in his campaign to quiet fears of how he might use the extensive appointive powers of the office by announcing that he would form a commission of distinguished citizens to advise him on appointments. His appointees in fact have uniformly been well qualified. He has also accelerated the trend of modern Virginia governors to appoint members of ethnic minorities to government posts and advisory boards and commissions. Thirty-five African-

Americans have been appointed to top administrative posts; Governor Baliles had appointed ten.[25] Two blacks are members of the governor's cabinet for the first time since the first minority was appointed by a Republican governor in 1978. Only two blacks have been appointed to policy and advisory posts in the governor's thirty-seven-person office, however, and Wilder's closest political advisers are all white. Ever protective of his prerogatives as the state's first minority chief executive, Governor Wilder responded to a legislative proposal to remove the authority of the governor to appoint large numbers of middle-level managers by indicating he had no objections as long as the new policy did not take effect until his successor took office.

As the state Senate's lone black member in the 1981 redistricting session, Wilder was able to persuade only two other members that a district line drawn through the minority community in Norfolk diluted the black vote. The Justice Department predictably rejected the plan for the reasons Wilder had cited.[26] Ten years later, Governor Wilder was positioned to veto a Senate redistricting plan that created only one additional majority-black district beyond the two existing ones. With the use of his veto he achieved two political objectives—the creation of two more minority districts for a total of five out of forty Senate seats and the retirement of two of his conservative Democratic adversaries due to the radical changes in the makeup of their districts.

Wilder also used his gubernatorial powers to persuade the legislature to increase from 61 percent to 64 percent the black majority in a new congressional district stretching from Richmond to Norfolk. In order to increase the black population majority and improve the prospects of Justice Department preclearance of congressional redistricting, Wilder's plan strengthened a future Republican challenge to Rep. Owen Pickett, the same man whose U.S. senatorial ambitions were derailed by Wilder in 1982, by removing more of his black electoral base in Norfolk. The election of a black candidate from the new district in 1992 would give Virginia its first black representative in more than a hundred years.

The Presidential Bid

Governor Wilder's aspirations for the national Democratic ticket evoked markedly different responses from Virginia's citizens. Two-thirds of black voters approved of his candidacy while almost 60 percent of white voters disapproved. The disapproval of his candidacy by the majority of the electorate obviously contributed to the plummeting of the governor's approval rating to an all-time low for a modern Virginia governor—30 percent—and the lowest for current chief executives in the southern and border states.[27] Other factors contributing to the low rating were the governor's race, his combative and vindictive style, and voters' disenchantment with his budget cuts.

Virginia's fiscal distress has been seized upon by Governor Wilder as a political asset for someone like himself adhering to the state's traditionally conservative approach to budgetary matters. He describes his approach as "fiscal responsibility with compassion." Unlike President Bush, Wilder says, he kept his no-new-taxes pledge and made the tough decisions to balance the state budget.[28] Contrasting the governor with former Massachusetts Senator Paul Tsongas, David Broder suggests Wilder "uses ideas in a much more typical politician's way—to rationalize and accommodate his ambitions." [29]

In announcing his candidacy for the presidency, Wilder addressed the concerns of those critics who suggested that Virginia would be shortchanged: "I will not shirk from . . . [my] commitment [as governor] one iota, nor fall short on my promise [to Virginia] one scintilla." In fact, his presidential aspirations had already contributed to a crack in his inner circle of advisers. Laura Dillard, who first worked as a student intern in Wilder's lieutenant governor's office and later as press secretary during the gubernatorial campaign, served as press secretary for the Wilder administration until the month before he announced his presidential candidacy. Speaking the night before he made that announcement, Dillard described the governor as isolated from the criticism that he was neglecting the state as a result of his national ambitions. Four years is "too short a time," she said, "to have a chief executive who hedges his bets." [30]

Given the one-term limitation on Virginia's governors and his low approval ratings within the state, Governor Wilder could reasonably conclude he had little to lose by seeking the presidency in 1992. He has not been a hands-on chief executive and would most likely not become one even if he were not involved on the national scene. A divorced, single parent of grown children, he exhibits boundless energy in meeting with and speaking to groups in and out of state. Nevertheless, not quite four months after announcing his presidential candidacy and before a single caucus or primary vote had been cast, Wilder withdrew from the presidential race. Ever mindful of politics as theater, Wilder made his surprise withdrawal announcement at the end of his televised State of the Commonwealth address to the state legislature.

Governor Wilder conceded that he could no longer balance the demands of running for president and managing the nation's twelfth-largest state in tough economic times. Faced with a difficult budget session of the legislature, Wilder followed the lead of New York's governor, Mario M. Cuomo, who chose not to enter the Democratic presidential race because of the budget challenges facing his state. The decisions of Governors Wilder and Cuomo confirm the rigorous challenges a presidential campaign poses for a sitting governor of a large state. Even the relative late start by modern standards of the 1992 Democratic presidential race did not change the situation for the two governors.

Governor Wilder's decision to withdraw from the presidential race was made easier by the political realities of a failed campaign, or perhaps more accurately, a campaign that never really got started. He was last in the polls in New Hampshire, and his early 1992 request for federal matching funds was lower than that of any other Democratic presidential candidate. In his statewide races in Virginia he had been able to take the black vote for granted and to reach out to moderate white voters; nationally Wilder had to direct his campaign strategy toward the black voters who had supported Jesse Jackson's candidacies in 1984 and 1988. Whereas he began his campaign with an emphasis on fiscal conservatism, he increasingly was making appeals primarily to black voters. Wilder's withdrawal left the Democratic party without a black candidate in the presidential primaries for the first time since 1980.

Conclusion

Political accomplishments can be understood only as a complex interaction of events, personality, and the conditions for governing. As a governor of consolidation, Wilder made the most of a situation ideally suited for his political style and ambitions. The state budget shortfall of the first two years precluded the possibility of an achievement or activist administration, and allowed Wilder to define himself politically as different from his progressive predecessor and the Republican president, both of whom reneged on pledges of no new taxes. Despite Wilder's fiscal conservatism, however, voter resentment of his presidential ambitions and public displeasure with his reputation for political feuding were widely viewed as factors affecting the outcome of a number of state Senate contests in the 1991 off-year elections.[31] Republicans increased their representation from ten to eighteen in the forty-member body by defeating seven Democratic incumbents and winning the seat of a retiring Democrat.

Doug Wilder's historic rise to the governorship in Virginia was made possible by his capacity to understand and work with whites. A recent study suggests that the light-skinned Wilder benefits both from looking white and from appealing to whites in ideology.[32] It is difficult to measure how much that analysis explains Wilder's electoral success, but the record leaves no doubt that he has always reached out to white voters. His home since the mid-1970s has been in a stable, racially integrated neighborhood, and whites have been included in his ever-widening circle of associates. Meanwhile, during this same period, Wilder, who was never a civil rights activist, was the most prominent spokesman for black Virginians in his party and in the halls of state government. Not noted for his substantive accomplishments in the Virginia Senate, he overcame vetoes by two Republican governors eventually to win approval of his bill establishing a state holiday for Martin Luther King, Jr. He has also spoken consistently and with passion to the plight of urban, black males, and he chose an African-American with experience in Jesse Jackson's National Rainbow Coalition to manage his presidential campaign. Over the many years of never having lost an election, Wilder's major political contribution has been in running and winning with biracial coalitions, not in governing. The record of his first two years as governor has yet to transcend that legacy.

Notes

1. Larry J. Sabato, "Virginia's National Election for Governor," in *Virginia Government and Politics: Readings and Comments,* 3d ed., ed. Thomas R. Morris and Larry J. Sabato (Richmond: Virginia Chamber of Commerce and Center for Public Service, 1990), 116-138.
2. *Richmond-Times Dispatch,* December 3, 1969, A-1; Donald P. Baker, *Wilder: Hold Fast to Dreams* (Cabin John, Md.: Seven Locks Press, 1989), 80.
3. Margaret Edds, *Claiming the Dream: The Victorious Campaign of Douglas Wilder of Virginia* (Chapel Hill, N.C.: Algonquin Books, 1990), 36-39.
4. Larry Sabato, *Virginia Votes: 1983-1986* (Charlottesville: Institute of Government, University of Virginia, 1987), 60-109; Dwayne Yancey, *When Hell Froze Over* (Dallas: Taylor, 1988), 364-375.
5. Interview with state Senator Joseph V. Gartlan, Jr. (D-Fairfax), Fairfax County, Virginia, May 20, 1991.
6. Edds, *Claiming the Dream,* 218-220, 224-226.
7. Sabato, *Virginia Votes,* 84; Sabato, "Virginia's National Election," 116-123; Edds, *Claiming the Dream,* 239.
8. Steven Daniel Johnson, "Charles S. Robb and the Reserved Governorship" (Ph.D. diss., University of Virginia, January 1990).
9. Erwin C. Hargrove, "The Presidency: George Bush and the Cycle of Politics and Policy," in *The Elections of 1988,* ed. Michael Nelson (Washington, D.C.: CQ Press, 1989), 153-157.
10. Edds, *Claiming the Dream,* 46; in a secretly taped telephone conversation between Wilder and one of his Hampton Roads supporters on October 9, 1988, Lieutenant Governor Wilder indicated Senator Robb was "fin-

ished" politically, making his endorsement "suspect." He emphasized that he neither wanted nor needed his endorsement for governor (*Washington Post*, June 9, 1991, A-19).

11. Interview with L. Douglas Wilder, *Playboy*, September 1991, 72.
12. Juan Williams, "One-Man Show," *Washington Post Magazine*, June 9, 1991, 14.
13. *Richmond-Times Dispatch*, January 16, 1990, A-1.
14. *Richmond-Times Dispatch*, January 21, 1990, B-1; February 16, 1990, A-6.
15. *Richmond-Times Dispatch*, August 17, 1990, 1.
16. *Richmond-Times Dispatch*, January 10, 1990, A-1.
17. *Richmond-Times Dispatch*, September 5, 1990, B-1; September 27, 1990, B-1; April 4, 1991, A-1.
18. Interview with L. Douglas Wilder, *Playboy*, September 1991.
19. Jeff E. Shapiro, "Money Picture's Cloudy, but Wilder Is Making Political Hay Anyway," *Richmond-Times Dispatch*, January 16, 1990, A-5.
20. *Washington Post*, November 30, 1990, B-1; August 22, 1991, B-1.
21. *Washington Post*, May 15, 1990, B-1; *Richmond-Times Dispatch*, May 15, 1990, B-1.
22. Edds, *Claiming the Dream*, 146-150.
23. *Richmond-Times Dispatch*, January 23, 1990, A-1; February 10, 1990, A-8.
24. *Washington Post*, February 20, 1991, A-1.
25. Margaret Edds, "Wilder's Record: More Style Than Substance, Analysts Say," *Virginian-Pilot and Ledger-Star*, September 14, 1991, A-1.
26. Thomas R. Morris, "Virginia and the Voting Rights Act," *University of Virginia Newsletter* 66 (June 1990): 7-8.
27. TV-6/Mason-Dixon Virginia Poll, September 1991, pt. 1: Wilder Candidacy.
28. *New York Times*, March 6, 1991, A-1; *Washington Post National Weekly Edition*, January 14-20, 1991, 13; *Wall Street Journal*, December 19, 1990, A-18; Rhodes Cook, "Wilder Campaigns on Message of Fiscal Responsibility," *Congressional Quarterly Weekly Report*, November 16, 1991, 3400-3405. Despite the claims of the Wilder administration, Virginia is listed by the National Conference of State Legislatures as one of thirty states increasing taxes. Virginians will pay $33 million in additional income taxes over the next two years as a result of the state's decision to reduce personal deductions in order to conform with the federal tax code (see *Virginian-Pilot and Ledger-Star*, September 14, 1991, A-10).
29. *Richmond-Times Dispatch*, March 31, 1991, F-7.
30. *Richmond-Times Dispatch*, September 13, 1991, A-2.
31. *Richmond-Times Dispatch*, November 6, 1991, A-1; November 7, 1991, A-1; *Washington Post*, November 7, 1991, A-1.
32. Ruth Ann Strickland and Marcia Lynn Wicker, "Comparing the Wilder

and Gantt Campaigns: A Model for Black Candidate Success in Statewide Elections" (paper presented at the annual meeting of the North Carolina Political Science Association, Winston-Salem, April 1991).

CONTRIBUTORS

Thad L. Beyle teaches political science at the University of North Carolina at Chapel Hill. He is the editor of the annual *State Government: CQ's Guide to Current Issues and Activities* (CQ Press, 1985—), *Gubernatorial Transitions, the 1982 Elections* (1985), *Re-electing the Governor, the 1982 Elections* (1986), and *Gubernatorial Transitions, the 1983-84 Elections* (1989). He is coeditor of *The American Governor in Behavioral Perspective* (1972), *Politics and Policy in North Carolina* (1975), and *Being Governor* (1983).

Elmer E. Cornwell, Jr., is professor of political science at Brown University and serves as the parliamentarian of the Rhode Island House of Representatives. He is the author of *Presidential Leadership of Public Opinion* (1965), coauthor of *State Constitutional Conventions: The Politics of the Revision Process in Seven States* (1975), and a contributor to *Gubernatorial Transitions: The 1983 and 1984 Elections* (1988).

Robert E. Crew, Jr., is associate dean of the College of Social Sciences and a member of the faculty in the School of Public Administration and Policy at Florida State University. His most recent book is *Politics and Public Management.* His current research focuses on gubernatorial leadership.

Richard W. Gable is professor emeritus in the department of political science at the University of California, Davis. He is a long-time observer of, and writer about, California state government, especially gubernatorial transitions in the state. He has also studied, written, and worked in the field of development administration and has taught, researched, and consulted in more than a dozen countries. Recently he was on the Board of Regents of the University of California.

Samuel K. Gove is director emeritus at the Institute of Government and Public Affairs, and professor emeritus of political science at the

University of Illinois, Urbana-Champaign. He has written extensively about state politics, with a special interest in the politics of higher education.

Dennis Hale teaches political science at Boston College. He is the editor of the *United States Congress* (1983) and coeditor of *The Nature of Politics: Selected Essays of Bertrand de Jouvenel* (1989). His essays and reviews have appeared in the *Journal of Politics, Administration & Society, Polity,* and the *Political Science Reviewer.* His current projects include studies of tax reform in Massachusetts and of contemporary American citizenship.

Ruth S. Jones is professor and chair of the political science department at Arizona State University. She has written and consulted extensively on state-level campaign finance and public campaign funding. Her writing has appeared in the *American Journal of Political Science, Journal of Politics,* and *Western Political Quarterly,* as well as numerous edited volumes.

Katheryn A. Lehman is in the Ph.D. program at Arizona State University, specializing in state and local politics, including the role of the media in elections. She has presented papers at meetings of the American Political Science Association and is currently contributing to a book about county government.

Thomas R. Morris teaches political science at the University of Richmond. He is the author of *Virginia's Lieutenant Governors: The Office and the Person* (1970), *The Virginia Supreme Court: An Institutional and Political Analysis* (1975), and coauthor of *Virginia Government and Politics: Readings and Comments,* 3d edition (1990). He has written articles on state attorneys general, state constitutional law, and the impact of the Voting Rights Act in Virginia. He was most recently a research fellow at the Virginia Center for the Humanities in Charlottesville.

Russell D. Murphy is professor of government and department chair at Wesleyan University. He is the author of *Political Entrepreneurs* (1971) and with John Grumm of *Governing States and Communities: Organizing for Popular Rule* (1991), as well as articles on city politics and government. His current research deals with the ways state constitutions and city charters limit the scope of electoral politics and the discretion of elected representatives.

Richard Murray teaches political science at the University of Houston and directs political surveys for the *Houston Chronicle.* He is the coauthor of *Progrowth Politics: Change and Governance in Houston* (1991) and *Texas Politics: An Introduction* (1992). His current research focuses on black/Hispanic coalitional efforts.

Gregory R. Weiher teaches political science at the University of Houston and is director of the Center for Public Policy. He is the author of *The Fractured Metropolis: Political Boundaries and Metropolitan Segregation* (1991). His current work focuses on social welfare policy and state allocation of public resources.

Carol S. Weissert is assistant professor of political science at Michigan State University where she teaches state politics and policy. Her recent research includes state legislative behavior, legislative effectiveness, and health policy. She has served on the staff of the National Governors' Association and the Advisory Commission on Intergovernmental Relations.

INDEX